America and the Pacific Rim

America and the Pacific Rim:

Coming to Terms with New Realities

Gerald L. Houseman

ROWMAN & LITTLEFIELD PUBLISHERS, INC.

ROWMAN & LITTLEFIELD PUBLISHERS, INC.

Published in the United States of America
by Rowman & Littlefield Publishers, Inc.
4720 Boston Way, Lanham, Maryland 20706

3 Henrietta Street
London WC2E 8LU, England

Library of Congress Cataloging-in-Publication Data

America and the Pacific Rim / Gerald L. Houseman
p.   cm.
Includes bibliographical references and index.
1. Pacific Area—Relations—United States.   2. United States—
Relations—Pacific Area.   3. Asia—Politics and government—1945-.
4. Asia—Economic conditions—1945-.   I. Title
DU30.H68   1995   909'.098230825—dc20   94-44145   CIP

ISBN 0–8476–8022–3 (cloth: alk. paper)
ISBN 0–8476–8023–1 (pbk.: alk. paper)

Printed in the United States of America

To
Penelope Lyon
in Loving Memory

Contents

Preface

The Pacific Rim is a term that has only come into being, at least in any political sense, in the recent past. Its greater history as a term, if it was a term at all, was more likely to be associated with studies of geology, marine biology, or oceanography. One might have envisioned the tremendous capacity for earthquakes or volcanoes shared by such disparate places as Indonesia, Japan, California, New Zealand, and Chile. The term had no cultural, social, political, or even historical relevance.

But what, precisely, is the Pacific Rim? There is no absolute authority on this question. If we treat the term literally, it is meaningless in all but a strictly geographic sense. One of the books that includes this term in its title seems to acknowledge this as it uses the western rim as its subject, including Australia and New Zealand with the usual cast of Asian countries, but not the eastern rim. We can make a little more sense of this since the cultures of most of these countries may—we must say may, not do—have some common characteristics. There are still some real problems, however, if we must include Australia and New Zealand, since these are primarily Western cultures; indeed, they might even be called Western inventions. The Pacific Rim seems to make the most sense, then, when we confine the term to the Asian nations that border the Pacific and other nearby countries, which seem to have a lot to do with them in their cultural, political, and economic spheres.

This book, then, seeks to draw up some basic understandings of twenty nations—namely Bangladesh, Brunei, Burma, Cambodia, China, Hong Kong, India, Indonesia, Japan, Laos, Malaysia, Nepal, Pakistan, the Philippines, Singapore, South Korea, Sri Lanka, Taiwan, Thailand, and Vietnam. This rather long list is nonetheless workable because similar forces seem to be at work in all of them—cultural forces, industrialization, economic development, modernization, an increased importance of international trade and diplomatic relations, and to a considerable extent, a growth of military power and arms stockpiling. These matters are all concerns, as they should be, for Americans who are pondering our economic, diplomatic, cultural, and military future. It can also be seen that this area of the world is undergoing rapid and dynamic changes, and the pace is so great that even specialists have a hard time keeping up with these.

All of these points demonstrate the reasons for writing this book. We need to be able to take stock of this part of the world and to think about it; having said this, I am sure that this work will become dated in five years or probably less time than that. This area of the world will continue to be fascinating to watch, however; for, assuming that the dangerous security threats in the region do not materialize, the story of development in each nation will keep unfolding. It will be interesting to know whether these nations, largely bereft at the moment of anything resembling a social welfare system, evolve in familiar patterns or whether some new pattern, perhaps one that is clearly Asian, exerts itself in these societies.

One might ask, why stop with these countries? Why not reach further, into such obvious and nearby lands as North Korea, Afghanistan, Iran, Papua New Guinea and the Pacific islands, or those new republics of Central Asia that seem both fractious and dangerous? The short answer, of course, is that you have to stop somewhere. In all of these cases except for North Korea, which presents special problems, it can be said that a quite radically different set of cultural, social, political, and economic conditions appear to exist which would move our analysis beyond a concrete and tangible unity. This book has already bitten off a lot without taking on such wholesale problems. In addition, there is some evidence, though it is still relatively scant, that the area taken up by these countries could emerge into a unified economic bloc at some distant time in the future. There is also the usual political science commitment to empirical generalizations, and these become less and less likely as our area of inquiry expands. Even with this bloc of twenty nations the comparative phenomena from country to country cannot invariably be emphasized in the same ways.

This book has been influenced by two other major considerations, one that is broad in purpose and one that is personal. The personal one is mostly a matter of my own study and research interests and their evolution. When I first went to graduate school, it was my hope and intention to work in the field of comparative politics. Indonesia was the nation that held my greatest interest and, indeed, I wrote some papers about this country and studied it, along with other subjects, in Australia. My career path then moved quite differently, however; although I was always able to keep a hand in comparative politics, I was required for a number of reasons to concentrate upon American political phenomena. Only since 1989 have I been able to fully return to the comparative field and devote myself to Asian studies. This is a change that has been both exciting and intellectually challenging, and it is hoped that this sense of new awareness and challenge is felt by the reader.

The broader consideration is a belief that, just as the television specials and many new books indicate, sometimes in a hyped way, the next century will be a Pacific century in which the destiny of America will be shaped profoundly by the events that occur in the countries that are the subjects of this effort. Whether this will eventually be a more profound shaping than has occurred from our other connections, such as Europe or Latin America, remains to be seen and, in any event, it would be a difficult matter to intelligently interpret in this way. It is sufficient to say that what occurs in Pacific Asia will almost certainly affect the United States and its economic, social, and political futures.

This book project relied upon a larger group of people than has been the norm for my works. It is safe to say, however, that it could not have been completed without this array of great helpers. Three of these are faculty colleagues in Fort Wayne: John Bell, James Lutz, and Sushil Usman, and another is a friend and colleague of many years, Sally Merrill. I am also indebted to Uma Balakrishnan of St. John's University, Kent Calder of Princeton University, Cal Clark of Auburn University, Steve Douglas of the University of Illinois, Richard Jankowski of the State University of New York—Fredonia, Bill Liddle of The Ohio State University, Linda Lim of the University of Michigan, Richard Merritt of the University of Illinois, Maria Chan Morgan of Earlham College, Srinivasan Narayanan of Edith Cowan University in Perth, Australia, Mappa Nasrun of Hasanuddin University, Indonesia, Lucian Pye of MIT, Neil Richardson of the University of Wisconsin, Doh Shinn of Sangamon State University, Narendra Subramanian of MIT, and the late Aaron Wildavsky of the University of California—Berkeley.

Students, both graduate and undergraduate, have been particularly helpful in this project in various ways. Some have offered suggestions and some have opened windows to their culture. These include Julianna Abdul Latif, Aida Basarudin, Notrida Gani Baso Mandica, William Eichenauer, Nidavanh Hanlotxomphou, Bick Do, Keiko Kurosawa, John Kurtz, Donald Larson, Laura Lineback, Farah Meor, Lissma Mohd. Yatim, Lakshmi Padmanabhan, Anis Ramli, and Shirin Safinas Mohamad. Special thanks and credit go to my research assistant, Ardeth Maung, whose many contributions, including the whole of chapter 8, have been essential. There was also the reliable, thorough, and necessary assistance of Barbara Blauvelt, Debra Haley, Marci Irey, Joyce Saltsman, Deb Sewards, and James Whitcraft.

I lost my greatest collaborator and supporter, Penelope Lyon Houseman, my wife, in a Jakarta hospital on March 6, 1994. She has been responsible for most of the inspiration and any successes found in my work. She has been a good and even great scholar in her own right, working in such diverse fields as childrens' literature, the history of science, the study of names, Hindu philosophy, botanical art, and the history and culture of South and Southeast Asia. It is difficult to imagine carrying on without her, but it is she to whom this book is dedicated, with my love.

Chapter 1

Awakening to the New
Realities of Asia

Anyone who visits Asia today can feel the quickened pulse of the movements of people and trade. You can see it in the congested airports and in the fact that it is often hard to find a flight. Many of the air carriers—Thai, Korean, Malaysian, Singapore, or whatever—are having to add planes, routes, and schedules to accommodate the huge demand. You can hear this pulse beating in the department stores of Hong Kong or Tokyo, on the well-groomed university campuses in Penang or Taipei, or in the harbors of Jakarta or Colombo. One of the very best places to learn about this new Asia, however, is found just by lying on your bed in your hotel room in the old and romantic port city of Malacca, on the west coast of peninsular Malaysia, and simply scanning the horizon. If you look past the Island of the Pregnant Woman and glimpse the far reaches of your view, you will see ships going back and forth every minute or two. In nearly all cases, these are tankers working their way through the Straits of Malacca, taking their cargo to Yokohama or perhaps Singapore from the Middle East while the "empties" move in the opposite direction.

This is because Malacca, an ancient crossroads for people as disparate as Indians, Arabs, Chinese, or perhaps Portuguese, lies close to the center of the Asia-Pacific Rim region, an area that contains over half of the people in the world and huge amounts of capital and natural resources. This part of the world, like so many, fits into a rather arbitrary and surely somewhat artificial grouping; but it is a workable concept, all the same, and it lends itself to the raising of questions and analyses that are worthwhile and meaningful in helping to assess our own place in the world.

The economies of these nations have grown significantly over the past decade (or two or three, in the case of Japan), and they now

1

provide great challenges and opportunities for the United States and the rest of the world. Arms suppliers have also been busy in the area and, in some cases, arms races have assured that, in the near future at least, this region will be unstable in such locales as Kashmir, Cambodia, Burma, Sri Lanka, and along the frontier between the two Koreas. Diplomacy will therefore be important in this area for a long time to come; and it is obviously in our interest to learn of the peoples and cultures of this part of the world to help us to work, negotiate, trade, and live well with them.

This is a region of the world that has known many miseries, and in the case of some countries, these miseries continue—wars, in many cases internal ones carried out by various factions of the populace; disease; environmental pollution, hazards, and damage, including horrendous deforestation; famine and perennial food and water shortages; overpopulation; and a lack of such basics as literacy or medical care. The recent histories of some of these nations, such as China and India, have often created images of perennial need when in fact both of these countries have enjoyed past periods of substantial prosperity. It is also sometimes overlooked that many of the poorer nations of Asia, such as Burma, appear to have adequate nutrition levels, for the most part, and have historically been self-sufficient in production of rice, the major staple of most Asian diets.

Most of these nations have known colonial rule and, for better or worse (and most of us would certainly say worse), their societies have been partially shaped by this. But the colonizers, even in the relatively long stretches of dominance, such as that of the British in India or the Dutch in Indonesia, finally made but a small imprint upon the thousands of years of customs, values, and ways of what proved to be the *temporarily* dominated peoples. The union jacks and tricolors all came down in the years immediately following World War II, leading to self-rule experiments of greatly varying success (see Table 1.1).

The World War II period in Asia, the 1930s and 1940s, saw Japan attempting to militarily dominate virtually all of this region. The idea of "coprosperity," which was a part of the ideology of Japan's military rulers, would have allegedly led to an economic and trading sphere in which all would prosper even though Tokyo would be the political, military, and economic center of this universe. The seriousness of Japan's vision was underscored by its conquest of present-day Korea, Taiwan, Hong Kong, Thailand, Malaysia, Singapore, Indonesia, Burma, Brunei, Vietnam, Laos, Cambodia, substantial parts of China, and a threat to, though not conquest of, India. The hatred and mistrust

Table 1.1
Independence from Colonial Rule

Country	Date of independence	Colonial power
Indonesia	1945	Netherlands
Philippines	1946	United States
India	1947	Britain
Pakistan[a]	1947	Britain
Burma	1948	Britain
Sri Lanka	1948	Britain
Vietnam	1954	France
Cambodia	1954	France
Laos	1954	France
Malaysia[b]	1963	Britain
Brunei	1984	Britain

[a]including present-day Bangladesh
[b]including present-day Singapore

wrought by this period can undoubtedly be found in remnants in the area even today.

It has been decided, for a variety of substantial reasons, to treat what we call Asia and the Pacific Rim as a region composed of roughly twenty nations. All of these countries are of at least some recognizable importance in the region and in the world, and all play some role, however marginal, in the politics, trade, development, and security concerns of Asia and the Pacific Rim. It is also safe to say that the United States has an interest in the activities and policies of these countries because of our own needs, whether these be in the area of economics, security, or diplomacy.

This seems to have been the case throughout the history of the United States. Even before America obtained its independence from England, entrepreneurs and traders were lured to the East by what they believed were the riches of the Orient. And they were often right. The spices, silks, and other products that had so excited Europeans during the Age of Exploration, when Spanish, Dutch, English, and Portuguese merchant vessels tried to find the best routes to Asia, remained a matter of keen interest even at this much later time. The fabulous mansion of trader John Brown of Providence, Rhode Island, was built from the profits of his China venture, and he was hardly a unique case. The opening of Japan to world trade in 1854 was realized through the efforts of Commodore Matthew Perry and his American fleet. The taking of the Philippines as a colonial possession by the United States in 1898 most certainly demonstrates American assertiveness in this part of the world. Just one year later, the United States unilaterally declared that an "open door" policy would govern world trade relations with China. This was aimed at maintaining the integrity of Chinese self-rule, but it was also a promotion of U.S. trading interests in that nation. The energetic construction of naval power by leaders such as Theodore Roosevelt and Daniel Mahan was bent toward the domination of not only Latin America, for which the United States is perhaps best known, but also many parts of Asia in which it was believed we had a strong interest. This same Roosevelt's insistence upon building the Panama Canal, which was opened in 1912, was greatly motivated by a U.S. interest in facilitating trade with Asia.

It was the Pacific War of 1941–45, however, that perhaps most fatefully and finally established a U.S. presence in the Asia-Pacific region; and the United States has never abandoned this interest since, despite such setbacks as the recent denial of renewal of Philippine base leases and, much more horrendously, the ignominious military defeat in Vietnam in 1975.

The Vietnam War and its outcome have proved to be influential in shaping American attitudes toward the Asia-Pacific region. Even those who supported the war effort with considerable enthusiasm often now appear to be less interested in supporting an American presence in the region. Some of these opinions are undoubtedly shaped by the bitterness and divisiveness that have been legacies of the Vietnam experience; but other motivations have also come to the fore. The absence of the Soviet Union from the political arena has brought on a more relaxed view of the world and the U.S. role in it. There is also a realization that some of the members of the Asia-Pacific community, such as Japan, South Korea, and Taiwan, have become much more wealthy nations than they used to be. And this leads to the conclusion that if security problems remain, these countries are quite able to take care of their own defense needs.

Today, most assuredly, it is the role of the United States in the world economy, rather than military or security matters, that seems to hold the center of our attention. Trade disputes and rivalries with Japan are a persistent focus of the media, the public, and policymakers, and these issues are often presented in stark and dramatic ways and, all too often, misleading ways as well. It is not merely Japan, however, that is the focus of trade disputes and problems. In various ways, the United States has its problems as well with China, South Korea, India, Taiwan, and many of the burgeoning economies of the increasingly assertive Southeast Asian nations. Security issues and concerns are still around and some subsidiary problems of diplomacy are almost always showing up. Some of the latter include tourism, the presence of a variety of U.S. interests and concerns in these various countries, and the often touchy issue of immigration. Overriding all of these concerns, however, is the quite obvious need to promote intercultural and international understanding so that we can learn to live with these peoples and nations in the world community.

A Classification of Asian Nations

Drawing up any classification scheme incorporating countries as subjects is an exercise usually fraught with methodological perils. The many features that make a nation unique will militate against classification. The criteria employed can be flawed or inappropriate. The analogies developed as a basis for classification do not always hold up under the rigors of analysis. The data supplied to the classifier can be misleading or even wrong; many nationally generated statistics about incomes, growth of the economy, inflation, or other major concerns may be motivated as much or more by propaganda purposes of a given regime as by any commitment to the development of hard data. Countries often like to make themselves look good (see Table 1.2).

There are many other problems involved with the classification of countries into various categories, and the literature of comparative politics is replete with the difficulties, some of which seem almost daunting, in such an effort. It is nonetheless important to establish a very rough set of categories for the twenty national entities that are the concern of this book. The five categories are:

The Three Great Nations—Japan, China, and India

These three stand out from the other countries in the region because they are, first of all, bigger and more important. Japan is easily *the* economic power of Asia. China, the most populous country in the world with well over a billion people, covers a huge land mass, is rich in both human and natural resources, and is a military force of considerable conventional and nuclear power. It is also increasingly becoming an economic power because its development, particularly in the South and coastal areas, is proceeding very rapidly. India is also a military power of considerable nuclear and conventional importance, and in recent years it has been sending its forces into nearby countries for a variety of reasons. It represents a major threat to Pakistan and some of its other neighbors. India is slated to become the world's most populous country by the year 2050. Its economic growth, generally considered to be slow through most of the years since independence, has started to boom into double digit annual rates recently, though this fact must be tempered by the presence of a very heavy-handed regulatory apparatus, a population crisis that has zoomed out of control, a deep inflation problem, and a weak currency.

In addition to the large populations of these three, their economic strength, and major military strength in the region (and Japan can also be included in the latter, despite its constitutional prohibitions against a military buildup), it is a fact of life in Asia that many of the other nations in this community must pay heed to what any of these three do or might do at any given time. It is often observed that all three of these great nations are capable of pushing their neighbors around because of their economic and/or military might. It is therefore a matter not only of paying heed to what these major members of the regional community may do, but also of sometimes carrying out policies that are to the liking, and often the outright advantage, of these three.

Needless to say, these three have problems with one another. Japan has given India notice that it believes it is becoming too great a military power. India and China have had border confrontations in the past, though these have not occurred for many years. China and Japan cast a wary eye upon one another because China has some cause to worry about Japanese economic dominance while, equally clearly, Japan must be vigilant about a big neighbor who has been aggressive in the recent past and also possesses nuclear weaponry and sophisticated weapons delivery systems.

The "Four Little Tigers"—Hong Kong, Singapore, South Korea, and Taiwan

These four countries have astounded the rest of the world over the past decade or a little longer with their tremendous economic growth rates and their great strides in development. They enjoy relatively high standards of living not only by regional but also by worldwide measures. They have managed to raise health standards dramatically, eliminate a great amount of poverty, and promote employment, housing, and education. In all four cases, a large trade surplus has been established with the United States and often with other markets as well (though never with Japan). In three cases—Hong Kong is the only exception—these are military powers to be reckoned with, though they are small and weak by comparison with the three great nations of Asia. Most importantly, they are excellent test cases of development, so that they are likely to see some of their methods and policies copied by other countries; this in fact is already occurring.

The Less-developed but Fast-growing Economies—Malaysia, Indonesia, Thailand, and the Philippines

Three of these nations—all except Malaysia, which seems to have a unique status just below the "four little tigers" but well above the other three listed here—can still be regarded as poor by the standards of the developed nations or of the "four tigers." But they are all making progress, sometimes very substantial progress. Thailand and the Philippines have both recently experienced some political instability and some adventurism on the part of some of their military leaders, but both countries have managed to establish and maintain reasonable to good economic growth rates. Indonesia, which has had the same "New Order" regime since 1965, has made significant upgrades in education, health, and especially housing in recent years. Some destabilizing factors, nevertheless, seem to be at work in this case. All four of these countries are presently seen as excellent prospects for foreign investment and continued social and political progress. Indonesia is also a major military power in its part of the world, and Thailand is seen as a major investor and exploiter of natural resources in neighboring countries.

The Less-developed Countries—Bangladesh, Burma, Cambodia, Laos, Nepal, Pakistan, Sri Lanka, and Vietnam

These are nations that still fit the descriptions we often apply to the term "Third World nation." Their economies are heavily reliant upon agriculture or other primary industries such as fishing, logging, or mining. Their currencies are weak, and so are their trading positions vis-à-vis most other countries. The people may not enjoy many modern conveniences nor health safeguards, such as sanitation facilities or clean drinking water. Growth rates—except for the recently spectacular case of Vietnam—are generally not impressive, though some of the nations on this list have seen good growth at times in recent years. In some cases, such as Bangladesh, there are fairly acute deficiencies in nutrition and health levels. In several of these nations, political instability of one kind or another obtains, and there is clearly a tendency, excepting the special case of Sri Lanka, for the military forces of the country to assume a large political role. It is true that some of these countries, most notably Pakistan and Vietnam, are military powers in their regions and because of this their neighbors must be watchful. Pakistan is also a nuclear power.

These classifications leave us with only one nation left over, the tiny sultanate of Brunei, which occupies some delta land on the island of Borneo, which it shares with Indonesia and Malaysia. Brunei has less than a quarter of a million people, who enjoy a high standard of living because of oil wealth. In the region as a whole, Brunei is neither a major power nor a major player.

These twenty nations will be the consistent focus of this book, and it can be seen that there are considerable variations within their classifications as well as between them.

Asian Political Cultures and Their Impact

The vital core of the task of understanding Asian societies is the development of an understanding of Asian political cultures. Such a task is of course a challenge for many reasons—language and other cultural barriers, a much different set of religions than those with which we in the West are familiar, customs and mores that draw upon Asian religions but which can depart from them or adopt them selectively, and most certainly, the complications brought about by Asian exposure to Western customs and values, which can yield sometimes strange mixes of behavior or attitudes.

There are practical considerations as well. Most Asian specialists, for example, tend to study one country only. The reason for this is that Asian languages are difficult for many of us to master, and, not remarkably, we often deem it to be very important to know a nation's language if we are to study that society in a professionally competent manner. It is also true that many Asian languages are not related to one another in terms of such matters as cognate vocabulary or grammatical structure. This means that one must start from scratch every time she or he seeks to learn an Asian language. By contrast, European specialists have the luxury of finding their way around Europe rather well if they have learned just one of the important languages of that continent. Latin Americanists enjoy this same advantage. The study of Asia does not seem to work in this way.

Furthermore, nearly all Asian countries contain significant ethnic or racial minorities who often speak a language different from that of the dominant language group. This means that, even in those cases of success in which a specialist has learned a language, it is often not possible to converse with, nor adequately study, other peoples in the country who may be politically, socially, or economically just as important to know about. Linguistic diversity is a major characteristic of such nations as China, India, Indonesia, Pakistan, Burma, Malaysia, Singapore, and the Philippines. Even in those instances in which a nation is tied to a common language, such as South Korea, there can be important differences in dialects. Not surprisingly, there is a tendency to forego learning a native language if a nation makes extensive use of English, as do nearly all of the South Asian nations—India, Pakistan, Bangladesh, and Sri Lanka, for example—as well as in Malaysia and Singapore. One of America's most respected political scientists who has made a long and successful career of being an India specialist is a man who knows none of the indigenous tongues of that great subcontinent.

Religion and Culture

The religions of Asia (Table 1.2) are also quite demanding for anyone who seeks to understand these cultures. Many of the basic moral precepts are easily and naturally understood by anyone who has been exposed to the religions of the West or of the rest of the world. You should treat your neighbor with kindness, honor your parents, achieve various measures of self-improvement, and refrain from such activities as theft or murder. The way in which these moral precepts enter into the day-to-day lives of Asian peoples, however, is a complex matter indeed, since it can often be a long step from stated belief to adopted practice. And, as in the West, not all of the adherents to a system of belief necessarily agree upon their mythology, theology, or overall meaning. One Hindu, for example, may tell you that a certain god or

Table 1.2
Major Religious Groups of Asia

Country	Christian %	Muslim %	Buddhist %	Hindu %	Largest Other %
Bangladesh	0.5	85.9	0.6	12.7	—
Brunei	8.0	64.2	13.1	0.9	13.3[a]
Burma	5.6	3.6	87.2	0.9	—
Cambodia	0.6	2.4	88.4	—	—
China	0.2	2.4	6.0	—	20.1[a]
Hong Kong	17.7	0.5	17.1	0.2	47.4[a]
India	3.9	11.6	0.8	78.8	2.0[b]
Indonesia	11.0	43.3	1.0	2.1	40.2[c]
Japan	3.0	—	59.6	—	22.4[c]
Laos	1.8	1.0	57.8	—	34.5[a]
Malaysia	6.2	49.4	6.4	7.4	29.8[d]
Nepal	—	3.0	6.1	89.6	—
Pakistan	1.8	96.8	—	1.3	—
Philippines	94.3	4.3	0.1	0.1	—
Singapore	8.6	17.4	8.6	5.7	53.9[a]
South Korea	30.5	—	15.5	—	27.5[a,c]
Sri Lanka	8.3	7.2	66.9	16.0	—
Taiwan	7.4	0.5	43.0	—	48.5[a]
Thailand	1.1	3.9	92.1	0.2	—
Vietnam	7.4	1.0	55.3	—	17.3[c,e]

Source: *Economist Book of Vital World Statistics*
[a]Chinese folk religion
[b]Sikh
[c]New religion
[d]Tribal religion
[e]Shamanism

goddess is significant for a certain reason while another may hold that the reason for this is entirely different. A person who subscribes to the Confucian philosophy may say that this means that he or she is not very religious; but another Confucianist may speak of religious precepts or may even pray in front of the image of Buddha. As this suggests, one religion or philosophy may have some effect upon another. Buddha is sometimes regarded as an avatar of the Hindu god Vishnu. The traditional dress of Hindu women in North India has been affected by Muslim customs. Millions of Asians rely upon a combination of Taoist, Confucian, and Buddhist beliefs. In South India, it is not unusual to see a bejaj, a kind of motor scooter set up to carry passengers, decorated with the images of the Hindu gods Shiva and Vishnu alongside a picture of Jesus Christ. And in the outer islands of Indonesia and the Philippines, it is not unusual to find Islam or perhaps Christianity mixed together with beliefs and practices stemming from animism.

Clifford Geertz, Lucian W. Pye, and other experts point out that knowing the basic principles of an Eastern religion is helpful, but knowing how these translate into everyday practice is the key to understanding Asian cultures. Theft and various forms of corruption are condemned in all countries, but a little payoff here or there to get things done is often considered a standard way of doing business by both the giver and receiver of the sum (see Table 1.3). Fines can be negotiable matters. Use of such influences as family or business connections or political power is not always seen as illegitimate. And

Table 1.3
Extent to which Certain Asian Nations are Free from Bribery, and Other Improper Practices in Public Life

Country	Corruption prevalent	Not prevalent
Singapore		95
Hong Kong	65	
Japan	62	
Taiwan	47	
Malaysia	45	
South Korea	38	
Thailand	23	
Pakistan	17	
India	16	
Indonesia	15	

Source: Responses of executives; answers quoted out of 100; World Competitiveness Report, *Far East Economic Review,* 5 November 1992, p. 12.

the traffic patterns of Asia often seem governed by laws of their own, including the laws of chance.

Generalizing about Asian Values

This comparative look at political cultures also raises the question of the usefulness of "Asian culture" as a category capable of being generalized. There are great variations from country to country in all of these matters, and any generalization will usually require some exceptions to be made here or there. For this reason, "Asia" or "Asian" must be often seen as little more than a term of convenience; and this particular frustration will unquestionably appear over and over again in works like this one.

It is possible, all the same, to set out some broad principles of Asian values that appear to have validity, as long as it is remembered that these principles are nuanced and detailed in various ways from region to region and country to country.

Authority and Order

There appears to be a clear preference for these values. Confucianism is often said to be one of the premier influences that has brought this value into being, but strong support for authority and order are evoked by the other philosophies and by a sense of security, predictability, a certain kind or amount of efficiency, respect for parents or for elderly people in general, and perhaps some advantages for community stability and for commerce. Another reason, surely, is that this is a traditional value in many Asian societies, and traditions that are bound up with authority and order are not likely to be scrutinized or questioned except perhaps at times of great social or political upheaval. This quest for authority and order is in evidence in all social relationships, and this may be especially true in the case of the family.

Family

Family, however this may be defined, is crucially important in Asia. In some cases this can mean the nuclear family as we know it in the West, but in most cases the family is an extensive set of relationships. It is much more likely, for example, that a first cousin will be a person of importance to you in Asia in a way that this is generally unknown in the United States. Aunts, uncles, and particularly grandparents are very important in a person's life, and maintaining family ties is something that is expected and is usually carried out. Family connections can be important in business, and, in many cases, a patriarchal scheme is at work in which it is assumed that upon the death of the father (or grandfather, as the case may be), a son—perhaps the eldest, perhaps the one who has shown the most business acumen—will take over the shop, the company, or, in some cases, the multinational corporation. Chinese families that are scattered throughout Asia are known for their ability not only to work well within the economies of countries where they are an ethnic minority, but to also take advantage of family connections in businesses in other parts of the city, the nation, or, not unusually, the Asia-Pacific region. Such a family might have one branch in Bangkok, another in Hong Kong, and others in Taipei or Jakarta. Divorce rates in Asia are generally low, though there are rather high rates found among Indians, Malays and, increasingly, Japanese families. Respect and care for parents is supposedly an ingrained Asian value. (Singapore has just made this a legal obligation.) Family celebrations and holidays are of great importance, and this fact alone can militate against cross-cultural marriages, such as the union of a person of Indian background with perhaps a person of Chinese background (though this, too, increasingly seems to happen). Children are treasured, and because of this, they are treated very well in a typical Asian family.

Attitudes toward Women

The position of women in most Asian communities is clearly one of second-class status, at least by Western standards. They are expected to agree with the mandates of the husband and to work harder than any of the members of the family. Having said this, it is also true that women in Asia generally take on the role of family manager, including—and perhaps especially—the role of financial manager. It is no exaggeration to say that women are the traders of Asia. In traditional settings such as villages, it is women who do the buying and selling of products on a scale most men would not dream of; and it is women who understand very complex systems of pricing, barter, and other details of exchange. Some Asians claim that the position of women is different from that experienced in the West because of certain social customs and trade-offs. Muslim societies, it is pointed out, provide care and protection for their female members in ways not known elsewhere. A female child is assumed to be under the protection of her father and, after she reaches adulthood and marriage, of her husband; but other men are expected to step in and take up this role if it becomes necessary. The death of a father or husband, or perhaps a divorce, will place a woman under the protection of a brother or an uncle. In all events, a Muslim society provides for some male or another to be in charge of providing a secure life for a woman. The fact remains, of course, that women are often badly treated in Asian families and communities. They are sold for a negotiated dowry price in India, or they are required to carry out onerous kinds and amounts of work in this or that country. In China, the one child rule used for population control purposes has sometimes resulted in the murder of female children. Women are often denigrated in the proverbs and sayings and social customs of countries. Deliberately ignoring a spouse or bride-to-be, or making her wait to find out important things, or not notifying her about absences or trips contemplated, can be common occurrences. Recent years, however, have seen the organization of women's rights groups and occasional mass demonstrations in support of them in India, Japan, Malaysia, Pakistan, Taiwan, and other countries.

Anti-bureaucracy and Anti-regulation Attitudes

The fact of the matter is that Asian politics are seldom an arena of public debate over the questions of business or social regulation. There is nonetheless a discernibly deep-rooted skepticism about the role of government in the life of a citizen. The authoritarianism of governments, even when they consist of a formally democratic structure as in Japan, India, Bangladesh, Malaysia, or the Philippines, undoubtedly is a major contributor to such attitudes. The intensity of bureaucratic meddling and a strong bureaucratic presence in many Asian states is a reflection of the truth that in many countries it is the government that is not only the largest single employer, but often the source of nearly all of the good jobs. There seems to be a fatalistic feeling that bureaucracies are omnipresent and inevitable, and therefore the approach to them should be one of avoidance or of making the necessary compromises, whether these be payoffs or other considerations, so that government meddling in one's life can be minimized.

In some of these nations, and particularly those of South Asia, an entrepreneur who is working hard to make perhaps small amounts of money will describe himself or herself as a socialist. That is because the politics of the nation are often fashioned around the idea that the people and the nation share socialist values. How this set of values is translated into policy, however, may be quite another matter. India, for example, is the scene of a kind of politics in which all of the major parties and politicians regard themselves as socialists; but the practices of this kind of politics and of these politicians often belie this claim. It is undoubtedly the case that many laws and policies do reflect a certain kind of socialist bias, but the enforcement of these is sometimes haphazard or perhaps totally unsynchronized with the original legislative intent. A millionaire Indian business magnate may also call himself a socialist—this would not be considered remarkable—but this definition would probably reflect a strong belief in keeping up contacts in the government who supply his company with business contracts.

Communalism

Many Asian villages and whole regions are organized around communal values and interests. The *kampong,* a word that can mean village or community, is found in both peninsular and western Malaysia and in Indonesia, and its counterparts can be found throughout Asia. China has a great deal of its life, urban or rural, built around communal ideas, but it can be argued that these are imposed and enforced from the seat of government in Beijing, and there is a great deal of evidence that indicates that these arrangements do not reflect actual social or political preferences. It is the case, on the other hand, that much of Asia's rural and village life, and sometimes its urban life as well, is built around communal principles. Historically, and to a great extent even today, the *kampong* survives on an egalitarian sharing of resources, whether these be sugarcane, fish, or cigarettes provided by tourists. In Sarawak and Sabah, the Malaysian states found on the island of Borneo, a "long house" often provides a home for every member of a village so that they all literally live together and enjoy a socialistic way of life. Even in the great cities of Asia, however, it is possible to find groups of people, squatters or otherwise, supporting and living with such principles in a great number of ways. This might be enforced by such ties as a common origin in some village or region, or by the tradition of caste, or by some religious or other cultural tradition.

Sometimes overlooked in analyses of Asian socialism and communalism is the importance of the cultivation of wet rice. The sharing of water resources necessarily imposes limits upon anyone seeking to deviate from well-established patterns of agriculture.

Communalism is also found in the life-styles of various Asian cultures. In Burma, for example, it is not uncommon for persons or families to spend perhaps three hours a day socializing and enjoying the company of friends or neighbors. Dropping by a home of a friend informally and unannounced is a common and expected event. And this applies to such places as India, Indonesia, Thailand, or rural Malaysia.

Western Influences upon Asian Political Cultures

There can be little doubt that Western influences must also be factored into any analysis of Asian political cultures. The colonial experiences of China, India, Indonesia, the Philippines, or Burma have made their mark on political and social institutions, both governmental and nongovernmental. The tremendous bureaucratic bias found in the politics of India, Sri Lanka, or Malaysia, for example, is owed, at least in part, to the traditions of British rule. The picture in Asia today, several decades after collapse of the various colonialisms, remains one in which Western cultural influences can be said to be in evidence, especially in such locales as capital cities or administrative or financial centers. This is even the case, though surely on a more limited basis, in nations like Burma or Indonesia and, until recently, China, where the policies of government eschew the values, traditions, and many of the influences of the West. In the case of Burma, even the adoption of Myanmar as the country's name recently is an attempt to downgrade a name associated with "the British days."

It is safe to say that, by and large, Asian societies have embraced not only the technologies, products, and marketing techniques usually associated with the West, but have in most cases opted for a life-style that embraces some of the ways of the West. Thus, urbanization, product specializations, manufacturing, trade, career choices, types and modes of education, communications, tastes in music, and even some family practices and traditions have taken cues from Western and industrialized nations' experience. Asian families generally aspire to have their share of washing machines, videotape players, and other luxuries and conveniences associated with the West, though this hardly means that Western values or philosophical premises about life-styles are necessarily accepted.

Probably the greatest resistance to the intrusions of the West are found in the area of family life and traditions. The customs of marriage, courtship, child-rearing, and extended family ties are rooted in strongly held values and folkways, which, so far at least, seem only slightly affected by Western attitudes. Japan's increasing divorce rate may somehow reflect this, though this is not certain. It should also be remembered that Asian societies do not particularly admire some Western ways; recent years, for example, have seen editorials and articles in magazines and newspapers warning against adoption of the casual approach to sexual relationships considered endemic in the West but unsuited for Asia.

The casual observer visiting Asia can hardly be unaware of a great variety of Western influences. The presence of well-known consumer product names like IBM, Ford, Coca-Cola, Kentucky Fried Chicken, Levis, or McDonalds can make this obvious enough; but the adoption of a consumerist lifestyle by many Asians will be apparent to any tourist who roams the many malls or shops of Hong Kong, Bangkok, Singapore, Tokyo's Ginza district, or even certain parts of what we still call Communist China. Films and television programs, and even news programming from CNN, seem to have the greatest of any American influences in the region. Their popularity is reflected in everything from T-shirts to music to popular attitudes.

Religion and Values

Religious belief will obviously affect the values of an Asian individual or family, and in some cases—Islam or Jainism are good examples—it can represent an entire way of life. The political impact of religious socialization cannot be overestimated, since this can be a powerful animator of political intensities. But religious belief can also affect a variety of attitudes that shape an Asian's life in indirect ways. Attitudes toward political questions about the Middle East can surely be affected by a person's attachment to Islam. Attitudes about Buddhist priests and their political role will unquestionably vary from one kind of religious adherent to another. During the days of America's military involvement in Vietnam, some of the South Vietnam leaders were hostile to such priestly political activity. Hinduism and Buddhism are often, though not invariably, associated with pacifist attitudes and stances on political issues. Buddhism is sometimes thought to

accommodate socialist ideology and practices in such nations as
Burma, Laos, Cambodia, and Vietnam, but this idea seems to fall
apart in such cases as Thailand and Tibet. Quite clearly, some governments or political movements are closely entwined with a particular
set of religious beliefs. A belief in God is one of the five principles of
pancasila, the set of national goals adopted by Indonesia upon gaining
its independence. And certain political parties and groupings in South
Asia are committed to fundamentalist Hindu, Muslim, or Sikh goals.

The Study of Political Culture

A broad panoply of approaches to the study of political culture have
been developed over the years by political scientists and others, and it
is worthwhile to know that there are many acceptable paths to this
kind of research and study. Basic to almost any approach adopted,
and self-evident at any rate, is the belief that cultures must be taken as
givens and on their own terms; for difficult as it may be to avoid our
own reactions and feelings about values and practices of other peoples,
it is quite futile and in fact frustrating to cling to one's own ethnocentric
sets of judgments. Our concern is not so much to make judgments in
any event, but to become aware and informed about the world around
us. This commonsensical supposition, which even today is not necessarily honored nor shared, was a guiding principle for the first great
social anthropologists, like Franz Boas and Ruth Benedict. Fortunately, it guided some influential European historians like Stamford
Raffes, whose direct influence upon several Southeast Asian nations is
still felt. Adoption of this view, of course, does not mean that we can
always escape our ethnocentrism, since we are bound to hold many
premises and values that are virtually ingrained; but we can try.
And such an effort is far more likely to lead to success in gaining
understanding of cultures quite different from our own.

Beyond this rather obvious point lie the questions of method, which
are more controversial amongst social scientists and which, in the
absence of vigilance and care, can result in work that may well fall
short of the aims of scientific research. (Social and political scientists
lay claim to the mantle of science not because we possess the precision
of the methods of the "hard sciences" of, say, physics or chemistry,
but because we use the basic scientific approaches of hypothesis
followed by testing followed by findings.) A basic problem in this effort
is that the term "political culture" has some slippery and imprecise
qualities and still fails to enjoy any unanimity of definition. It is true,

however, that Gabriel Almond helped us along in this quest when, several decades ago, he came up with the seven characteristics found in all political cultures that define their political life: interest articulation and aggregation, socialization, communication, elite and leadership recruitment, rule-making, rule-execution, and rule-adjudication.

This set of categories does not enable us, unfortunately, to give a name or classification to the various political cultures we are likely to find in the world, and so work continues to go forward in this area of political theory. We have seen a variety of approaches made to political culture that have had varying degrees of success. Clifford Geertz, a noted anthropologist, has used "thick description" as a method of studying a society, which basically means that he believes that the best way to understand a culture is to know about it in as detailed a way as possible. Lucian W. Pye, a political scientist who has studied China extensively and is the author of a classic study of Burma, uses an intuitive approach that takes advantage of his own extensive personal background in Asia and is combined with the application of psychological insights. From such work it is inferred, for example, that there may be a connection between such phenomena as child-rearing practices and the dominant kinds of actions and traditions that animate a nation's politics. Another prominent scholar, James C. Scott, combines the insights of a political scientist with fieldwork of the kind usually undertaken by anthropologists to elicit the motivations and values of peoples, such as Asian peasants, who must rely upon their cleverness and their inner resources to deal with, and actively resist, authorities.

All of this work, in one way or another, is controversial. "Thick description" is said to be not reliably scientific, and, in any event, it can be bound up with trivia. Pye's use of psychology, because it is intuitive and has a potential for going off in many different directions, has also been deemed suspect. Perhaps the best example of recent controversy in cultural studies based in Asia is that found in the work of Niels Mulder. He likes to study Asian cultures as settings for values that largely fulfill human needs. When a member of a given society revolts against such norms in the name of modernization, socialism, or some other such cause, it is felt by Mulder that this is a symptom of the individual's moral lapses rather than those of the nation or culture. A major problem with this is that sometimes oppressive governments in the Philippines or Thailand are given support for their "Moral Recovery Program" or "Duties of the Populace." Mulder believes that Western intellectuals are excessively critical of these or other regimes because they approach such regimes from the standpoint of an alien set of traditions, something the early anthropological giants warned against. This is admittedly an oversimplification of Mulder, but his work is analogous to some of the work of political scientists in Asia, Latin America, and elsewhere.

The array of approaches to political culture has left an aura of dissatisfaction within the political science discipline. Political scientists, above all, like to get at questions of power and resource allocation—in other words, questions about what Harold Lasswell called who gets what, why, and how—as well as questions of political values. A model of political cultures developed by anthropologist Mary Douglas and political scientist Aaron Wildavsky, with refinements by Michael Thompson, is sometimes considered an answer to these concerns. This model sets up four basic categories of values and political culture which lend themselves to critiquing, evaluating, and manipulating (for study purposes) the work of teaching or researching comparative political values (see Fig. 1.1). This model is misleadingly simplistic at first; but work with the four categories can elicit both subcategories and extrapolations that sometimes result in a useful development of propositions about cultures. Obviously, there are problems with the model that can show up in both research and teaching environments, but these have benefits as well, including the

Figure 1.1
The Douglas-Wildavsky Model of Four Political Cultures

Number and variety of prescriptions (grid)	Strength of group boundaries (group)	
	Weak	**Strong**
Numerous and varied	Apathy (Fatalism)	Hierarchy (Collective)
Few and similar	Individualism (Competition)	Egalitarianism (Equality)

Source: Aaron Wildavsky, "Choosing Preferences by Constructing Institutions: A Cultural Study of Preference Formation," *American Political Science Review* 81 (March 1987): p. 6.

challenges of refinement and fashioning of substantive materials to flesh out the model.

Interestingly, and significantly in terms of our purposes, an attempt has been made to apply the Douglas-Wildavsky model to Asian political cultures. Maria Chan Morgan of Earlham College, in a provocative conference paper, used this model in an attempt to explain the economic successes of the four Asian "tigers," namely Hong Kong, Singapore, South Korea, and Taiwan. Morgan sought to examine the values of Chinese culture and to apply these to the social settings of three of these four nations; in the case of the fourth, South Korea, it can quite easily be maintained that some similar cultural values obtain in that society as well. Making use of the cultural literature on these nations and then bridging it to the Douglas-Wildavsky model, she notes that these "tiger" societies have some overriding goals. These are meritocracies, Morgan points out, in that competence and efficiency are rewarded and recognized, but wealth is still accorded the highest social status, and the wealthy have enormous political influence even if they do not actually wield political power. Moreover, the role of the government in the economy varies a great deal among these countries, but government intervention is expected to conform to the market rather than act against it.

This paper then goes on to claim, somewhat tentatively, that people in these countries share a cultural bias both for hierarchy and competitive individualism, two of the opposite blocs obtained in the Douglas-Wildavsky model. This argument, overall, is persuasive, since it draws upon relevant literature, makes necessary adjustments and qualifications that almost always appear to be needed in model application, and, just as importantly, comes up with conclusions that coincide with the direct experience of those who know the four countries.

It is a long step, however, from introducing a few approaches and models of political culture to the adoption of one particular model as the most suitable for this study. It is therefore necessary, in pursuing this particular study project, to remain open to the value and qualities of a variety of approaches and models, taking the most appropriate approach that is suggested by the relevant and given circumstances and factors. This, incidentally, is not the stance that will be taken on models of economic development, because one of these appears to be more useful and appropriate than the others.

The dynamics at work within present-day Asian societies must necessarily be seen as forces that are both traditional and modern in nature. Traditional emphases upon family, life-styles, established habits of commerce and trade, religion, and social interaction are challenged by the universalities of an increasingly broader community. This community is urban-oriented, Westernized (though it might be more accurate to say modernized), aware of technological and social changes, and, quite often, in communication with the rest of the world and its tastes and values. The MTV (Music TV) channel on cable television, for example, is now seen in most countries of the world; and news events of great importance seem to be reported almost simultaneously to every corner of the globe. Middle class Indians organized "CNN parties" during the Gulf War so that the latest information on that event could be quickly digested and discussed. Fax machines, video cameras, and communications technology innovations bring us all closer together. The long-range effects of these changes are difficult to gauge in terms of their impact upon Asian societies, but no one seems to doubt that they will have important effects.

Further Reading

Beer, Lawrence W., ed. *Constitutional Systems in Late Twentieth Century Asia*. Seattle: University of Washington Press, 1992. Although this is not truly a comparative set of contributions, the studies found here point up the legal and cultural norms and values of various Asian societies.

Betts, Raymond. *Uncertain Dimensions: Western Overseas Empires in the Twentieth Century*. Minneapolis: University of Minnesota Press, 1985. Much more of a cultural rather than political history of French and British colonialism between the two world wars.

Borthwick, Mark. *The Pacific Century: The Emergence of Modern Pacific Asia*. Boulder, Colo.: Westview, 1992. New, informative and up-to-date history of Asia, which includes selections penned by noted Asian scholars.

Douglas, Mary, and Aaron Wildavsky. *Risk and Culture: An Essay on the Selection of Technical and Environmental Dangers*. Berkeley: University of California Press, 1982. One of the first works in which the Douglas-Wildavsky cultural model is presented.

Geertz, Clifford. *The Interpretation of Culture*. New York: Basic Books, 1973. Analyses structural-functionalism and behaviorism and the problems of applying these to the study of culture; a well-known work by a scholar whose frame of reference is often Asia.

———. *The Social History of an Indonesian Town*. Westport, Conn.: Greenwood Press, 1975. Important case study which traces the fate of a town from the Dutch colonial period, through economic boom and bust, then Japanese occupation, and finally urbanization.

Khoo, Gilbert, and Dorothy Lo. *Asian Transformation: A History of South-*

east, South, and East Asia. Singapore: Heinemaan Asia, 1977 (rptd. 1992). A good short introduction to the history of these regions during their colonial eras.

Pye, Lucian W. *Asian Power and Politics*. Cambridge: Belknap Division of Harvard University Press, 1985. An heroic effort to summarize the cultural-psychological panoramas of Asia carried out by a well-versed Asianist.

————. *Politics, Personality, and Nation-Building: Burma's Search for Identity*. New Haven: Yale University Press, 1962. One of the earlier attempts to apply psychology to cultural norms, this is still often cited and referenced.

Scott, James W. *Weapons of the Weak*. New Haven: Yale University Press, 1987. Analyzes techniques of evasion and resistance to avoid direct confrontations with authority; the subject is peasants in Malaysia.

Taylor, Robert. *Asia and the Pacific*. New York: Facts On File, 1991. Valuable two-volume library reference set examines the political and socioeconomic lives of the peoples of the various regions of Asia; broad in scope.

Chapter 2

Issues of Asian Economic Development and Trade

Economic development is an issue in both the political sense and, much more narrowly, in a social science methods and philosophy sense; and it is a major concern in the study of Asian societies if for no other reason than the great economic progress that has been established in the region over the past decade (and, in the case of Japan, over the past three or four decades). This growth and development is a continuing story of great accomplishment; the year 1995, for example, is expected to be the first year in which all of the twenty countries featured in this book will see the growth rate outstrip the population rate.

However successful this story of growth is, however, it must be said that, to a great extent, it was not really anticipated by those experts who, we assume, are knowledgeable about such things. That is because the recognized theories of development preceded much of the actual development that occurred in Third World nations—or, perhaps more accurately, former Third World nations. And this literature, from the pristine viewpoint of hindsight, which we now enjoy, often missed the mark as it proffered advice to the world on how to achieve living standards that would provide people a measure of prosperity and well-being. The further point must also be made that only parts of Asia, hardly all of it, have succeeded in this quest for a substantially better life for their peoples.

Invariably there appears to be a difference between conceptualization and what occurs in practice. The hard work of economic and political development, in Asia at any rate, seems to have been carried out in quite different ways within the various countries that have known success. South Korea, for example, has relied upon a very close, almost corporate-state, kind of hand-in-glove cooperation between the industrial giants of the country and the strong arm of the government's marketing and planning apparatus. Taiwan is quite the opposite case; regulation and government involvement appear quite minimal or nearly nonexistent as portions of the development story. Hong Kong has operated in a very similar vein. Japan and Singapore, in rather different ways, have used the power of government to focus upon the international marketplace and bring about a strong growth of exports.

It is simultaneously inaccurate to think of the successful cases of Asian economic development as something that has occurred on a country-by-country basis. Regional cooperation of various sorts has been going on. Among these is the strong role played by Hong Kong and Taiwan firms in the development of capitalism in southern and coastal China. There are some cases of regionwide investment by multinational firms—IBM, Dana Corporation, and some electronics, garment, and shoe firms provide examples—and this has introduced a comparatively new kind of measure of development and growth, which has not been confined to one nation. Most particularly, as Ronald Donen points out in his book, *Driving a Bargain,* Japanese firms have been investing in manufacturing enterprises in the region, particularly in Southeast Asia, so that their products can be fabricated at substantially lower costs than would be the case in Japan. This has had a major impact in the region. (Anyone who understands W. Arthur Lewis's model of economic development would readily appreciate why this activity is occurring, but more about this later.)

Any scrutiny of Japan and the four "tigers"—Hong Kong, Singapore, South Korea, and Taiwan—will show that all of these have arranged, in one way or another, to rein in population growth and to heartily support education at all levels; but while such factors as these may help to explain the success of these economies, not all demographers, economists, political scientists, or others would agree that these are totally determinative. It does seem significant, all the same, that these trends are occurring in those nations, such as Malaysia, Indonesia, Thailand, and even China, which seem to be next in line for modernization and a relatively high standard of living. There can also be little doubt that higher literacy rates, reduction of the number of dependent people relative to the productive population (a problem now looming large in Japan), the large participation of women in the labor force, and some reduction of pressures on educational institutions or health agencies, to cite two examples, can give governments and business firms some room for social and infrastructure improvements generally considered vital for solid economic growth. In the case of the four "tigers," the fact that the fertility rate has been more than halved since 1965 has probably gone a long way toward helping to insure this growth. Japan's earlier success in this sphere demonstrates that this is a pattern for the future, and the still-struggling economies of India or Bangladesh or other nations show that high fertility rates coincide with slow economic improvement rates.

The four "tigers," which necessarily serve as a major part of our focus upon economic development, have used education as a very important part of their plans for national prosperity. All of these nations, and, quite significantly, Malaysia, Indonesia, and Thailand as well, have made both financial and infrastructure commitments to education in order to improve the skills of the populace. Singapore, South Korea, Taiwan, China, and Malaysia are well known in the United States for their large contributions to the international student numbers in its universities. Hong Kong is now embarked on a very large expansion of education at all levels, and this includes the founding of several new universities. The shadow of 1997, when China is supposed to take over the colony from Britain, does not seem to have impeded these ambitious goals.

The results of all of these efforts can be seen in high literacy rates, skilled work forces, and a concomitant consumer purchasing power that aids in everything from heavy manufacturing to consumer services. And the "tigers" are experiencing relatively small amounts of social dislocation, alienation, and crime, even by Asian standards; this seems especially the case when comparisons are made with nations like India, Cambodia, or even the Philippines.

The development of highly skilled work forces has meant that there is an increasing emphasis on carrying out the routine work tasks, such as assembly manufacturing, in "offshore" locations; in most cases these are less-developed nations like Indonesia or Thailand. The "tigers," then, are increasingly seen as centers for company headquarters operations or for such activities as research and development.

Theories of Economic Growth and Development

The literature of economic development is replete with theoretical works aimed at explaining the processes and results of growth patterns—or their lack—in Third World countries. Neo-Marxists, such as Paul Baran and Paul Sweezy, for example, have held that development is well-nigh impossible for poor countries because the surplus wealth achieved by the hard labor of the workers and peasants is invariably drained off by the capitalist economic and political powers of the world, namely, the multinational corporations and their Western neo-imperialist sponsors such as the United States, Britain, or Germany. Such writers as these also hold that the various and general responses to Third World needs made by the West (and, for that matter, by Japan) are inappropriate as vehicles for development, growth, or much-needed social and political change. Baran, Sweezy, and others of similar viewpoints have traditionally been able to construct a quite devastating case against this state of affairs and, at the same time, to have some effects of diminishing hopes for improvement. Working against their theoretical contribution, of course, is the fact that a number of previously underdeveloped nations, like the "tigers" but also like such countries as Brazil, Mexico, and Chile, have managed by some means or another—the methods and results are hardly uniform—to break out of the cycle of dependency and to achieve significant strides in real wage gains and in raising living standards. These successes tend to militate against the Baran-Sweezy view; but these thinkers should not be easily dismissed, for their analysis still seems to describe much of the Third World, perhaps especially in the nations of Africa and Central America, but also in Asia as well.

There are many other levels and modes of analysis, however. At the level we might call the least remarkable, Donald Gordon has quite conclusively made the case that even in the absence of natural resources, it is possible to match the resources of education with the institutions of private property to take advantage of the findings and resources of science and technology. Japan has done this in what historically must be considered a relatively short time span and, most assuredly, it is not a nation blessed with much in the way of natural resources. Singapore is an obvious second case. Gordon's work provides proofs, to the extent that such exist in the world of economics, for a bit of common sense that, when mulled over, is not that amazing.

Thinking Derived from the Cold War Era

Unquestionably the most celebrated work of its time in the arena of economic development was that of Walt Whitman Rostow. In the mid-1960s, a time of considerable idealism about Third World countries and their futures, which proved, like so many things in our politics, to be a mere passing fad, Rostow demonstrated that he had spent time and thought on the subject. It is safe to say, however, that the growth patterns we see in Asia today have drawn nothing from Rostow. He emphasized the importance of an agricultural base, hardly the kind of concern possessed by city-states like Hong Kong or Singapore (though both of these do have some agriculture), nor, for that matter, by South Korea, Taiwan, or present-day Malaysia.

Rostow's stages of economic development of a nation appeared at the time to possess cogency and logic, but it is now possible with hindsight, always a great help, to see that Rostow's work was far too taken up with answering the Communist world and the threat it seemed to pose in poor nations. The archaic and basically unusable characteristics of this work show up in measuring a nation's progress by its commitment to automobile use, which might well be considered an untenable measure today. Policies of Japan, Singapore, and, more recently, Thailand, demonstrate that the automobile is seen as a threat to the environment and even to economic growth. Most unfortunately, however, from the standpoint of the developing nations is the fact that Rostow's emphasis was often thoughtlessly applied by aid agencies, banks, and the International Monetary Fund (IMF) in setting up guidelines for a nation's political leadership. The result, far too often, was a neocolonial form of economic imperialism which, in the long run, could be said to have done little if any good. The IMF in recent years has become notorious for imposing stringent belt-tightening measures on countries in order to deal with such problems as debts owed to international, and often private, banks. These austerity measures do not always work well for a nation's people and they almost certainly work to the disadvantage of incumbent political leaderships (not that this is always bad). These policies have undergone change; but in all events, it appears clear that little of Rostow has ever been drawn upon for economic development guidelines by nations who were the objects of this thought and work, which is probably fortunate for them. In the final analysis, Rostow's work, which was seen as a possible alternative to Marxist challenges by its author, is as wholly ideological as the dependence theories of the neo-Marxists. It is now a museum piece in development theory.

Understanding Asian (and World) Economic Development: The Work of W. Arthur Lewis

Despite the failures we can now clearly chart in the work of neo-Marxist dependency theorists or in the work of Rostow, we have some good resources with which to carry out the tasks of analysis of economic development. Sometimes overlooked among economic thinkers is the late Nobel laureate W. Arthur Lewis, whose legacy provides a rich reservoir of both theoretical and practical contributions that seem to grow more pertinent as the years go by. Lewis's work so impresses this author, in fact, that it will be used as a basic organizing principle of this book.

Lewis, who began life as a citizen of the Third World, was a prescient observer whose work possesses a clearly predictive capacity. He offers an explanation that, when it was written in 1954, could hardly have foreseen the dynamic growth now taking place in much of Asia. His work possesses significance not only for Asian nations, however; his thesis can be used to discover development trends in Latin America or other parts of the world, and in the final analysis, he tells us much about the current economic condition of developed nations, such as the United States, as well.

In his landmark 1954 article, "Economic Development with Unlimited Supplies of Labour," Lewis showed us how labor and investment patterns work internationally. He set out a model of some complexity; from it can be derived two basic requirements for a nation to become the desired recipient of capital investment, whether that investment happens to be domestically or internationally based.

The first of these is wage levels, which reflect that a surplus pool of labor exists that can be profitably exploited. The second requirement relates to living standards and, most especially, to nutrition levels. The workforce must be sufficiently skilled and must have enough physical energy to put in a day's work in a factory, shop, or other workplace. Until a nation achieves these characteristics of low labor costs coupled with adequate nutrition levels, the international investment community will largely shun it. The four "tigers" of Asia, to return to our often-cited examples, achieved these basic requirements and conditions at least a decade (or longer) ago, and in fact these countries are now too expensive for such low-tech investments as shoe or umbrella factories and may be too expensive now for some high-tech or skilled worker needs as well. Japan, of course, moved past such points at an even earlier date. But Indonesia and Thailand, to cite two good current examples, have moved into the Lewis theory's orbit only recently and should probably be considered optimal investment locales. Many other Third World nations—Bangladesh, for example, or non-Asian nations such as Haiti or Ethiopia—are still far behind the curve simply because they are too poor for achievement of adequate nutrition levels (see Table 2.1). Their day for investment and development is still awaited.

Most casual observers of international economic affairs are aware of these trends. It is assuredly true that much of the developed community of nations—the United States or Britain can serve as examples—have found themselves grappling with an out-migration of jobs in conformity with the characteristics of Lewis's paradigm. A major concern for these nations, for which there is no obvious solution, is how to get around such trends which, incidentally, are predicted by Lewis's work. Only unique skills, products, cutting-edge technology, and very innovative managements serve as hopes for the future in dealing with this crisis.

What makes the work of Lewis most useful today, however, is that it enables us to take better and more precise bearings on the status of any given country. Such a country may be a Japan that loses a garment

Table 2.1
The Lewis Model of Economic Development
Applied to Present-Day Asia

	High Wage Level Nations	Low Wage Level Nations
Nations with adequate nutrition levels (2,210 calories or more per person per day)	Brunei Hong Kong Japan Singapore	Burma China Indonesia Malaysia Pakistan Philippines South Korea Sri Lanka Taiwan Thailand
Nations with inadequate nutrition	--	Bangladesh India Nepal

Note: 2,210 calories is the standard adopted by the World Bank. Wage levels are extrapolated from GDP per capita figures.

factory to Taiwan, which later loses the same manufacturer to perhaps Indonesia; but it might not stay there, either, if nutrition levels rise in Bangladesh or some other prospective labor market. As Table 2.1 tends to show, it is possible to develop classification schemes that incorporate virtually every nation, not merely Asian nations, into a position somewhere along the spectrum of developed, developing, and potentially developing countries. It is a rather good compass for finding our way through the thickets of trade, production, employment, sales, and economic growth figures.

Admittedly there are problems with Lewis's theory. It does not take political stability and change sufficiently into account. Burma, for example, fits in Table 2.1 in the category of nations with adequate nutrition levels and low wages, the very criteria called for by Lewis for optimal conditions for development; but the political situation in that country strongly militates against foreign investors even now with that nation's policy of no longer being closed off to the outside world. Lewis' theory also ignores a wide range of factors that are well-known as important to development, such as education, health standards, and population growth. Above all, it seems to make no allowances for the nuances of political culture. Recognizing such drawbacks does not necessarily make the model deficient, however; it tells us that we can attempt to solve such problems in various ways—and probably conceptualize these with other models—while also utilizing this worthwhile roadmap of world economic development.

Third World (North-South) Issues in Asia

The burgeoning prosperity of much of Asia in the last decade or so has tended to obscure the fact that much of the region remains poor and undeveloped for a variety of reasons ranging from political instability, inefficiencies imposed by various regimes, or even civil wars to those endemic with nations caught in the cycles of poverty, malnutrition, disease, ignorance, and, quite often, population growth which is out of control. Asia is therefore not immune to the kinds of problems nor the array of arguments offered that are characteristic of the debate we have generally referred to as the North-South conflict.

North-South is a somewhat misleading term, for it is hardly the case that all of the wealthy nations of the world are "North" anymore than it is true that all of the poor countries are in the planet's "South." Realizing that this is simply a term of convenience, which is also the case with the term "Third World," it is certainly true that the set of issues related to rich nation-poor nation relationships has received a great deal of attention in forums such as the United Nations General Assembly or, with less intensity, in the U.S. Congress. In the list of countries with which we are concerned in this text, the nations of the "South" include Bangladesh, Burma, Cambodia, Indonesia, Laos, Nepal, Pakistan, the Philippines, Sri Lanka, Thailand, and Vietnam. Two of the three superpowers of the region, China and India, should also be considered poor nations as measured by living standards. Brunei and Malaysia are rich enough that they can join Japan and the four "tigers" on the list of countries excluded from the "South" category. It is, in fact, the success of Asian economies that is causing the North-South division to be increasingly obsolete.

Although there is a list of issues which we can cite as specific North-South differences, it is accurate to say that above and beyond such specifics is a concern of the "South," or "Third World," nations that the developed countries of the "North" are too uncaring and unconcerned about the fate of their fellow citizens of the planet who have been unfortunate enough to live in circumstances brought about through a combination of such factors as natural handicaps of climate and lack of resources, imposed handicaps brought about through colonialism and economic and political exploitation, and historical antecedents of various types and seriousness that have helped to bring about the status of "underdeveloped" or "less-developed" country. The charge of unconcern is too often verified if one looks at the opinion polls, priorities lists, and actual practices of the rich and developed nations. Polls, for example, seldom show concern about Third World poverty among the top concerns of American, British, German, or French respondents. "Third World" can even be a negative or pejorative term in some quarters, even among foreign affairs experts or policymakers. In the case of the United States, a very strong tradition of isolationism and feelings about "taking care of our interests at home" have historically been important, and events of the magnitude and smashing nonsuccess of the Vietnam War tend to reinforce such attitudes. This isolationist stance, like so many historically important forces, is grounded in the quite practical approach of the United States in the nineteenth century, when noninvolvement with the world was not only feasible but often desirable; but attitudes do not necessarily change as quickly as can technologies or objective situations.

The major specific issues of North-South politics include (1) the question of how and whether development of a country can or will take place; (2) the issue of methods employed by a nation's political leadership in order to bring this development about; (3) the policies and attitudes of the "South" nation's leadership toward the developed nations, especially those who may see themselves as aid donors or useful partners in trade; (4) the responsiveness of the poor nation's leaders to economic policies suggested by the wealthy nations and, more often, the agencies that are given the task of helping with development goals. The latter would include the International Monetary Fund (IMF), the World Bank, some international aid agencies, and, very often, privately owned banks and finance sources located in New York, Tokyo, Frankfurt, London, Milan, or other centers of Western and industrialized nations' commerce; (5) the foreign policy alignments established by the poor nation's leaders; (6) observance of human rights by the poor nation's leaders; and (7) most marginally, the issue of corruption in the "South" nation. Invariably deemed as important is the attention of the client nation to the property interests of investors from the "North" who may have bought lands, built factories, or have provided other facilities. A takeover of such entities by the state or by politically well-connected local interests can invite economic, political, or—in very hard circumstances—military retaliation.

Africa and Latin America seem to have yielded more tales of these kinds of interventions in the years since 1945 than is the case in Asia. Ghana, Zaire, Guatemala, El Salvador, Nicaragua, the Dominican Republic, Jamaica, Panama, and Chile can all provide dramatic examples of U.S. or Western intervention in a very direct way into their internal affairs. Asia can, of course, provide cases, all the same. The United States responded in a mighty and determined way in Vietnam, Cambodia, and Laos in order to change the course of events in those countries. It must be admitted that this course in the years since the war probably was changed in serious and important ways, though not necessarily to the liking of U.S. policymakers or the U.S. military. The years 1950–53 saw U.S. (and, officially, U.N.) intervention in South Korea in order to defend that nation against North Korea and, as it turned out, China as well. It is also clear that such countries as Thailand and a former U.S. colony, the Philippines, have had to submit to certain pressures over the years, though these may now be in abeyance more than at any time in the recent past. Taiwan is also a state that, because of what it has perceived as acute military and other pressures from mainland China, has locked itself closely into a strong embrace with America. The early years of our postwar relations with Japan also were undoubtedly characterized by a variety of bows to U.S. insistence upon this or that policy or practice. Most controversially, it is claimed that the Central Intelligence Agency (CIA) was involved, at least peripherally, in the events that led to the great bloodbath of 1965 in Indonesia, when at least 250,000 people died in the turmoil of establishing a government that, all observers will agree, is much more to the liking of the United States.

A primary focus of the nations of the "South" in the post-World War II period has been a foreign policy built upon the premise of nonalignment with any great power. This was a policy described by leaders of India—who often considered themselves the founders of "neutralism" or nonalignment—as one that is based upon certain moral requisites of nonviolence and, more than that, a positive commitment to world peace. Nonalignment was also an attractive stance during the Cold War years, however, because it gave leverage to Third World nations who sought aid or trade advantages. They could go to the West or to the Soviet Union or other members of the Eastern bloc with requests for help, and in most circumstances they could count on some measure of aid from some source.

Nonalignment worked in different ways for different nations. India, it has been generally claimed, was nonaligned with some tilt, for geopolitical reasons, toward the Soviet Union and against the West. There was some feeling of ideological oneness with the USSR, but as time went by, there was also a belief that "the enemy of my enemy is my friend," a reflection of the fact that the Soviets and Communist China did not get on well. China had invaded Indian border lands in the Himalayas in 1962, and India keenly felt threatened by this. The United States has typically been critical of India's foreign policy and has been aligned, even by treaty obligations for a time, with Pakistan, India's greatest enemy. In Burma, by contrast, a Marxist view of the state's role in the economy has been predominant, but there has been an ambivalence toward China, actual war against Communist insurgents, and an adamant policy of isolationism and noninvolvement with the rest of the world. In Indonesia, nonalignment was extremely important until 1965; the national leader at the time, Sukarno, was in fact considered one of the international architects of such a policy. After Sukarno, however, Indonesia maintained nonalignment as an official policy though it clearly bent itself toward the West. His successor, Suharto, is currently the official head of the NAM (Non-Aligned Movement), which has a formal organization. Nonalignment can therefore even involve a significant amount of alignment. Singapore, to cite another example, is officially nonaligned, but it has offered the U.S. Pacific fleet a kind of home to replace the bases lost by the refusal of the Philippines to renew American leases there.

Some nations of the Asia-Pacific region have eschewed nonalignment altogether. Japan, the Philippines, Taiwan, Thailand, and, for a time, Pakistan, have allied themselves with the United States by formal treaty. In all events, however, it must now be said that nonalignment has lost much of its clout and even any rationale of substance since the Soviet Union and most of its Eastern bloc allies have disappeared altogether. This means that new approaches to the North must be devised in order to win support and help for the cause of development. This process is now well under way, but it comes up against the hard reality that the developed nations, all of which have experienced economic downturns in recent years, are less inclined to provide aid or trade advantages. It is therefore generally expected that it will take some time for South nations to work out policies and approaches that will help to bring development issues to the fore again; in the meantime, the major response of both Third World and developed nations to this dilemma seems to be an almost rapacious thrust into the resource bases of the Third World—mining, deforestation at a very rapid rate, the depositing of toxic materials in the Third World by the West in ways that would be unacceptable in their own countries, the sale of body parts such as kidneys and lungs, and the building of factories that will employ cheap labor, most of which are devoted to low-tech products and industries.

Labor in Asia

Labor conditions in Asia can obviously vary from country to country as well as from industry to industry. Peasants carrying out rice farming in China are not going to enjoy the perquisites of bank employees in Tokyo, and the workers involved in jute processing in Bangladesh are not likely to know the benefits or advantages of Hong Kong office workers. To a great degree, the wages and conditions of workers are determined by skill levels, the relative abundance or scarcity of labor, the kind of industry with which they are associated, the state of the economy, and other objective factors.

Within these frameworks, some opportunity can almost invariably be found for improvement of the lot of workers. Strong financial performance of the firm that employs the workers, a demand for certain skills, a steadily improving productivity of the workforce, or even reduced profit margins, among many other factors, may be the source of real or prospective labor gains.

The natural response—and one that, incidentally, is recognized in a variety of national and international human rights covenants—for workers seeking to maximize their economic position is to organize a labor union. The right to organize, it is fair to observe, is generally held to be a rational and efficacious approach for employees who want to use their collective power to negotiate, bargain, and perhaps strike for the purpose of wage gains or improved conditions.

This does not mean, unfortunately, that Asian governments or employer groups necessarily subscribe to the remedy of labor organization. Active resistance, which can be forceful and violent, is often the response. International civil liberties organizations have condemned any number of Asian governments for their failure to recognize such basic rights as organizing and the use of the strike as a bargaining tool. The International Labour Organization (ILO), a UN special agency, has also taken significant and strong positions in support of the rights of Asian workers. In recent years it has become an easier task to track labor movements and labor conditions in Asia because of better popular press coverage and because of a Hong Kong monthly, *Asian Labor Monitor,* which is specifically concerned with this area.

The support of the law or, perhaps, of a national constitution for the rights of labor does not, alas, appear to be an altogether important factor. The countries that are avowedly socialist, such as China, Vietnam, or Laos, can hardly be looked upon as protectors of workers' rights. Nor can Indonesia, for example, where a top-ranking official was recently quoted as saying that the right to strike was guaranteed by the legal system, but that the government finds such actions intolerable. The Malaysian government has hinted on occasion that it might invoke the Internal Security Act to deal with long strikes, though the rights of unions might be in better shape there than in many Asian societies.

South Korea has only legalized unions since 1987; before then, workers could be (and were) shot for organizing strikes. But repression of the labor movement continues, and a recent statement by a leader underscored this when he said that his union's major accomplishment is that it still exists. Burma's Federation of Trade Unions exists only as an exile organization. Unions do enjoy varying measures of freedom, however, and even economic power in India, Sri Lanka, Singapore, the Philippines (now that Marcos is gone), Japan, and other countries.

Generally, Asian labor unions must be considered a weak force, and the absence of a free and respected labor movement, in the many places where this is the case, tells us that the nation's political economy is immature and even backward in certain respects and that, above all, this important mark of a free society must develop if a nation is going to provide a decent political and economic life for its citizens.

Asia's International Trade Relationships

Perhaps the most major focus on Asia today, as far as Americans are concerned, is on trade. The persistent U.S. trade imbalances with Japan have received ample publicity and a strong measure of public concern in both countries in recent years. Animating much of the debate on this issue is a clear concern of the publics of both countries that this trade imbalance be rectified, because it is generally believed that this is a matter of mutual concern and mutual benefit. Complicating the issue even further, however, is the fact that the status of the total balance of payments is even worse than the trade imbalance, largely because Japanese investors and financial interests have bought huge amounts of American private and especially government debt. The persistence of this trend, fueled by a seemingly unmanageable U.S. federal budget deficit, has created fears on both sides of the Pacific because it causes vulnerabilities in the international economy.

The U.S.-Japan trade and balance of payments issues will be taken up at greater length; but it also should be noted that the United States is now faced with mounting trade deficits throughout much of the rest of Asia as well (see Table 2.2). China is owed more on the tally sheets than any nation in the region except for Japan, but there are also significant amounts of U.S. indebtedness to South Korea, Taiwan, Singapore, Hong Kong, Malaysia, and other nations. There are also serious trade disputes with India, which seems to be perennially listed by the U.S. Commerce Department as a violator of the rules and norms of international trade.

Understanding the trade issue can of course be difficult, and economists, business people, government officials, and other experts voice sharp differences over the proper policy course and, almost as often, over the facts and realities of trade. It is claimed, for example, that

Table 2.2
Current Trade Surplus/Deficit and
Total Foreign Debt of Asian Countries in Mid-1993

Country	Surplus deficit	Total foreign debt
Bangladesh	$0.31 billion	$11.9 billion
Brunei	+1.5	0
Burma	-0.66	4.8
Cambodia	+13.30	60.5
Hong Kong	+1.30	0
India	-3.60	73.5
Indonesia	-4.20	70.1
Japan	+117.70	0
Laos	-0.07	0.7
Malaysia	-1.70	15.8
Nepal	-0.28	1.7
Pakistan	-2.17	22.3
Philippines	-0.90	29.8
Singapore	-3.82	0
South Korea	-4.60	40.2
Sri Lanka	-0.36	6.1
Taiwan	-7.90	0
Thailand	-7.06	27.3
Vietnam	-0.44	15.3

Sources: Individual government data, World Bank, and various publications.

Japan, Korea, India, or some other nation is unfair in its trading policy in this or that way because it will not allow imports to compete with some domestic product or, on the other hand, this alleged violator is known to engage in "dumping," that is, the illegal and wholesale exporting of goods, often below costs of production, in order to gain marketing advantages. Classification of products can also be an issue. The American auto industry and the United Auto Workers Union (UAW) claim that minivans should be regarded as trucks and therefore subject to higher import taxes. Japanese manufacturers, eager to maintain lower tariff duties, claim that these vehicles are passenger cars. It is also the case, however, that the United States and virtually all of the players in the international trade arena have some protected industries which, for one reason or another—often a matter of political as much as economic influence—have been given some degree of immunity from the international free market. How much finger-pointing and complaining can be done, then, is sometimes a matter of conjecture. Justifications for such protection can be found, it seems; some industries are considered important to national security, or perhaps it is believed that protection of a certain kind of farm crop is important to the future of a country in some way or another. South Korea, for example, provides protection against imports for its domestic rice producers, and may feel that this is necessary as well as politically expedient.

The focus on U.S. trade with Asian nations should not obscure other important dimensions of international commerce. It is certainly true, for example, that the European Community (EC) is an important trading bloc and an economic force in the region. Oil imports from the Middle East must fit into any major equations about Asian trading patterns as well, and it is certainly the case that the poorer nations have been badly hurt by the great escalation in petroleum prices, which has taken place on the world market in the period since 1973. This was the year of the great Arab oil embargo against the West, which in turn was brought about because of a war against Israel.

Most significantly, Japan has fostered relations with other Asian nations, which are its number one set of trading interests in the world. Several factors contribute to this thinking: the proximity of Asian nations, the intertwining of Asian economies, and the fact that in recent years this trade has been immensely profitable, perhaps more profitable than with any other region of the world. In addition, the barriers against Japan in Southeast Asia and other parts of this region are relatively small and insignificant when these are compared to the restrictions established by the European Community or the United States. Japan's dealings with the United States include, to cite one significant but not untypical example, a "voluntary quota" on the number of cars that can be exported to American destinations. Such obstacles, though not unknown, are less likely to appear in the rest of Asia and when they do, they tend to be less important barriers. Recent years have seen Japan winning an increasing share of the market in nations like Malaysia, Indonesia, Singapore, and Thailand. Moreover, it is taking the offensive in opening up new markets in the area in places like Vietnam and Burma. Assessing the U.S. trade position in Asia, therefore, requires a look not only at bilateral relations with Japan or perhaps Taiwan but also at the fact that the United States and its export or potential export companies are steadily losing ground there in the markets now being established on an intraregional basis. The dynamics of intraregional trade can be illustrated by the example of Malaysia. This fast-growing economy was once more or less built around a trading position that was close to a one-third Japan, one-third EC, one-third United States arrangement; but in the past few years, there has been a significant tilt in favor of Japan.

The nations of Southeast Asia and, to a much lesser extent, South Asia, have taken up the task of promoting trade among themselves. Six countries—Brunei, Indonesia, Malaysia, the Philippines, Singapore, and Thailand—have created ASEAN, the Association of Southeast Asian Nations, which is seen as a potentially important trading bloc. Other nations of the region—Japan, China, Australia, Burma, and Vietnam—see themselves as associated members of the ASEAN bloc, but this matter has yet to be sorted out. ASEAN has a long way to go in order to establish a cohesive trading bloc, but it has already set up a secretariat—in other words, a bureaucracy—and is cooperating on matters such as airline regulations, education, and tourism programs. There are many obstacles to overcome, including territorial disputes (chiefly over the Spratly Islands, which may contain oil reserves), and, most importantly, the present patterns of trade, which are directed toward Japan, the EC, and the United States, rather than toward other ASEAN member states.

The Lack of a U.S. Response to the Asian Trade Challenge

A rather large amount of anecdotal and hard data evidence suggests that American-based companies have only on relatively rare occasions mastered the tactics and strategies of trade with Asia. Agonizingly symbolic of this fact was the disastrous trade promotion trip to Japan made in early 1992 by then-president George Bush and a retinue of company executives from a variety of industries, most notably automobile. The ungainly group of three dozen executives, along with the president and trade officials, were unable to impress Japan's Prime Minister Kiichi Miyazawa nor, apparently, anyone else with the need to develop more imports of American products. The pledges obtained to buy more American cars were small concessions indeed and, in any event, these pledges have not worked out well. The *UAW Washington Report* of February 19, 1993, quotes Honda's president, Nubuhiko Kawamoto: "We were pushed to set a big target. Now Mr. Bush is gone. The person at MITI (Japan's Ministry of International Trade and Industry) is gone. Only the figures remain." The U.S. trade deficit with Japan grew to a record $44 billion in 1992, although U.S. car producers have recently been able to console themselves with some sales to China and a bigger market share in their own country.

A persistent theme that is broadly hinted in the American business press, as well as in other forums, is that American-based companies are unwilling or reluctant or unable to enter the international arena to aggressively market their products. If this is the case, it means that another serious obstacle to competitiveness exists, one that is inherent in practices or perhaps attitudes of the business community. This is not an unlikely proposition, however, since recent decades amply afforded American firms an opportunity to conduct business and to be prosperous even if the global market was ignored. This experience stems, perhaps initially at least, from the post-World War II period, when the United States was by far the biggest and most dominant consumer and industrial market in the world.

Since a global business view now is required of companies seeking to remain viable and effective, an informal survey of businesses in the Fort Wayne, Indiana, area was set up in 1992 with the idea of testing the awareness, determination, and export-sensitivity of local firms. Obviously, this was an attempt to uncover any attributes or deficiencies, in aggregate terms, that might indicate the kinds of abilities local companies might have in pursuing international business.

The focus, then, was on exports. Most decidedly, there was not even a hint of focus on international investment that might result in plant relocations or job losses, which we consider very undesirable. The emphasis, indeed, was on enhancing job prospects in the region through the possible promotion of awareness of export sales. Undergirding this task was the fairly certain assumption that the Fort Wayne area, with its many factories and other kinds of businesses, would be producing goods that would be attractive to consumers or other buyers abroad. We therefore utilized the *Harris Guide* to Indiana business, which provided the names of more than four hundred firms in the area. Many of the companies listed in this guide—retail establishments, for example—could not be realistically expected to be interested in exports. Manufacturing concerns, on the other hand, might be prospective or actual exporters. We were able to find twenty-three companies listed that seemed to be promising prospects for our survey because of the kinds of products they offered.

Surveying the world in late 1992, we came up with the interesting observation that the only region of the world currently involved with economic growth—and dynamic growth at that—is Southeast Asia. This leads to the hypothesis that a company that is aware of export opportunities will know not only that the rest of the world is in a slow-growth or recessionary mode, but also that some real opportunities may be available in the only part of the world still experiencing rapid growth.

Unfortunately, there are some stereotypical images of Asia that are still at work, dated as these may be. Asian countries are still considered, by people who are ill-informed about the world, as backward, poor, undeveloped, and lacking in much hope of growth or prosperity. Add to this some confusions about geography and one can see that any number of problems quickly emerge; so it was not surprising to us that in conducting this survey, we were asked where Southeast Asia is, or what it is ("do you mean Japan?"), or, at other times, we were met with some other indicator of a lack of awareness.

Ten of the twenty-three firms surveyed said that they do some business in Southeast Asia. This included four magnet wire firms (a major product of the Fort Wayne area)—Rea, Phelps Dodge, Essex, and General Electric—and such firms as Lincoln National Corporation (insurance), Fort Wayne Wire Dye, and Dana Corporation (automobile parts and heavy equipment). A couple of these firms admitted they only "do a little bit" of business in that part of the world. Significantly, some manufacturers of rather popular consumer products—sophisticated toys, for example—indicated that they do no business in the region and have no plans to do so. One firm, which has no export business of any kind, stated that it was interested in opening up some export business in Eastern Europe or Russia in another five years or so; which made us ask, why not try to make some money *now* in the world's hottest market?

Only one firm in the sample, Midland Corporation, carried out a significant amount of business in Southeast Asia. This company sells cellular phones in the region, and has been marketing them there for the past fifteen years. "We recognize the market and its potential," said Leonard Goldstein, the president of Midland. "We have invested in an office and a warehouse in Singapore and it has been good for us. It is a unique kind of operation, but it is also a unique profits opportunity." But Goldstein and Midland represent the great exception in this survey, both in terms of international awareness and export profitability.

A conclusion we seemed unable to avoid after conducting the interviews is that many American-based companies seem content with simply holding their present market share of the business in which they are involved; this is probably a quite deliberate strategy, given the tough business climate they must face today, but it is also an inherently defensive strategy. It is not unusual for companies devoted to this approach to be run over by a dynamic foreign-based (perhaps Japanese) rival. In the meantime, the World Economic Forum has reported that the United States has declined as a trading nation in the world from second to fifth place, and this decline occurred in just a single year, 1991. The U.S. position improved thereafter, but much of this gain was due to the decline of the dollar against other major currencies.

American businesses are not entirely at fault in this situation. Many firms—producers of flat glass, rice, tobacco, and even automobiles and their components—can work hard to develop Asian markets and still find, to their dismay, that they are shut out by policies that amount to protectionism. Japan is not the only example of this because many Asian countries have taken their cues from Japan's apparent success. This means they seek to export to the United States and the world while they close off domestic markets.

A final note should be made about the problem of Americans' perceptions and expectations about their economy. It seems clear that the United States enjoyed a dominant position in the world economy from 1945 well into the 1970s, and this position was in some ways almost immune to the ebbs and flows of the rest of the world. Globalization of the American economy, a long-lasting and more natural phenomenon than the dominance of earlier years, is seen by many people in threatening terms. But an appreciation of the nation's position and of the challenges faced is more likely to lead to rational and competitive responses than fear or a longing for the past.

Further Reading

Bosworth, Barry. *Saving and Investment in a Global Economy*. Washington, D.C.: Brookings Institution, 1993. Makes the case that the trade difficulties and balance of payments problems of the United States are caused by domestic failures, such as the big federal budget deficit and the low savings rate, rather than any particular practices of foreign governments.

Frieden, Jeffrey A., and David A. Lake, eds. *International Political Economy: Perspectives on Global Power and Wealth*. New York: St. Martin's Press, 1991. Introductory readers can provide a student with some grounding in this subject; the essays, as is always the case with books of this type, are uneven, but those dealing with Asia are of some value.

Lewis, W. Arthur. "Economic Development with Unlimited Supplies of Labour." *Manchester School* 22 (1954): 139–91. Landmark analysis of development economics, which serves as one of the organizing principles of this book.

Porter, Michael. *The Competitive Advantage of Nations.* New York: Free Press, 1990. Strongly heralded and lightly condemned from time to time, Porter takes a comprehensive approach to this time-honored question. Lengthy but very informative.

Prestowitz, Claude V., Jr. *Trading Places: How We Are Giving Our Future to Japan and How to Reclaim It.* New York: Basic Books, 1988. Controversial examination of bilateral trade issues written by a former Bush administration trade official accused of Japan-bashing.

Schneider, Harold K. *Economic Man: The Anthropology of Economics.* New York: Free Press, 1974. Makes the case against alleged social science condemnation of economic man and calls for rigor in analysis of these interdisciplinary complexities.

Schumacher, E. F. *Small Is Beautiful: Economics As If People Mattered.* New York: Harper and Row, 1973. Many critics would argue that this work is both irrelevant and out of date; but Schumacher's worldwide following on his views of development economics will at least make reading him a thought-provoking exercise.

Todaro, Michael P. *Economic Development in the Third World.* 4th ed. New York: Longman, 1989. A text with a comprehensive approach to North-South issues.

Tyson, Laura D'Andrea. *Who's Bashing Whom? Trade Conflict in High-Technology Industries.* Washington, D.C.: Institute for International Education, 1992. This is of more than passing interest since Tyson is the chair of President Bill Clinton's Council of Economic Advisers. A firmer stance toward Japan and other nations on trade is suggested through an approach she calls "cautious activism."

Chapter 3

Security and Human Rights Issues

Security Problems of the Asia-Pacific Region

The Middle East and, more recently, Eastern Europe, where ethnic and religious divisions have boiled over, are the major centers of attention in the world when the world's security problems are reviewed. War and the threat of war seem almost endemic in those regions. Latin America and Africa certainly have their share of such problems as well. And disasters that imply political instability and security problems, such as mass starvation in some African nations, also receive attention, as they should.

Asia seems relatively quiet to anyone who observes the world through the lens of the evening news broadcast. Most of the news from Asia concerns economic growth, trade disputes with the United States and other Western nations, and various matters such as what happens to Hong Kong after 1997 when China is to take it over by treaty arrangement, or whether the two Koreas are thinking about talking to each other again or have shut off their dialogues. There are also sundry matters pertaining to art, religion, tourism, stock markets, or fashion, all of which have received increasing attention in the West in recent years. And even when security topics do appear in the papers or on television, they seem to be concerned with policy issues such as Philippine base closings, Japanese defense budgets, or the role of Thailand's military leaders. None of these subjects are likely to have a sensational impact.

Crisis news does appear, of course, even though it appears only now and then. India's religious riots, Pakistan's endemic civil conflicts, Cambodia's tense brink-of-civil war negotiations and problems, the violent repressions of student demonstrators in China and Burma, the systematic destruction of society and culture in Tibet, strife in Sri Lanka and Kashmir, and nuclear arms buildups by China, India, and Pakistan are all topics or potential topics for news analysts from any media. Most importantly, Asia is presently confronted with an arms race that exposes some of the many tensions which may not be that obvious to the casual observer of the scene but lie just below the surface.

The U.S. Role in Asia

The United States is the major player in the matter of Asian regional security. It is the mightiest power that deploys military personnel and weaponry in the region, and its presence is considered vital by many of these nations—Taiwan, South Korea, Thailand, and most certainly Japan, to cite some of the more obvious examples. The United States is in fact committed by treaties, either bilateral or regional, to the defense of these nations. It seems equally clear, however, that many nations in the area who are in no way formally committed to any obligations with the United States, and to whom America has no formal commitment either, are nevertheless counting on the presence of the United States either as a security factor or perhaps as a power balancer. A list of such dependent nations would be very long indeed, but it is safe to say that it includes Indonesia, Malaysia, and Singapore; and even though they have denied the United States the right to maintain bases there anymore, the Philippines surely wants to see a continued U.S. presence in the Western Pacific.

The Vietnam War, almost anyone would agree, was the traumatizing event for the United States in recent Asian history. It was surely one of the most disastrous military and diplomatic episodes ever to occur in the two centuries of America's experience as a nation. The heavy loss of life and the waste of time and resources remain haunting factors to Asian experts and specialists, the foreign policy-defense establishment, and the American public. The humiliating and debilitating scenes of the final American retreat—the helicopters lifting people off the roof of the American Embassy in Saigon—has seemed to indelibly remain with many Americans since those ignominious days of 1975.

However one may feel about the Vietnam War—and there can be no doubt that this is a matter that continues to divide American society in a variety of ways—cannot necessarily help any of us in answering the obvious and logical next question: what do we do now?

It makes sense, as a starting point, to say that the United States needs a coordinated and general policy position in the Asia-Pacific region. A broad set of policy guidelines for this area would include complementary diplomatic, economic, and military positions. These would have to be flexible enough to deal with changes, foreseen or unforeseen; but they should be stable and thoughtful to the point that they could serve as a reference guide to policy preferences and actions.

Such an approach would not be altogether new. Such presidents as Theodore Roosevelt, Harry S. Truman, Lyndon B. Johnson, and Richard M. Nixon have set up general policy doctrines for the Asia-Pacific region. These had varying degrees of success and failure, though all of them saw the United States as a major power—and major player—in Asia. The shortcomings of Theodore Roosevelt are usually considered a set of problems of his era—ethnocentrism, visions of grandeur, and a great overestimation of exactly what the United States could do in the region. Truman was criticized for not drawing the American line in a forward enough position, which, it is claimed, led to adventurism by North Korea and China in the 1950–53 Korean War. Johnson and Nixon are both seen by many observers as men afflicted with some of the same problems that affected Theodore Roosevelt; Johnson believed in the false hope that the Vietnam War could be won, and the Nixon Doctrine was developed in the false hope that some American position in Vietnam could be salvaged. Both were wrong.

A new and comprehensive policy position for the United States in Asia will require an awareness of today's commercial and defense realities. A more modest appreciation of U.S. power in the region seems to be called for, one in which the nation can play a role tied to coordination rather than dominance. This is in keeping with the downscaling of the U.S. defense role now being carried out on a worldwide basis and with the relatively new, but nonetheless real, economic power of Japan, China, and other Asian nations. There is some good evidence that the Clinton administration understands this set of factors; its strong sponsorship of APEC, the Asian Pacific Economic Cooperation organization, which is headquartered in Singapore, has been a major new policy thrust.

Potential Flashpoints

Another major question to ask when security problems and issues are broached is, who fears whom? and why? And in the Asia-Pacific region, the potential for conflict is evident in a number of possible and, unfortunately, quite plausible scenarios.

Perhaps the greatest threat in the region is suggested by the March 1993 announcement of the government of North Korea that it was no longer committed to the cause of nuclear nonproliferation. It has since indicated to the UN's International Atomic Energy Agency that it may not go ahead with planned nuclear armament programs; but this nation no longer considers itself bound to refrain from the development of nuclear materials and weaponry. It has even renounced the armistice it signed when the Korean War ended in 1953. This can only be bad news for South Korea, Japan, and other nearby countries. North Korea's inability, or perhaps we should call it failure, to join the prosperity parade found so often and obviously in Asia may be one of the frustrations motivating this hostile behavior; but whatever the cause or motive, North Korea's renunciation of its commitments, coupled with its obvious determination to develop nuclear capability, is a worrying and destabilizing influence.

The continued confrontations of India and Pakistan, mostly over the issue of the future of the states of Jammu and Kashmir, are fraught with danger. Both of these major Asian powers possess nuclear arms and, in all probability, the means to deliver them. This is why border incidents or sectarian organizing in the Kashmir area are so potentially lethal. The two sides to this dispute harbor feelings that go all the way back to the partition of India into two entities by the British colonial rulers in 1947, and these are exacerbated by insistence upon one religious preference, either Hindu or Muslim, over the other. The Indo-Pakistan border region also is the home of the Punjab, a state that stretches across both countries and is the stronghold of the Sikhs, still another religious minority with a distinct set of premises about political as well as spiritual life. Sikh and anti-Sikh violence has been costly and tragic since the early 1980s.

The ever-present threat of a return to civil war in Cambodia, though it is not characterized by a threat of nuclear weaponry, brings nightmares to the people of the nation, to people of the Southeast Asia region, and to anyone who is aware of the Holocaust-like slaughter of millions by the Khmer Rouge army and its leader, Pol Pot, in the 1970s. This carnage was one of the most costly, in terms of the scale of lives lost, ever to occur in the history of Asia. A return to such violence would be a very great tragedy for Cambodia, for the region, and for the world. Anyone aware of this threat tends to hang on the news from Cambodia, which always seems to be emphasizing the great delicacy of putting together a ruling coalition that will somehow insure that there will be no return to this unfortunate country's apparently tremendous capacity for violence. Grim forebodings, therefore, accompanied the withdrawal of the Khmer Rouge from the capital city, Phnom Penh, in early 1993; and though it was later invited to join a coalition with a newly elected government, it has remained isolated, hostile, and violent.

These three locales—the front lines separating the two Koreas, the Indo-Pakistan border, and Cambodia—are probably areas of greatest potential for violence and for a serious and very troubling impact upon the rest of the world.

Substantial military postures have been taken by a number of Asian nations in recent years. Five of these powers—China, India, Japan, Indonesia, and Pakistan—have a capacity for causing major trouble in the Asia-Pacific area if they should choose such a course.

The Asian arms race extends to smaller powers as well. Malaysia has increased defense spending by 125 percent since 1987, Singapore by more than 100 percent, Thailand by as much as 70 percent, and the Philippines by almost 50 percent. Complicating this scene is the new-found sharpness of competition in the international arms industry. American defense contractors are looking almost anywhere for a market as a result of the cuts enforced by the Clinton administration and, earlier, by the Bush administration. Russia, in need of business of any kind, is using its rather sophisticated arms industry as a means of raising hard currency and food imports. Other suppliers—Britain, France, Germany, and China are good examples—are making their bids as well.

The Russians have a price advantage because of deep discounts they have made, and so far the evidence shows that this is appreciated. Both Malaysia and Thailand, which have never made such deals in the past, are currently considering major purchases of Russian aircraft and weapons.

Whether this ambitiously pursued buildup of forces throughout Asia will result in confrontations or calamities is an open question. Opponents of the Cold War arms race claimed that building and setting weapons systems in place would eventually bring about their use. They were wrong about nuclear weapons (at least so far, but we are not entirely out of the woods yet), but they were often right about conventional weapons systems.

More optimistic observers point out that the surge of arms purchases in Asia is undoubtedly tied to the many new-found national arenas of prosperity that are found there. The heaviest purchasers in recent years, such as China, Japan, Singapore, Malaysia, and Thailand, are nations whose economies can accommodate large increases in defense spending. Is such an assertion too simplistic? We cannot be sure, but a large arms cache could at least encourage future governments who have more adventurous leaders. It is therefore difficult to take much comfort from the expansion of a military presence in the region. Americans, however, can hardly carp about such developments as long as their country continues to be a major arms supplier to Asian nations.

Human Rights in Asian Societies

Some concessions must be made to cultural differences when human rights matters are considered. Many Asians and Asian observers, Lucian W. Pye among them, insist that privacy rights, to cite one example, are perceived somewhat differently in Asian societies. There is a feeling that seems to question why privacy is needed and even may go so far as to inquire about what it is that one might be doing that might require the exercise of this right. It is also true that police powers seem greater in most Asian countries than we may regard as comfortable from a Western point of view. Japan, which by most any standard must be considered a democracy, nonetheless gives its police the power to hold a suspect for ten hours before a formal criminal charge is required. And most countries in the region look upon humiliation as a major, perhaps even dire, form of punishment to an extent perhaps not appreciated in the United States or Europe.

Regardless of such contrasts, it is generally held by the international community that certain standards must be met by any country that wishes to have itself included within the family of respected nations. Torture, slavery or bondage, crackdowns on political dissent or media freedom, a widespread use of military forces to carry out what most of the world might regard as civilian functions, phony elections, or gross inequalities in treatment by the authorities are some of the practices that appear to be universally condemned and that fall short of observance of common standards of decency.

A major problem in Asia, and one that is met throughout the world, is the imposition of one set of national or cultural values at the expense of another. At the moment, for example, China is continuing to carry out its systematic eradication of Tibetan culture and norms. Minority groups or cultures are faced with persistent problems as well, in such countries as India, Pakistan, Indonesia, Burma, Thailand, and even modern Malaysia and Singapore. Not all of these cases are of the same level of seriousness, of course; the pressures, for example, against the Malay minority in Singapore are hardly of the same kind faced by Tibetans or by the Karens in Burma.

Pressures in support of human rights have now become an important and worldwide phenomenon. The United Nations and its various subunits pass resolutions or even establish embargoes against regimes that fail to recognize this basic set of human needs. Private groups like Amnesty International employ letter-writing campaigns that are sometimes successful. And groups such as Asia Watch publish studies that demonstrate the problems of political prisoners or of establishing the right to dissent from official lines set by authoritarian or totalitarian governments.

The Clinton administration has given a new emphasis to the role of the assistant secretary of state for human rights, an emphasis unknown during the 1980s. It has called for attention to human rights issues in various international forums and it has tied trade issues to human rights concerns in the cases of nations like Indonesia, Burma, India, and China. This means that compliance with human rights standards or at least some movement toward compliance is expected if these countries are to continue to enjoy "most favored nation" status. MFN status confers the benefit of lower trade barriers in the United States. Although President Clinton is clearly reluctant to remove such a benefit—which, after all, hurts our own trade prospects—the threat is nevertheless real for noncomplying regimes. This threat became somewhat muted during 1994, all the same, as the United States continued to extend MFN status to such countries as China and Indonesia.

China is singled out more than any country in the region for its human rights abuses. This is because its treatment of some of its citizens falls far short of the standards generally expected by the world in the 1990s. Undoubtedly this is also because China is the biggest and most populous nation in the region (most populous in the world, in fact) and because the United States and other Western nations have never liked Communist governments. China has fostered cultural and physical genocide in Tibet. The government crushed the freedom movement in 1989 with violent repression of students and other protesters in Tiananmen Square in Beijing. Prison conditions in the country are often well below the norms expected for adequate food and other necessities of life, and inhumane treatment has been exposed and documented. Press freedom is unknown. Rights of political expression and association are not observed. And, most unfortunately, criminal trials are set up for the purpose of sentencing the person accused rather than determining the question of guilt or innocence. The liberalizations that have occurred in recent years in the economic sphere of life in the South and in coastal areas do not appear to have affected the political, legal, or perhaps even the human rights consciousness of the nation.

Cambodia is also an arena of gross government misrule. The Vietnam War, which greatly affected this nation once it was entangled by President Richard Nixon's invasion decision of 1970, brought in its wake a terrible instability that broke out into civil war. The Communist forces known as the Khmer Rouge, led by the tyrannical and murderous Pol Pot, slaughtered as many as one million citizens of the country in a bloodbath that ranks among one of the most abominable cases of genocide in history. These same forces could presumably be unleashed anew against a government coalition that is being held together by the most fragile of feelings and factors.

Burma is another of the great abusers of human rights. From 1962 to 1988, it was ruled by Ne Win, who imposed an insular view of the world and retarded the nation's seemingly natural tendency toward economic growth, prosperity, and ample food production. Things were already bad enough, then, when the military took over the state in 1988. Although apparently free and fair elections were held in 1990, elections in which the government lost more than 80 percent of the vote to the democracy movement, the military imposed its rule in place of the people's mandate. Leaders of the democratic forces, including Nobel Peace Prize winner Aung San Suu Kyi, were repressed by being imprisoned, killed, placed under house arrest, or forced to flee the country. Rangoon University was closed and student protesters were shot or jailed. And despite strongly generated international pressures against the regime, including severe criticism from the UN and a variety of respected figures ranging from the Dalai Lama of Tibet to Bishop Tutu of South Africa, political freedom appears far away for the Burmese people. Aung San Suu Kyi remains under house arrest and is separated from her English husband, who has been permitted only one short visit. In addition, it is quite clear that this government continues to follow a long-established pattern of unequal treatment for the nation's various minority groups, such as the Karens or the Shans, and it even carries out wars against these peoples that have been going on for decades.

While China, Cambodia, and Burma may be the worst cases, there are civil liberties problems in virtually every country in Asia. India and Pakistan have both permitted conditions of bonded servitude in which children and sometimes adults work for an employer under a debt contract for little or no pay and certainly no benefits. Sometimes the people living in bondage are not even supplied with adequate nutritional needs. Under few circumstances do such individuals find that their indebtedness ever gets paid off so that they can start living their own lives. South Korea and Taiwan have both moved toward democracy in fits and starts in recent years, but there are still many political rights problems for dissenters. Until recently, the Korean government suppressed labor unions, student organizations, and other kinds of social movements.

The colonial heritage of vast portions of Asia must also be considered a factor contributing to human rights abuses. This is a brutal historical legacy for any nation to bear, and on this general proposition it seems to matter very little whether the power in question was British, French, Dutch, or whatever. From an institutional standpoint, it seems clear, for example, that the heavy reliance upon bureaucracy and its disposition to sometimes rule almost by fiat is one of the British "contributions" to India and Pakistan. Many of the legal instruments of oppression that were developed to control the colonial populace remain available to the rulers of now-independent countries. A prime example is the Internal Security Act, a British legacy found in India, Malaysia, Singapore, and other countries ruled from Westminster. The Internal Security Act provides broad discretionary and emergency powers of the sort one might expect to find in a colony faced with occasional nationalist discontents. Suspension of habeas corpus rights, jailing of suspects without formal charges being made, the closing down of newspapers or other media, the removal of public officials from their posts, whether these be elective or appointive, and even the imposition of martial law are all possible under this extremely broad mandate. The invoking of the powers of the Internal Security Act is often simply allowed to proceed indefinitely, even when it is clear that an "emergency" period has passed. This makes it possible for a government to renew these powers in an expeditious way if this is deemed necessary. It should also not be forgotten that the United States ruled the Philippines from 1898 to 1946, and the results of that experience have often been extended; an example is the ill-fated Marcos regime, which was both corrupt and dismissive of human rights claims.

The recent worldwide surge of democratic forces has unquestionably had a salutary impact on the cause of human rights in Asia. The pressures of public opinion faced by a regime, both internally and internationally, are probably greater now than at any time in the recent past. The trend toward increasingly democratic systems in Asia—in South Korea, Taiwan, Thailand, the Philippines, and, increasingly, in Malaysia, has established better environments for the assertion and maintenance of human rights. And the consistent attachments to democracy seen in Japan, India, Sri Lanka, Bangladesh and other states can also be said to aid this cause.

There is a long way to go and a great deal to be done if human rights are to become firmly established in Asia, however, because commitments to these freedoms are often tenuous and subject to a variety of political currents that are not necessarily democratic. Surely, for example, the argument that a flowering of economic growth or of privatized and capitalistic institutions will lead to democracy remains unproved if not unconvincing.

The Right of Migration and Political Reactions to It

Asian migrations are a constant of Asian history. The peoples of Malaysia, for example, have been affected by a variety of patterns originating in India, Sri Lanka, China, the Indonesian islands of Sumatra and Sulawesi, and other places. Burmese people, as well as some of the minority groups within Burma, are said to be related to Tibetans, although the evidence for this has been challenged in recent years. Taiwan has an indigenous minority group that originated in the Pacific islands; and India has been the scene of vast migrations of people, some of them temporary and some permanent.

The movements of people across the face of Asia and, sometimes, out of Asia altogether, should therefore be appreciated in terms of a long-range perspective; and any analysis of such movements should bear in mind the natural tendency of people wanting to improve their lot in various ways. Foremost among these ways is simply looking for a better place to live, one that offers more opportunities than people have known in their former circumstances. Today migrations seem to be a topic in the media of virtually every nation. Unfortunately, this issue seems to be rarely discussed in unemotional or analytical terms. It seems to be framed, at best, in concerns about the loss of jobs and health standards and increases in government costs such as welfare

Table 3.1
National Signatures on Human Rights Covenants, June 1991

	1	2	3	4	5	6
Bangladesh						
Brunei						
Burma			x		x	
Cambodia						
China			x			x
Hong Kong						
India	x	x	x	x	x	
Indonesia					x	
Japan	x	x			x	
Laos			x	x	x	
Malaysia						
Nepal			x		x	
Pakistan			x		x	
Philippines	x	x	x	x	x	x
Singapore						
South Korea	x	x	x		x	
Sri Lanka	x	x	x			
Taiwan						
Thailand					x	
Vietnam	x	x	x	x		

Source: *Constitutional Systems in Late Twentieth-Century Asia,* Lawrence W. Beer, ed., (Seattle: University of Washington Press, 1992), pp. 41–42

1 = International Covenant on Economic, Social, and Cultural Rights
2 = International Covenant on Civil and Political Rights
3 = Convention on the Prevention and Punishment of the Crime of Genocide
4 = Convention on the Non-Applicability of Statutory Limitations to War Crimes and Crimes against Humanity
5 = Convention on the Political Rights of Women
6 = Convention against Torture and Other Cruel, Inhuman, or Degrading Treatment or Punishment

and education. And it is cast, at its worst, in ethnocentric or racist alarms supposedly concerned with national integrity, culture, language, or heritage.

Immigration, whether it is legal or illegal, is a perennial political and economic agenda item. If acute labor shortages exist, the task of filling positions with immigrants appears unremarkable and natural. This has been true at times in U.S. history and also in Western Europe in the earlier years following World War II. If, however, job markets are relatively tight, as they are now in Europe and North America, objections can be expected; and this is the case today in Germany, Italy, France, Britain, Spain, the United States, Canada, and many other countries. Recent events in these countries have been ugly and violent, and the response of governments has generally been to limit, tighten, or abolish the chances of immigrants.

Migration must also be seen, however, as a human rights concern. More than twenty years ago a writer on philosophy and ethics concluded that a right of mobility, a right of peoples to move peacefully across the face of the earth, is a right most of us simply "are not ready for." Recognition that migration is often a solution for the problems of people has been around since the beginning of time and it can be expected to persist into the future in spite of laws, measures, and programs taken by governments to thwart such movement. There is strong evidence, in fact, that a right of mobility is an internationally recognized human right. It is specified in one form or another in six national constitutions, from Mexico to Ghana to Japan, and it is set out in the UN Universal Declaration of Human Rights. It can even be found in the Magna Carta of 1215.

The patterns occurring within Asia today are perhaps precursors of political trouble in the countries which are the targets of migrants, but it should also be borne in mind that all, or nearly all, economic data shows a consistent association between in-migration and economic growth. This is because, in its own way, migration is a response of a felt need for people to fill jobs or meet other economic needs of a nation. If migrants or potential migrants feel that little or no opportunity exists in the purported land of promise, their preference will be to stay home.

What are these patterns? It is safe to say that they are many and varied, and it should also be pointed out that illegal immigration necessarily involves guesswork. Japan is clearly a target of migrants today, however, because it offers work opportunities that are better than those that are available in India, Pakistan, Burma, China, or perhaps even Korea. Singapore and Malaysia attract Indonesians from the south and a smaller but significant number of Thais and others from the north. And India, poor as it may be, seems to attract a large number of illegal immigrants from such nearby countries as Pakistan, Bangladesh, Nepal, and Bhutan.

Some migrations are forced. Chinese, Indians, Pakistanis, Cambodians, Vietnamese, the minority groups of Burma, and many other peoples have known—and continue to know—the horrors of forced migration in this century. A significant development today is that citizens of Communist or formerly Communist countries, who were never allowed to migrate by their governments, are now free to go elsewhere; and this has had a burgeoning effect upon migrant numbers. Some of the stories are heartbreaking; we read of refugees from Cambodia sitting in destitute camps in Thailand or of desperate "boat people" from Vietnam who try, often unsuccessfully, to find their way to the shores of Hong Kong, Malaysia, or Thailand. They are often returned to their country or, it is alleged, their boats are pulled out to sea and the people are set adrift. The repressive Burmese government offers Thai citizens $200 for each citizen of their country who is brought to them who is on a "wanted" list of political offenders.

The issue of immigration has had, and will continue to have, an important effect upon cultural and even governmental relations within Asia; but it is also very clear that this is happening with the United States and Canada as well. Half of the ten nations that are the greatest sources of migration into the United States are Asian: the Philippines, Vietnam, China, India, and Korea.

The years 1993 and 1994 have seen new concerns arise in the United States about illegal immigration from Asia. Chinese ships, often loaded beyond capacity with hopefuls seeking a new life, have sunk or have come under the jurisdiction of immigration authorities. In many instances, these are people who have paid smugglers as much as $30,000 to get them to America. It is undoubtedly the case that such incidents build upon anti-immigration sentiments, which have always been fairly strong in any event. These may take many forms in reaction to what is seen as a threat: demands for immigration curbs, stronger border patrol or immigration service personnel numbers or enforcement mechanisms, "English only" demands for school instruction language or even signs on commercial establishments, and, of course, violence.

The migration issue contains ironies. It is often the case that people who espouse the free market as the answer for U.S. economic concerns, such as Pat Buchanan or Jesse Helms, oppose an internationally free labor market. It is fine for business firms to migrate to find the lowest wages possible, but it is not all right for workers to try to find the best deal they can make if this requires movement. And not all of the hypocrisy is on the political right: many well-meaning and humanitarian types favor helping poor nations but do not want the citizens of those countries to come to our shores where they supposedly undermine labor markets.

The potential posed for troubling diplomatic relationships between the United States and any of the countries which are the homes of migrants—India, South Korea, the Philippines, or others—is very great, and this is simply because immigration laws are measured by such countries in terms of attitudes toward their peoples.

It is obvious that we must begin to deal with this grave and severe international problem, but we must do this intelligently. International organizations and forums are better arenas in which to air these matters than (for example) national or regional newspapers or talk shows. Much of the rationality required and desired will be lost when a migration issue reaches this level of public discernment. It is true that migration matters are taken up in a variety of UN and international publications and in at least one social science journal exclusively devoted to them, but the general publics of the United States and other nations have virtually no access to these. It therefore appears to be a good idea to establish an international conference devoted to human migration and to find solutions for the concerns and problems allied with it.

A special international conference devoted to these problems would be able to help us all to understand the advantages as well as the disadvantages wrought by migrations, the economic benefits as well as the downside, and the fact that these are related to a well-established human right of mobility. Most importantly, it might publicize the dangers of anti-immigration pressures and laws, such as racism and ethnocentrism and the repressive types of measures, such as identification card systems, which are used to prevent migration but which also pose other significant civil liberties problems.

The need for a conference, or some other means of stirring a broad public interest, is promoted by the fact that the United States undertook a broad review of its immigration laws in 1994; the results of this review could be bad for the causes of tolerance, the right of mobility, and relationships of the United States with Asian nations.

A Century of Asian Assertiveness

The new realities of Asia include an evolutionary democratization, an ongoing buildup of military power (especially in China, India, Pakistan, and Japan), dynamic though hardly universal economic growth, simultaneous influences of modernization and a return to basic religious and political values, strengthened regional links, and a broadening global perspective. Probably the greatest sign of the new Asia, as far as the rest of the world is concerned, however, is the trade challenge posed by Japan, the new "tigers," and the emerging nations who hope to soon join this select circle.

It is misleading, however, to think that Asian assertiveness is a new phenomenon. While it is true that popular and semipopular treatments of Asia refer to the twenty-first century as "the Pacific century" or whatever, a more accurate assessment will show that our century has been one of sustained Asian insistence upon the right to its own future.

The seeds of this assertiveness are found at the very beginning of the century. Perhaps the signal event was the victory of the Japanese in their 1904–5 war with Russia, which was the first occasion of outright defeat of a Western-originated attempt to impose its powers over an Asian nation. The fact that Japan went on to become an imperial force itself, and with disastrous results, does not alter the significance of their victory over the Russians. Much of the historical literature on twentieth-century Asia points to this victory as a source of pride and inspiration for virtually all Asian peoples, not only the Japanese. In the same era, the people of China were demanding an end to concessions to colonial powers such as Britain, France, and the United States, and in 1900 (and slightly before this date as well), the Boxer Rebellion was launched as a protest against a Chinese regime seen to be far too indebted to Western forces and their demands for control of the economic lives of the populace. Though the Boxer Rebellion failed and resulted in an even more supine role for China in the short run, its breadth and fervor were omens of things to come not only in China, but throughout the continent.

It is obvious that the independence movements of many nations also fit within this pattern of Asian insistence upon self-rule and control of their own national economies. The Indian Congress was well organized and moving toward its goal of self-rule by the 1920s even though Britain did not leave the subcontinent until 1947. Similarly, the victories for the cause of independence in Indonesia, Burma, the Philippines, Vietnam, and other nations can be seen as major forces that have shaped contemporary Asia.

However we may dislike it, it can be argued that Japan's militarism and its goal of a "coprosperity sphere" is also a major historical surge in the cause of Asian assertiveness and, whether one cares to admit it, the role of Communist movements and governments in China, Vietnam, North Korea, and other nations must be seen as an important effect of the belief of Asian rulers and peoples in finding their own political destinies.

It clearly is the case, then, that awakening to the new realities of Asia must involve an awareness of processes that have been occurring for a long period of time and that, for all intents and purposes, are still going on.

Further Reading

Amnesty International. *Annual Report 1993*. London: Amnesty International, 1993. This well-respected human rights organization issues a report annually which describes nonobservances on a country-to-country basis; virtually all of the countries that are the subjects of this book, unfortunately, are found in these reports.

Bonner, Raymond. *Waltzing with a Dictator: The Marcoses and the Making of American Policy*. New York: Vintage Books, 1987. Factual description by a provocative journalist. This work shows the interdependence of foreign policy and human rights issues in Asia.

Bradnock, Robert W. *India's Foreign Policy Since 1971*. London: Royal Institute of International Affairs, 1990. One of the many sources that describes the approach toward security issues taken by non-aligned Asian nations; a brief treatment.

Bruszynski, Leszek. *SEATO: The Failure of an Alliance Strategy*. Singapore: Singapore University Press, 1983. Sets out the reasons for the U.S. policy failures in Asia that led to the dissolution of the Southeast Asia Treaty Organization, one of the linchpins of Cold War strategy in the area.

David, Steven R. "Why the Third World Still Matters." *International Security* 17 (Winter 1992/1993): 127–59. Argues for increased attention to Third World nations in the post-Cold War era because it is believed that these are now often capable of threatening vital interests of the United States.

Gill, R. Bates. *Chinese Arms Transfers: Purposes, Patterns and Prospects in the New World Order*. Westport, Conn.: Praeger, 1992. Detailed description and analysis of Chinese arms transfer policies and their destabilizing effects upon Asia and the Middle East.

Klare, Michael T. "The Next Great Arms Race." *Foreign Affairs* 72 (Summer 1993): 136–52. Squarely faces the threat posed by the arms race in Asia and suggests policy responses including a continued U.S. presence in the area.

Lawyers Committee for Human Rights. *Malaysia: Attack on the Judiciary.* New York: Lawyers Committee for Human Rights, 1990. Interesting and brief case study of human rights and separation of powers controversy in a developing Asian nation.

The Pentagon Papers (as published by the *New York Times*). New York: Bantam, 1971. With many sources available on the reasons for the U.S. debacle in Vietnam, it might be best to start with this official set of documents and to analyze them from a current historical perspective.

Puckett, Robert H., ed. *The United States and Northeast Asia.* Chicago: Nelson-Hall, 1993. A set of articles which deal, for the most part, with security problems affecting the policies of Japan, China, and South Korea as well as the United States.

Chapter 4

Japan: Powerhouse of Asia—
and of the World

Political reform remains our top priority.
> Prime Minister Morihiro Hosokawa, quoted in the *Los Angeles Times,* August 1, 1993

Threats aren't going to work with Japan anymore.
> Prime Minister Kiichi Miyazawa, combined wire services dispatch of April 19, 1993

Visitors had seldom appeared in their land. That is why a blend of fear and curiosity greeted Commodore Matthew Perry and his crews as their three ships entered the harbor at Edo, now Tokyo, in 1853. The Americans surveyed the harbor and made note of the various water depths, shoreline features, and guides to navigation. The commodore told his hosts that he would return in a year; and he did, this time with many more ships, all of which were outfitted with heavy guns capable of leveling the imperial capital city. For better or worse, Japan would never be the same again. This event, the great "opening" of Japan by Perry, meant an end of centuries of virtual isolation and the beginning of commercial, diplomatic, and many other kinds of associations with Americans, other Asians, and the peoples and nations of the world. How this "opening up" actually occurred is quite often left out of treatments of U.S.-Japan relations, but it should not be seen as something to which the Japanese gave their voluntary assent.

The importance of Japan in the world's political economy is now well established. This is understood by any casual observer of current events, by political and corporate leaders in America and in all other nations, and, most certainly, by the world's financial press.

A precise assessment of this importance, however, is another matter. Hyperbole or at least exaggeration are too often the order of the day, and articles and books on Japanese politics, society, business, finance, or the economy end on a note of sour despair or, just as often, in an atmosphere of "optimism," if that really is the word for it, which holds that Japan is really not quite the economic powerhouse, the financial whiz, the military threat, or perhaps the technological wonder that we have been led to believe. The unemployment and financial problems of 1993 and 1994 have tended to verify these arguments; but also supporting such approaches is a hostility of the American public toward Japan that has grown steadily in recent years.

The truth often lies elsewhere; Japan, after all, is a great and complex society, one that is made up of what is too often seen as a homogenous population in which everyone seems to think in the same way. There is a tremendous amount of social homogeneity, to be sure, and this is much stronger than that found in most large nations that are of political, diplomatic, economic or military consequence. And there may be less emphasis upon individualism as a value than is generally the case in the West; but Japanese people are residents of a highly advanced and sophisticated country that leads the world in many spheres, not all of which are entrepreneurial, economic, or technological (see Fig. 4.1).

Japan is seen, for example, as one of the cleaner advanced nations

Fig. 4.1
Japan

Gross national product per capita	$35,000
Gross domestic product growth, 1992	0.1%
Gross domestic product growth rate anticipated, 1995	2.5%
Annual population growth rate	0.3%
Infant mortality per 1,000 births	4
Literacy	100%
People per doctor	610
People per telephone	1.5
Population	125.2 million
National capital	Tokyo
Major trading partners	U.S.A., Germany

Sources: United Nations, World Bank, and various publications

because it is attentive to environmental concerns. It is considered a world leader in some of the more delicate and complicated arts such as dance, theatre, or elegant tea ceremonies. It is a land in which public transportation, which saves energy resources and better supports the environment, plays a vital and significant role in the lives of its highly urbanized people. It has developed educational and scientific establishments that are acknowledged as world leaders. Most importantly, it is the home of the world's oldest and most continuous monarchy. The title and role of the emperor has been with the nation for thousands of years, perhaps originating around 660 B.C.E. Somewhere in the mists of time, the nation's myth of origin tells us, a sun goddess created the islands of Japan; and the imperial office itself was created in heaven so that the emperor cannot be seen to be a mere mortal. In today's rational, secular, and scientific world, this may merely appear to be an inexplicable anomaly, something that is much closer to theology than to the science of government; but in the still unexplored reaches of the psyche and the fundamentally important ethos of political symbolism, this continues to exercise a hold on the minds and certainly on the hearts of the populace.

Another anomaly, though this one is sure to be gone soon in the throes of Asian political and economic progress, is that Japan is alone among the seven great economic powers of the world in having developed from Eastern roots. The story is a familiar one to those who have paid some attention to national histories of the planet's great political actors. For 264 years, from 1603 to 1867, feudal Japan lived through the Tokugawa era, when local dynasties or shoguns, occasional internal hostilities, and perhaps best known, the cult of the samurai warrior were dominant. This was also a period of a very insular Japan, which turned away Portuguese traders or anyone else; a few Dutch managed to hang on to trading posts. The culture of the nation seemed insular by its very nature during this period, though this was aided by the geographic position, which places Japan at the edge of the Asian continent.

In 1868, the Meiji restoration took place, an event that saw the return of the emperor to a real seat of power and a much more unified Japan; but Japan had already been "open" to the world as of 1854, the year of Perry's none too subtle return to Tokyo with war ships. The takeover by the Meiji dynasty and the end of the Tokugawa era provided an even greater spur to Japan's quest for modernization, Westernization, and development. This regime, in power until 1945, presided over the greatest industrial and technological metamorphosis

Asia had ever seen. It created the formidable and challenging economy and world presence we know today. For a very long time, and perhaps even in some ill-informed quarters today, the outside world regarded these developments with a mixture of curiosity and disdain. There was quite naturally an interest in the phenomenon of an Asian nation undertaking a tremendously ambitious effort to become a twentieth-century industrial power. The early factories, service establishments, and even streetcars sent out this message. Simultaneously, it was generally held to be the case that while Japan was good at imitating product innovations or technological breakthroughs, it would not—indeed, could not—become a significant world leader in such sophisticated realms as manufacturing, finance, distribution, diplomacy, or even in its traditional area of interest, the military, because it was so utterly dependent upon learning how other nations perform these tasks. Therefore, the reasoning went, it was not possible for Japan to ever move ahead of the rest of the world because Japan was always learning from it. We should know now, if this was not known before, that this idea is absurd, not only in any application to Japanese culture, but in attempting to apply such a wrongheaded lesson to any nation or people.

Today the facts are clear enough. Japan is the world leader in research and development, and this has resulted in a wide variety of industrial products and consumer gadgets that the rest of the world likes to purchase. Japanese business interests have made big splashes in America not only with cars, electronic consumer products, and other product sales, but they have also made highly visible purchases of such entities as downtown Los Angeles office buildings, New York's Rockefeller Center, the Seattle Mariners baseball team, and movie companies such as Columbia Pictures. Japanese business concerns, stock markets, and banks, which are the world's largest, are influential the world over; and even such popular culture items as films, music, dance, and food have had a broad international impact and acceptance.

The nation has come a very long way since it picked itself up from the destruction and despair of 1945. The world's first country to suffer from nuclear destruction had to abandon dreams of Asian leadership and domination, which had been at the center of Japan's war aims. A "coprosperity sphere," as Japan termed it, was to have been developed in China, the Pacific region, and Southeast Asia, with Japan performing the role of economic and military leadership. The terms of "coprosperity," however, were never altogether clear. The reach of Japan's military effort demonstrated determination to impose its will on the Asia-Pacific region. Troops landed in, and captured, some of the Aleutian islands off the coast of Alaska as well as Indonesia, Malaysia, Singapore, Hong Kong, the Philippines, New Guinea, hundreds of Pacific islands, Burma, Thailand, Cambodia, Laos, Vietnam, and important parts of China (as well as Korea and Taiwan, which had been taken over by Japan at earlier dates). Japanese planes were able to fly far enough to bomb parts of Hawaii, Australia, and India. The end of World War II saw Japan making a quick turnaround, taking its cue from its history of rapid growth and industrialization to rise to its present position of world leadership. Japan's populace was apparently determined, in the shadow of the American occupation, to help its nation to resume the important place it had held in the international arena prior to the outbreak of war.

Sometimes overlooked by observers of Japan's recent history and politics is the fact that a rather strong peace movement emerged from the rubble of war. Suffering through the unparalleled calamity of nuclear attacks undoubtedly contributed to this development; when Japan's militarist tradition is considered, however, this balancing factor must also be taken into account. It has been a stabilizing agent within Japanese society, and it has also been a force on behalf of continued adherence to the constitutional prohibitions of military buildup. As the statistics for almost any country seem to show, and as Paul Kennedy's historic study of military powers tends to confirm, the national and policy refusals to get involved in defense spending on a major scale, as measured by percentage of gross domestic product, has contributed mightily to Japan's postwar prosperity. This reluctance to establish a big defense capability may fade, however, as the country's security needs seem to grow and as the U.S. position in Asia continues to adjust to a smaller role in regional protection.

The prosperity of Japan seems recently to have started to fade, though most observers believe this is a temporary state of affairs. The early 1990s have brought a steep drop in stock market and real estate prices, higher levels of unemployment (though still below levels of those found in the West), big reductions in corporate profits, and a recession that is serious by Japanese or perhaps any other standards. Firms that have generally offered lifelong employment, which typically are the larger companies, are changing this policy. And one of the best-selling books in Tokyo in 1993 has the title of *Honorable Poverty*. There is little question that the rolling thunder of the W. Arthur Lewis model, which states that jobs will move to lower-cost labor areas, is also having some effects, even though Japanese businesses seem to make a greater effort than their American counterparts to preserve jobs for the country. There can be little doubt, in all events, that this tight economic picture has increased pressures upon the nation's political processes, which at the moment seems to have taken on a new and unfamiliar instability. The system, all observers agree, is shot through with staggering amounts and kinds of corruption as well. Whether these developments will have significant effects upon trade negotiations with the United States and other economic partners remains an open question; but the general expectation is that, in the long term at least, they will not.

Public opinion verification of the feelings of national malaise appeared in an Associated Press report of April 18, 1993. It should be remembered that most samples of Japanese opinion taken in recent years demonstrated a mood of optimism about economic matters and national destiny; but a widespread disenchantment has set in. More than 44 percent of adults, a record number, now believe that their nation is moving in the wrong direction, a figure nine points above a year earlier and twenty points above three years ago. Only 31 percent of respondents believe that their country is still headed in the right direction. Responses about national problems indicated broad concerns about the economy, the environment, and foreign and defense policies. Significant and perhaps even devastating was the response of a full 70 percent of the people who complained that their government does not represent the views of its citizenry. This was a jump of nine points in a single year.

This sense of malaise was reflected in the crisis that overtook Prime Minister Kiichi Miyazawa's government in the summer of 1993. Thirty-six members of his party, the Liberal Democrats, defected and joined the opposition parties to bring down the government on a confidence vote. These defectors have formed their own group, the Japan New Party. Miyazawa resigned after the resulting elections saw his LDP fail, for the first time in modern history, to win a majority in the Lower House of the Diet, the national parliament, which is one of the nation's crucial centers of power. (The others are the more or less permanent leaders of the bureaucracy and the leaders of corporations and the keiretsu, which are described below.) Miyazawa's hopeful successor, Morihiro Hosokawa, lasted only eight months, though he achieved some significant reforms of the election process and of political financing. His successors, Tsunomo Hata and Tomiichi Murayama, helped to set a record for changes of government in a single year. In the case of the latter, a Socialist who heads an LDP-dominated coalition, it is fair to say that much cynicism greeted his appointment. A Socialist who leads his erstwhile political enemies appears, to some at least, to be more interested in power than in policy making.

The Economy and the "Politics of Compensation"

The Japanese economy is a marvel to behold, according to much of the economic literature and, most assuredly, the popular press. It sometimes appears to outsiders to be a synchronized machine, scientifically and thoroughly tested before it was ever set into motion, and it has hummed along in a precise and all-consuming way under the prodding of a tough-minded, homogenous, and hardworking population. The popular images of Japan have probably contributed to a misunderstanding of the nation and its processes, to say nothing of its goals. Japanese society does seem to have institutions and approaches that are unique and that would probably be impossible to imitate for members of other different political cultures, but it also meets with problems and failures just as any society does.

A major factor in Japanese economic direction has been the continuous leadership of the Liberal Democratic party, which until 1993 had won every national set of elections (save for one election for control of the Upper House in the Diet) since it was created by a merger of parties in 1955. This ruling party, as one might expect, has been a conservative force that, it is fair to say, is dominated by elite interests such as the larger corporations and financial institutions, the very powerful bureaucracy, the military, and influential politicians who seem to control factions of the party—and therefore of the Diet—even after they have served as prime minister.

Conservatism of this ruling party and its leaders should be viewed in a context that is different from that which is applied to such parties in the West and perhaps elsewhere; in the context of Japan, it only means some reverence for tradition and an awareness of the need to protect the overriding and substantial interests of influential persons and groups. It is not a conservatism set out in the sometimes strident ideological way found in Western countries, such as the United States, Britain, or France.

The LDP should of course be seen as a force that helps the cause of employers against labor unions, the position of industrial leaderships bent upon combination in ways that would violate American antitrust laws, the solvency and profitability of banks and other financial institutions, and the support and facilitation of export-oriented businesses. It would be quite wrong, however, to see LDP leaders or parliamentarians as persons committed to some sort of abstract "conservative" vision of the future. The LDP, in short, has been largely focused upon a practical and case-by-case approach to policy issues and concerns. Whatever works for Japan and its ruling interests has been the test for policy measures. Whether a publicly owned or privately owned entity performs a particular economic or policy function, for example, is not seen in Japan as a particularly important question or matter for concern. It is unlikely that a politician or policymaker would raise such a point or perhaps even express such a preference. To some extent, this is reflected in the kinds of institutions that have been established in the country; they may be private or governmental, but on many occasions a policy agency is quasi-governmental in nature; that is, it has a mandate of authority on certain policy matters, but it is a mandate that flows from a mixed base of public and private institutions and actors. Perhaps the best example of this kind of arrangement is found in industrial policy and planning, which will be explored in greater detail.

The tendency to view issues and policy concerns from a nonideological standpoint carries over into matters of social policy. Contrary to some popular notions expressed from time to time in the United States about the nature of the Japanese political economy, there is a social net in the nation which provides a measure of security for its citizens. It certainly is not, to be sure, the broad scale or type of arrangements found typically in countries like Germany, the Netherlands, or Sweden; but it does amount to a welfare state of limited scope. Japanese workers and citizens can depend upon limited government support measures for such social maladies as disability, old age, and unemployment. There is even a health care system, although it tends to be tied to employment.

Through more than thirty-five years of LDP rule, the government was concerned with the kinds of measures—and the kinds of controls— one might expect a traditional and somewhat elitist leadership to foster: economic and trade measures, budgetary controls, close attention to the letting of contracts and what Americans call "pork barrel," or highly political, favors and projects, public works, and a rather careful balancing of important interests such as finance, industry, the bureaucracy, the military, and agriculture. On a few occasions, however, the LDP leadership has turned to measures, improvements, and adjustments that promote the general welfare and that include even the poorest elements in society. Health care or disability protections, housing measures, education, and care for the aged, for example, may receive attention and, more importantly, a permanent kind of improvement when the LDP decides the time has come for such socially oriented laws. The LDP's rather deliberate policy role of developing such measures is called "compensation" by Kent Calder, a Japan scholar, because he believes that this kind of attention to social measures reflects a belief that the hardworking and deserving members of the Japanese public have earned the right to expect a better life, which provides opportunities not known in the past.

Three factors seem to have been at work in promoting the idea of "compensation" along with the accompanying measures: first, the steady and occasionally spectacular rise in real wages that Japan has enjoyed since 1955 has made such provisions of social welfare policy possible. And there is a practical consideration to this point as well, for any populace probably expects to share in the wealth it knows it has created. This should not be taken to mean that there is broad satisfaction with LDP or employer welfare schemes, however, since a strong current of Japanese opinion claims that inequality has been the order of the day. Second, a strong social homogeneity exists in Japan, which prevents certain barriers from intruding into social policy making. There are minority and immigrant groups in Japan, but these are relatively small in number and are politically unimportant. In certain respects, then, there seems to be a strong communal aspect of Japanese life that manifests itself in social policy. This is not a particularly socialistic impulse; it is more a matter of seeking to appreciate each person's contribution to what is broadly seen as a socioeconomic success story of recent decades. Last, a minimal net of social protections is seen as one of the features expected of a modern, sophisticated, and technology-oriented society, and this is recognized in Japan. Japan's social welfare system, after all, is not one of the more extensive (nor expensive) sets of protections one might find in the community of advanced and wealthy nations, though it compares very well with the United States.

The enactment of social welfare measures or improvements has been only an occasional matter, however; perhaps it is only a small stretch to say that these seem to have been developed as a kind of afterthought or tidying up of the nation by its LDP governments. The principal opposition, the Japanese Socialist Party (JSP), has typically had a more egalitarian agenda; it had never won national power until the formation of the new coalition of 1993, and, at this writing, it holds the office of prime minister for the first time. It has had the satisfaction, if one might call it that, of seeing some of its agenda enacted by LDP governments from time to time simply because the government sometimes took an opposition idea and put it into effect. There must have been frustrations experienced by the Socialists because of this, but the practice demonstrates some of the communalist, corporate, and cooptative forces that can almost always be found in some aspect of Japanese politics.

The result of this nonideological, rather all-inclusive, quite attentive (to domestic concerns, at least), and, until now, stable pattern of government is that Japan enjoys one of the highest standards of living in the world—higher, in some respects, than that which is known to the American people—and that there is a measure of sharing of this enjoyment. True, Japan is hardly a socialist or egalitarian society; no informed observer would broach such a thought. It does have more income equality, however, than that which is found in the United States, whether this is measured by executive compensation, income of various groups within the society, or contrasts of the high and low ends of the income scale. There can be little doubt that many Japanese people are satisfied with the policies and direction taken by LDP governments historically despite its bad poll standings of recent years.

Some dark clouds have rained on the LDP, all the same, because its long turn at the helm has brought about at least three severe problems. Perhaps the most obvious of these is the perennial and ever-broadening problem of corruption. Several prime ministers have been brought down or have had clouds over their careers because of favoritism, payoffs, personal misbehaviors of one sort or another, or fraud, and there seems to be no end of this issue in sight. The revelations continue to pour out in the press and the electronic media, creating a national despondency, shame, and disgust that have caused the LDP position to recede and, finally, to disintegrate. Second, the recession that has plagued Japan since 1990 is taking its toll on jobs, incomes, opportunities, life-styles, and perhaps above all, on the optimism that once seemed to guide the nation's economy. Companies such as Nissan have closed plants and ordered layoffs as the depressed local and international markets fail to respond to the usual enticements of Japanese-made consumer products. When this recession will end and what kinds of permanent damage will be caused by it are still matters of conjecture at the time this is written. There is certainly some evidence that the inevitability of the W. Arthur Lewis model, set out in an earlier chapter, is one of the forces at work. Last, and perhaps surprisingly to critics of Japan and its stance on trade policies, there has been a rather broad-scale resentment and criticism of these policies because the Japanese public believes that the failure of foreign goods to penetrate their market has been expensive for them. The Japanese public still appears committed to a rather high savings rate by international standards—certainly this is the case in comparison with the United States—but it is nevertheless a community of consumers as well, and there is a marked eagerness to truly participate in international, and not merely domestic, markets for goods and services. A measure of satisfaction might be supplied to the Japanese public, however, by the knowledge that theirs is a country respected throughout Asia as a leader in the cultural, political, and economic challenges being made to the rest of the world today by Asian nations.

This national pride must be seen as tempered, all the same, at least when comparisons are made with the United States. A 1981 Gallup International Poll, the most recent we have on this subject, shows that while 96 percent of the American public responds positively to a question by saying that they are "very proud" or "quite proud" of their country, the Japanese respond in this way only 62 percent of the time. And, in a related poll result, which bears witness to the Japanese commitment to at least a minimal kind of welfare state, a 1987–88 Gallup international sample showed that when persons were asked which is more important, freedom or equality, freedom was the choice of 37 percent while equality ran not far behind with 32 percent. Americans, by contrast, believe that freedom is a more important value than equality by a vote of 72 to 20 percent. This may help to explain some of the policy results seen in the social welfare area in recent years in Japan, at least by comparison.

The 1993 Elections: An LDP Debacle

The great public dissatisfaction with the LDP came to a boil in 1993 when thirty-six members of the Diet joined the opposition forces to bring down the government on a no-confidence motion. This required the calling of national elections. The LDP failed to win a majority of Lower House seats, the key to parliamentary rule in the country, and this brought about the resignation of Prime Minister Kiichi Miyazawa and the end of his corruption-stained regime.

In the negotiations which followed this, an eight-party coalition was put together. This included the Socialists, but the prime minister,

Morihiro Hosokawa, was the leader of the New Japan Party, a group that had left the LDP. The Socialists dropped out of this coalition after only eight months, and a minority government—that is, one without a majority in the Diet—was formed by a new prime minister, Isunomo Hata. But Hata lasted only a few short months before an LDP-dominated coalition, headed by a Socialist, took over, creating an expectation of little more than caretaker government.

Some experts on Japan ask how much of a difference all of this makes. The shifting currents of coalitions, elections, or even party realignments seem to have less overall significance for Japanese policy, especially economic and trade policy, than the steadfast and continuing power of the bureaucracy.

The Governance System

It can be seen from the description of the culture set out so far that a great deal of consensual decision making, and of course a great deal of consensus building, are characteristic of the Japanese system of governance. There are opposition parties and policies, to be sure—not only the Socialists, but also the Democratic Socialists, the Communists, the significant New Party and the right-wing Komeito—but it seems clear that the quite practical LDP and its major opposition, the Socialists, have provided most of the debate and policy parameters for the political system. This is changing now, however, as all of the non-LDP forces seem to be banding together into a new and bolder opposition group.

In its own way, the elections process has helped to contribute to this framework of consensus building and quite often nonideological politics. This is partially explained by the fact that while most Diet seats are filled by politicians who represent single-member districts, there also have been a number of multimember electoral districts, which are called jiten. These multimember areas were abolished in a 1994 reform pushed through by Hosokawa. These districts elect four and sometimes five members to the national parliament. As any political scientist or close observer of political phenomena will almost instantly recognize, such a system has definite effects upon voting patterns, party loyalties, and results. A system of this sort lends itself to what is variously called bullet voting, single-shot voting, or slot voting. This merely means that someone who is most committed to a certain candidate will be very likely to cast only one vote in such a system rather than the four or five that are permitted. The effect of this kind of voting is that it not only helps the candidate supported, but it hurts all of the others. Smaller parties tend to like a system of this sort because it means that a concerted effort on their part will at least give them some chance to win a seat or perhaps two. This helps to explain the presence of at least four opposition parties in the Diet over the years.

Added to this significant experience is a highly personalized brand of politics that is perhaps without peer except in such classic cases as the machines of Chicago or of Albany, New York, or perhaps the politics of modern-day India. The following developed by individual candidates in their constituencies is one of considerable loyalty not only to the person involved but also, in the case of the LDP, to a particular faction of the party. Candidates who run good races but fail to get elected often go on campaigning on a more or less perennial basis, so that future elections can bring different results. This was even more likely to occur in the now-abolished multimember districts. Such an effort is supported by strong attachments that individual voters and groups have for these candidates. Such personal kinds of loyalties tend to insulate the system from ideological considerations, and the Japanese electoral and governance systems seem to generally reflect this.

The overall approach to Japanese politics and governance, then, might be seen as practical and businesslike; for however supportive of ideological stances a particular group of voters might be, they tend to be outnumbered by those who hold personal loyalties to certain politicians and the factions to which they belong. This approach also seems to lend itself, unfortunately, to a reciprocal back-scratching mentality that often leads to corrupt practices. Corruption, in fact, appears so rife and so endemic to the system that the events of 1993 and opinion polls are beginning to show that the general patience exhibited to date on such matters may be soon coming to an end. And the nature of this corruption indicates that it has taken on its deepest and most troublesome aspects at the very highest governmental levels. Several recent prime ministers have been touched in one way or another by this corruption habit—most, but not all, of which seems to be financial—and some of them have been directly implicated and have had to leave government under a cloud (though some of these still retain Diet seats).

It is not merely the habits of personalized politics that have sustained the LDP up until recently, however. A demographic trend, namely the aging of the population, helped the government party to maintain its grip. The weakening of trade unions, which has occurred in recent years, also was helpful to the government because the unions have generally given their support to the parties of the left. Most certainly, the strong economic performance of Japan over the past two decades or longer also gave the LDP a strong hand in national politics. The relatively bad economic performance of the country since 1990 therefore should be seen as a major factor affecting the changes of 1993. Whether these changes will move the politics of the nation off the consensual path, however, is a very dubious possibility. And the power of the bureaucracy to sustain rules and consensus building has held together through all of the recent turmoils; many observers think that this is the most crucial factor in the governance of the nation.

The Values of Japanese Political Culture

The values of Japan seem to take much of their shape, for Americans and perhaps most Westerners, from a variety of stereotypes. Among the reasons for this, of course, is simply a failure to understand the language, arts, politics, religion, morals, and values of what, by all measures, must be considered a complex society.

It might surprise some observers, for example, to learn that the northern island of Hokkaido has been influenced by a Gandhi-like figure, Andoshoiki, who lived there several hundred years ago. Nitobe Inazo, who was an influential figure until his death in 1933, wrote of bushido, a moral code that he believed should—and indeed did—direct the lives of the Japanese people, pulling them away from militaristic, authoritarian, and even commercial influences, practices, and values. Nitobe, who is honored by his appearance on the currency of the country, was a Quaker pacifist who worked for his nation and for the cause of peace in the academic world but also in the League of Nations. And Maruyama Masao was a political theorist who, most prominently at the time when Japan was immersed in the ashes of its first and only defeat in a war, combined a utopian vision of democratic development with practical suggestions that demonstrated his belief that Japan had been ready for democracy for a long time. It can be said, therefore, that some of the popular images of Japan should probably be set aside so that we can at least consider the pacifistic, democratic, and ultimately humane tendencies that exist in this nation.

The culture of a nation is surely reflected in its politics; and we have already seen that Japan is a society in which there is a heavy emphasis upon a personalized brand of politics at the local level and a pragmatic, consensus-building system operating at the top of the policy making system. Such a system, as might be expected, listens to interest groups, whether these be business associations (and there are four general-level business groups that are quite powerful), groups of rice farmers, the bureaucracy, the military, or even consumer groups and trade unions.

A further difficulty in analyzing Japanese political culture is found in the sometimes intense levels of Westernization that seem to have affected broad bands of society. Japan is in every way a modern state, and this means modern pressures of work routines, communications, transport systems, technology, and the administrative wherewithal to operate such systems. The social side effects of Westernization are also in evidence—in the whims and preferences of popular culture, whether this is in the form of music or art or dress, and certainly in the pressures felt as a result of increased marital breakup, mental illness and mental exhaustion, alcoholism, and changes in child-rearing practices. The development of a women's rights movement is also to some extent a reflection of attitudes that have migrated to Japan from the West and perhaps elsewhere.

Japan's political culture has been able to flourish and grow, at least in part, because of the advantage fostered by Article 9 of the American-inspired (and, for all intents and purposes, American-written) Constitution, namely the prohibition against development of military forces beyond the level of internal security needs. This has enabled the country to concentrate largely upon the civilian sector of the economy and the fulfillment of civilian needs. The result has not only been an economic advantage, but a psychological one as well. The culture is one that has been able throughout the post-World War II period to rely upon American protection, an arrangement that is sanctified by U.S. treaty obligations.

Religion is always recognized as a major cultural influence in any society, but Japan has moved toward increasingly secular trends in life-styles and belief systems. The major religions of the country are Shintoism, Buddhism, and Christianity, and these are all affected by a heavy influence of Confucianist philosophy. Shintoism enjoyed the status of official national religion from the 1870s until the end of World War II, when Emperor Hirohito renounced any claim to divinity. This religion is therefore closely tied to the myths of the monarchy and its origins, but it is also regarded as holding high respect for ancestors and for having some relationship to the nation's militaristic traditions. There are still more than eighty thousand Shinto shrines and temples found in the country. It is a Shinto ceremony that is performed at royal weddings. Shintoism overlaps with Buddhist beliefs and with Confucian philosophical tenets. But the most important trend in Japan today is toward secularism, and this is evident in the life-styles of the people and in occasional opinion poll results on religious faith.

Critics will sometimes say that Japan's culture is racist, and that Japan's long history (as well as its geography) of insularity has given its people a feeling of exclusivity or specialness. Undoubtedly there are racists found in almost any society, but whether Japan is any more racist than any other country is an open question. An analysis of Japan that has gained some currency says that its culture may serve the needs of its people well enough, but this is not a culture—since it is so very inward looking—that can provide much of a measure of world leadership. This sentiment, though sincerely argued, seems to go very far, probably too far, in judging the alleged strengths or weaknesses of Japanese society. It is a view that ultimately rests merely upon a suggestion rather than upon hard evidence. And such a claim appears to call for a context, perhaps in the form of a listing of the requirements for a culture aiming to influence and lead the rest of the world.

Individualism, it is fair to say, is not as highly prized in Japanese society as it is in the West. This is reflected in a great variety of cultural norms: a great respect for authority, a greater emphasis upon teamwork than upon individual effort, the strengths of family and business ties, and, even today, a respect for the customs and habits bound up in social traditions. The respect and politeness displayed by Japanese people in their everyday lives, and assuredly in such matters as the carrying out of business transactions, are well known to the rest of the world but perhaps not very well understood. But it is the value accorded such social mechanisms that helps to provide the society with some of the strengths that hold it together.

Japanese Culture Viewed from the West

There is little doubt that some of the misunderstandings about Japan that have developed in the West are bound up with a failure to know about the importance of such customs and, most importantly, the purposes and methods by which these are carried out. A further complication that adds to this sad state of affairs is the relatively small number of Americans, or of Westerners generally, who have learned the Japanese language, which is the major window for this kind of enlightenment.

Some of our mutual history also works against understanding each other. When a war occurs between nations there is often a legacy left over that promotes wariness and distrust. In most instances, it seems, this legacy is worse than that which has been experienced in the U.S.-Japan relationship; but this residue exists all the same and it becomes pronounced when events or circumstances occur that serve as reminders. The celebration of the fiftieth anniversary of the Japanese bombing of Pearl Harbor in Hawaii, the signal for the United States to enter the Pacific war, brought out a great deal of resentful and even aggressive sentiment in America, which has apparently not had enough time to dissipate. The visit to Japan by President Ronald Reagan upon completion of his term of office in 1989 and his two speeches there, which were rewarded with fees of more than $2 million, caused stirrings and mutterings about taking a delayed bribe that had been earned by making concessions to Japanese interests while Reagan had served in the White House. The visit to Tokyo by President George Bush in early 1992, which was adjudged a flop by those who had hoped for better trade concessions from the president's hosts, seemed to exacerbate an increasingly bitter national attitude on both sides of the Pacific. Other incidents have occurred from time to time that have caused bitterness—the Japanese insistence upon trying an American soldier in their courts on a murder charge rather than allowing U.S. military authorities to do this, or the shooting of a young Japanese exchange student in Louisiana who had simply gone to a home to inquire about directions.

A rather continuous decline in mutual respect has been noted in opinion polls. These show that the United States and Japan, who in many ways should be regarded as allies who need each other, are having serious problems and differences in perceiving the motives and goals of their historically close and important partner.

A *Wall Street Journal* report of December 29, 1992, for example, showed that the annual poll taken by the newspaper *Asahi Shimbun* revealed that only 30 percent of the populace, the lowest number since the end of World War II, believed that relations between Japan and the United States are good or fairly good. At the same time, a Harris poll taken in the United States listed a like number of Americans, 38 percent, who felt that relations were good or fairly good, the worst sentiment since this poll was originated in 1982. In addition, most

Americans stated that they believed their new president, Bill Clinton, should take a harder line on trade with Japan, and a majority of Japanese believed that, indeed, he would. As for the future, only 10 percent of the Japanese sample thought that relations between the two countries would improve in the near future, while one-third of the American public demonstrated a faith in such a hopeful development. Obviously, policies and perceptions on both sides of the Pacific seem to have gone awry, even though any expert conversant with the relationship would probably accept the premise that this is a vital friendship that is very worthy of preservation.

Any approach toward this preservation will require Americans to understand the attitudes and, to be sure, the grievances felt in Japan about trade and other issues. A good place to begin such an understanding might be with a book of Japanese comic strips reproduced by the University of California Press and entitled *Japan, Incorporated.* The stories found in this book, which are set in the decision-making echelons of Japan's industry, illustrate well the way in which such issues are seen and framed there. American quotas on Japanese auto imports, to cite a major example, are seen as a terrible imposition that has the effect of raising the prices of their products. (Chrysler executive Lee Iacocca is portrayed as a major villain.) Knowing about such perceptions helps to explain a great deal. For example, it is rather well known that Japanese industrial leaders now tend to look upon Southeast Asia as an ultimately more lucrative place to do business because it does not seem to pose the trade obstacles found in the much bigger but more difficult American market.

Knowing about grievances and opinions related to them does not, of course, mean that these points of view are necessarily correct or just; but an understanding of these is probably a good starting point for the rebuilding of what has been, overall, a good and valuable relationship.

Trade and Competitiveness

The ability of Japan to compete in international markets has become legendary. Automobiles, electronic products of various kinds, and vast arrays of industrial and consumer products, from freight trailers to computers, have made their appearance in the Americas, Europe, Africa, and Asia and have achieved broad and sometimes enthusiastic acceptance. Japanese goods are regarded as high in quality, durability, and dependability. And Japanese firms are committed to research and development, to teamwork in the planning, production, and marketing processes, and to awareness of new technologies and their potential.

In addition, the marketing and trading abilities of Japanese firms are envied in other countries. In some places and circumstances, the only response that has been successful at all in combating these firms is to simply not allow their products to be sold in the country. France, for example, has few if any Japanese cars, and this is probably not a reflection of the choices of consumers there. Critics of American trade policy of recent years believe that the United States has been too easy on the Japanese, allowing their country access to the great American market while being shut out of Japan. The terms and negotiations of trade, however, are not too well understood by the general public. It is a fact, for example, that the United States discriminates against foreign-made products in any number of ways, from government subsidies of one kind or another to outright tariffs or quotas. It is also true that Japanese trade commitments are usually kept, at least on paper, and that it is some other consideration—such as a requirement for extensive inspections or an imposed quality measure—that often results in the shutting out of American goods.

The 1992 election of Bill Clinton as president was heralded by trade policy critics as a turn for the better. We shall see whether this is the case. Clinton's campaign, and the unsuccessful campaign of Ross Perot as well, made frequent references to the heavy lobbyist machinery set in place in Washington by Japanese industrial and governmental interests. In many cases, a Reagan or Bush administration official who spent some years on trade policy or a related area—in the Commerce Department, perhaps, or as a member of the Federal Trade Commission—later took a job working for one of the Japan lobby groups. These people, plus a heavy amount of legal and administrative talent, were recruits to the Japanese trade cause; and their critics made the point that such a move, especially without much of a time gap between these jobs, must be viewed as unseemly if not downright unethical.

The U.S. position on trade issues is further complicated by the large government budget deficit. American needs for an improved trade balance vis-à-vis Japan and other Asian countries is not merely an issue of trade figures or advantages or disadvantages; for the balance of payments, which reflects the currency adjustments between nations, always includes a large red ink figure for the interest paid to foreigners, including the Japanese, who are holding U.S. government debt instruments. This means that even in a month in which there is a relatively good trade figure, even if it is a minus, the overall payments balance will be badly affected by government debt. Easing this crisis will therefore depend, in part, upon a better export performance. No turnaround is in sight at the moment, however, and the $50 billion trade deficit represents most of the foreign debt of the United States. Approximately three-quarters of this debt, incidentally, is represented by Japanese car sales.

Japan's economic performance is of course the basis for its strong surplus positions in trade and in the balance of payments. This remarkable record shows that, by and large, there have been dramatic increases in real wages, hence gains in living standards, from the 1960s to the present time. When it is remembered that Japan is merely a place that processes raw materials it has imported and then exports the finished products, it can be seen that a number of dynamic factors have been at work to produce these gains. Though arguments surely continue about this subject, it seems quite clear that the Japanese have relied upon a very strong savings rate—17 percent of average annual family incomes or more than that—to seed investments. They have also committed great efforts to research and development and to a good system of education. Great economic inequalities persist in the society, certainly, but these appear on the whole to be no greater than those now in existence in the United States. At this writing there appears to be no consensus about the damage and long-term effects of the great Kobe earthquake of January, 1995, in which more than five thousand people lost their lives.

Many analysts have given us descriptions of the structures of the Japanese industrial system and the governmental mechanisms committed to their support. Among the latter is the potent MITI, the Ministry for International Trade and Industry. The MITI often plays the role of coordinator of industrial policy for a given industry and, to some extent, for the rest of the Japanese economy as well. Its most dominant role is in international trade, where MITI can serve either as an offensive or defensive tool. It works to develop and finance industrial groups, which are representative of several or even many firms, in specific and selected areas of technology. In the past, MITI projects have included autos, high-definition television (a project that may or may not work out well), color liquid crystal displays, supercomputers, and a current project of substantial importance, the fifth-generation computer, which will supposedly incorporate artificial intelligence. The MITI typically provides funding for product development, below-market financing, price goals, marketing advice, and, quite often, government guarantees of certain amounts of purchases of the new product once it reaches the output stage. The United States has no equivalent agency since this would most certainly entail violation of antitrust laws and other statutes and, most certainly, violation of long-held and sometimes mystical beliefs in competitive enterprise, which now often appear outdated and dysfunctional for national purposes. The almost certain imposition of some sort of industrial policy by the Clinton administration may bring some agency, less powerful than its MITI counterpart, into play.

The keiretsu is a grouping of companies that seems to have a distinctively Japanese cultural origin. European nations sometimes have government-owned industries and will sometimes tolerate trading cartels of various kinds, but neither of these are in any way like a keiretsu. Keiretsus represent an effort to coordinate industrial partner-ships, sometimes referred to as "organizational synergy," which will prove to be complementary to the operations and aspirations of indi-vidual firms. There are three types of keiretsus: industrial, production, and distribution.

Most major industrial corporations in Japan are a part of one of six different groups, or keiretsus. These are formal associations (though they do not bind individual members to every nuance of their policies), and they are made up of several hundred companies organized around a major bank and a major trading company. Keiretsu members look to other firms within their group as their first-preference customers and suppliers. In most circumstances, the bank and trading company hold about one-third of the stock of each member company, and these member companies usually finance about 40 percent of their debt with this bank. Member companies usually hold some of the stock of each member company of the group, and strongly organized interlocking directorates are found honeycombing the entire keiretsu organization (see Table 4.1).

This, of course, means that each company not only has some sense of its own goals and direction, but a broader-based set of strategies and dimensions as well. Meetings are held, usually on a monthly basis, of group members in order to plot strategy against the other keiretsus and foreign competitors. It can be seen that the keiretsu is perhaps the premier mechanism that permits the Japanese to implement their long-term view on profitability and market share (which is often commented upon in the West as a strength of their system). From time to time, Japanese industrial leaders have criticized Western firms and econo-mies for failing to develop this long-term stance.

How this is carried out in practice is enlightening. In the case of

Table 4.1

A Comparison of Japanese and U.S. Industrial Performance:
Some of the Indicators of a Japanese Lead

Recent years have seen Japanese firms open up a wide lead in these six areas
of industrial operation:

Working stock and inventory
Time from order to shipment
Quality defects and rework
Average age of equipment
Annual investment per worker
Annual investment in research and development

NEC, which was the object of much keiretsu nurturing in the hope
that it would become a major producer of IBM-compatible personal
computers, a strategy was developed in which it was agreed that the
trading company would carry out research upon, and also develop,
export opportunities; the bank would provide financing and group
members would provide supplies on favorable terms; and, perhaps
most helpful of all, all of the firms in the group would be expected,
indeed required, to buy the new personal computer product for its own
use as soon as it appeared on the market. Such an arrangement not
only has the built-in advantages of the mutual supports described, but
also benefits from the lack of an apparent need for a good or immediate
"bottom line" number to show that this is a profitable idea. (A
Harvard Business Review article and some other sources have set out
the details of the rise of NEC.) In this way, a Japanese firm has a lead
time and a patience simply unknown in like-sized firms in the West.

Another major keiretsu function is to help, sometimes even rescue,
member firms who have run into difficulties. A classic case is the
Sumitomo keiretsu's valiant and successful attempt to save the Mazda
automobile company in the late 1970s when its rotary-style engine
proved to be a mechanical and marketing failure. Finances and supplies went to Mazda on very favorable terms from other group members, workers who lost their jobs with Mazda were absorbed by other
keiretsu companies, special efforts were made within the keiretsu to
buy Mazda products, and there was even a rather elaborate door-to-
door selling campaign launched with the frank appeal that the company
was in trouble and Japanese consumers should help to save it.

Production keiretsus are most generally found in the automobile industry, and these have proved crucial for the elaborate arrangements set up by car companies and their many suppliers. In this scheme, suppliers are sometimes asked to share in cost reductions and other sacrifices that must be borne by the car company. This was the case in 1993, when Nissan and other companies were hit hard by the world-wide recession. Such an arrangement naturally helps a company to maintain price levels that are otherwise not achievable.

Distribution keiretsus involve integration of companies and their product lines at every level from factory to retailer. These distribution groups control pricing at every level as well, so that their grip on the domestic economy is very strong. It is typically a distribution keiretsu that is being discussed when claims are made—claims that often or usually are valid—that the Japanese domestic market contains inefficiencies and barriers that make it impossible or near impossible for foreign producers to penetrate it.

Japan is a tough competitor in international markets because it can rely upon this very hard and fast infrastructure represented by MITI and the keiretsus. But it also erects trade barriers that are at odds with its claims of fealty to the free market and that have aroused ill feeling not only in the United States, but in many nations of the world, including Asian nations. An examination of tariff and quota structures set up by Japan seems to defy this description, because these are generally lower than those found in most of the major industrial nations. Only agricultural products enjoy the privilege of an umbrella that can be frankly labeled "protectionist."

Most of the effective trade barriers set up by Japan are of a subtler nature. The networks established by the distribution keiretsus, for example, are not a result of government policy but are based upon intensively coordinated and frankly exclusive efforts that in many ways are far more effective than anything a government might do. Formal barriers include import cartels, or monopolies, which have been organized with the blessing of MITI. These have been used to prevent imports of price-advantaged products as diverse as aluminum baseball bats and soda ash, which is used in making steel. An effective legal obstacle to imports is bureaucratic insistence upon a variety of inspections and inspections procedures; these are used against American cars, for example, on the matter of emissions standards, even though the United States has higher standards than those required in Japan. Testing and its attendant costs and delays, some of which can be onerous, are therefore required even though this is really not necessary.

Last, and perhaps most important, there is a "buy Japanese" movement of considerable power. This is formally sanctioned in a great variety of keiretsu and other commercial trading arrangements, but it is also a general preference found in Japanese industry and most certainly among the general public, which has grown to believe that an American label on a product means that it is probably of inferior quality. Apparently no amount of trade negotiations or concessions can really deal with this phenomenon, which of course has its counterpart, though it is probably a less effective one, on the other side of the Pacific.

What kind of stance should the United States take on trade issues with Japan? This is a question of considerable debate and controversy, and no consensus exists. The image of the Reagan and Bush administrations was one of consent to most Japanese wishes because of a strong-felt commitment to free enterprise ideology, but critics of these twelve years believe that this was a costly and even foolish approach. A stance that is unreasonably tough will also fail to work, however, and such pressures as Japanese holdings and purchases of U.S. Treasury bills probably provide a psychological barrier to our side's negotiators. It does appear clear that, for a variety of reasons, the Japanese have failed to provide a level playing field for trade negotiations, and that a certain amount of U.S. assertiveness is certainly in order. No amount of rhetoric now appears likely to impress the United States or, for that matter, the rest of the world with some idea that it is healthy for such trade dominance to proceed, willy-nilly, into the future. A perspective should be borne in mind, all the same, that incorporates the fact that the United States' international trade position in the past has held an even more dominant position than that which is centered in Tokyo today.

Perhaps a "triggering mechanism" approach could be taken by the American side; this was envisioned by the Gephardt amendment offered in 1986 and in the period just prior to the 1988 presidential election. It called for trade sanctions to take effect on a more or less proportional basis upon passage of certain deadlines. It could be argued that a "triggering mechanism" presently exists in the form of the annual Commerce Department listing of nations that are officially considered to be violators of fair trade, but this is not really a comparable kind of sanction. The difficulty with a "triggering approach'' is that it sets up a more or less inflexible stance that does not permit latitude to trade negotiators.

The approach that now appears to be emerging as the choice of the Clinton administration is one of setting targets and measures of improvement of Japanese imports of American goods. The president himself set out this idea in the Group of Seven meeting in Tokyo in mid-1993, and the reaction on the other side was muted, although there were the usual objections that a trading market cannot be mandated by government edict. Trade tensions have continued to build and Japanese surpluses have continued in the face of a strong demand for yen and a weakened dollar.

What is abundantly clear is that the United States needs to work more carefully and precisely on the development of appropriate trade strategies. The most promise lies in exports of quality products which Japanese consumers will demand to have admitted. This has many hurdles built into it, but various government incentives to export-oriented businesses, including incentives carried out at levels of government other than Washington, can have a salutary effect.

Management of Japan's trade policies is obviously more than a matter of determining stances toward the United States, even though we are the major foreign market. The European Community presents a different set of problems because the pressures within that organization are somewhat different from those of the United States, and also because Europe has had a rather more overt set of trade policies in recent years. Unification of the EC economies is a new force still to be reckoned with and understood; and no one can really tell where trends in this part of the world may lead. The newly found emphasis upon Eastern Europe and its purported investment opportunities is just one of the many dimensions of policy that will take shape over the next few years. The attitude of Japan toward Southeast Asia, by contrast, is proprietary if not patrician. This is not only because of geographic proximity. Three factors supply major characteristics to this region's future in trade. Its resources and development capacities are considered complementary to the interests of Japan. Its great and booming growth rates make the region desirable for investment and trade; and, significantly, the region has been organizing itself into a trading bloc as ASEAN, the Association of Southeast Asian Nations. Japan has a strong interest in providing some kind of guiding hand for this fledgling group, and certainly does not want to be excluded from its developing advantages. This accounts for Japan's leadership in a new entity—more potential than real at the moment—called the East Asian Economic Caucus, which will include virtually all of the nations of East and Southeast Asia.

Japanese trade policy seeks to coordinate these different parts of the world so that while one of them serves one set of the nation's interests, another can serve a second set. Simultaneously, planners and policy-makers must work within the framework set by GATT, the General Agreement on Tariffs and Trade, to which all of the industrialized nations subscribe. Ratification of GATT by the world's leading traders, including Japan and the United States, and the establishment of a regulatory body, the World Trade Organization, may lead to freer trade for the entire world; but Japan's success with nontariff barriers illustrates some of the limits of this hope.

Economic Management and Industrial Policy

General economic management measures taken by Japan have been considered very effective in the post-World War II period. Great gains in real wages and in living standards have been made on a year-by-year basis, and this has so much been the case that this growth has often been termed an economic "miracle." The operations of MITI and the various keiretsus, the relative tranquility of the labor move-ment, the high savings rates of both business firms and families, the psychology of "Japan, Incorporated," which is probably ordained by a homogenous society unfettered by serious levels of crime, environ-mental pollution, and a variety of socially dislocative and anomic forces, and the hardworking and responsible approach to life engen-dered by Confucian values can all be said to be factors in this miracle. For a brief period of time, it was also argued that Japan benefited from a thoroughly modern equipment and machinery advantage stemming from the nation's utter destruction in war, but the period in which this was a real advantage is long since past.

In addition, it is obvious that Japanese policymakers and planners have remained aware of the inherent weaknesses of their country. It has virtually no resource base and is therefore subject to the tides of the international economy to a greater extent than is the case with the United States or other countries. The yen has proved to be a powerful currency in the past two decades, and its strength can sometimes build to the point of discouraging Japanese products in foreign markets. (One of the perennial arguments against worrying about the impact of the Japanese on the international economy has typically been based on the hope for a more expensive yen; but this argument has lost ground as one goal after another—the 250-yen dollar, the 200-yen dollar, the 98-yen dollar, and so forth—has been achieved and has passed on. It has been plain for quite some time that the powerful position of the Japanese in international trade is based upon something more than an advantageous currency differential.) And, in all events, the Japanese economy, no matter how well administered it seems to be, is hardly immune to the downturn in the world economy that has characterized recent years.

The government apparently believes in the classical Keynesian formula of stimulation of the economy at a time of slack growth and unemployment and, conversely, of damping down economic activity when inflation becomes the major threat. It uses both fiscal policy—taxing and spending—and monetary policy, the manipulation of interest rates, to meet its various goals, and it shows little reluctance about such interventionism or about any worries engendered by arguments about disrupting free market forces. It should be added that the government often does like to deny that it is taking this or that action in order to provide a better environment for markets, but observers, both foreign and domestic, have long discounted such denials.

It is instructive, in this regard, to look at Japan's response to the rather severe recession of 1990–94, for this provides a typical example of the pragmatic approach taken by the government. Faced with a recent severe decline in stock exchange prices and in land values, the government developed a stimulus approach of considerable sophistication in terms of both policies and their timing. This began with an August 1992 announcement of a plan to spend the equivalent of $87 billion on stock purchases and public works. The first measure is a direct intervention into finance; the second, which is an alternative almost always available in infrastructure-poor Japan, is an attempt to put money into the economy and also to build some confidence into the activities of such groups as consumers and investors.

The next month saw the government-run social security system and the very extensive postal savings system, which is a powerful economic actor, authorizing an increase in their stock purchases. In December, they followed through on these commitments by having these agencies purchase $25 billion of securities, providing a boon to the economy through the enhancement of the capital positions of the companies whose shares were purchased. The next month, January of 1993, saw the Finance Ministry convincing the nation's banks to dispose of billions of dollars of bad loans, a move that is temporarily painful for any bank or financial institution but that is fruitful in the long run.

February saw monetary policy come into play. The Bank of Japan, the nation's central bank and chief monetary player, reduced its discount rate, the interest figure set for loans to the nation's banks. (This was set at 2.5 percent.) More importantly, the LDP leadership announced that it was looking seriously at a fiscal stimulus package of significant size. This was followed up, in March, by the announcement that the government would probably pump $105 billion into the economy to give it a strong jump start.

April brought more action. The Bank of Japan stated that recovery would be achieved by the following winter (1993–94), and the yen followed suit by establishing a record value against the dollar of 113.3. Later in the month, Prime Minister Miyazawa, visiting President Clinton in Washington in a meeting described as tense, said that Japan would definitely be pouring $116 billion of stimulus into its economy. He hinted broadly that the U.S. economy might benefit from this action more than it would from any trade concessions. Through all of this policy making, the hard realities of 1993 in Japan seemed to be coming into play.

Whether this set of actions will have the desired effects can only be proved by time and events; but the Japanese economy does possess a strong resilience. The director general and president of Keidanren, the Federation of Economic Organizations, which is based in Tokyo, wrote an op-ed article in the *Wall Street Journal* of December 28, 1992, in which he listed five reasons why the Japanese economy will bounce back from its early-nineties recession. These are (1) a continued high level of investment for the near future; (2) significant portions of this investment are geared toward a new wave of high-tech innovations, all of which have received substantial investment interest and support; (3) the savings rate remains high; (4) labor-management relations will continue to be cooperative and therefore beneficial to the entire economy; and (5) the financial institutions and system remain stable and dependable, despite some quite shocking scandals which have occurred recently. Whether this writer, Masaya Miyoshi, is correct or not in the long run, it is true that a great deal of Japanese economic and financial planning is built around such assumptions. And few observers located abroad are doubting that Japan will continue to play a major and perhaps decisive role in the international economy in the near future or perhaps beyond.

The decision of the Japanese government to pump $116 billion into the economy in early 1993 also offered an interesting contrast with what was occurring in the United States at about the same time—actually, within a span of one week. While the Japanese were prodding their not-altogether-weak economy, an economy about half the size of that of the United States, with this massive infusion of investment, the U.S. Senate was filibustering to death a $16 billion economic stimulus bill offered by President Bill Clinton as a part of his economic plan. The opposition claimed that the Clinton package was not needed to stimulate the economy and produce jobs. It will be interesting to see how such contrasting approaches, even given the many differences on the respective national economic scenes, will work out.

The major problem of Japan's need to focus upon economic revival has actually been as much political as it has been economic. The instability wrought by the dishing of the LDP by the voters in 1993, and by the subsequent short-lived governments, may have temporarily forced Japan's trading partners to put their plans on hold. But the continuity of policies and programs enforced by the powerful bureaucracy and the intricate industrial structure limits the effects of such troubles. The only recent event which has seemed to be well beyond bureaucratic control is the great and devastating earthquake of early 1995, which some domestic critics say was not as well administered in terms of emergency assistance as it might have been.

Foreign and National Security Policy

Policymakers and the general public have been content to live with the strictures of Article 9 of the Constitution, which forbids the rearming of Japan except for the limited purpose of providing internal security. The absence of large-scale expenditures on defense correlates, of course, with an outstanding record of economic growth and rising standards of living. This should not be surprising, since several studies of U.S. defense spending show that funds spent elsewhere in government or in the private sector would produce more jobs and a greater measure of national prosperity. In addition, Paul Kennedy's famous historical study that traces great military powers and their fates from 1500 to the present day shows that this kind of commitment is a drawback for a nation, whether this is measured economically, culturally, or just pragmatically. Japan's historically recent experience with militarism and its results also suggest that this can be costly as well as humiliating. The influence of Japan in Asia and the Pacific Rim, and in the world generally, is undoubtedly greater today than it ever was during the militaristic period of violent aggression, and it has paid many more dividends.

Sensationalist articles found in the popular press seem to continue to feed the fear of a revival of this militarism. This especially seemed to be the case during the fiftieth anniversary of the Pearl Harbor attack; but even respectable analysts occasionally spend time speculating about such a revival. The recent heavy buildup of plutonium reserves, for example, has alarmed those who are skeptical of Japan's motives, since this material is used for the manufacture of nuclear weapons. The closest-watching and best-informed observers of Japan, however, tend to discount the possibility of a militaristic revival almost totally, if not completely. Interestingly, they also seem to be increasingly discounting the possibility that Japan will be content to carry on its status as a military nonfactor in the world, and this assumes that such a position is simply not commensurate with the economic and political status now held by Japan in the world.

Guiding Japanese policymakers throughout all of the post-World War II period has been the existence of a strong security bond between their country and the United States, and this has been formalized in a mutual security treaty. And it has been realized in the establishment of large U.S. bases in locations such as Yokusuka and the island of Okinawa. For most of the years of this U.S. presence, the financing of such bases was entirely the responsibility of the Americans. These arrangements have meant that Japan has been able to exist on the rim of Soviet Asia through all of the years of hostility from Moscow because of the nuclear and conventional arms umbrellas provided by the Americans. This has obviated any need for a large-scale buildup of military forces even if the Constitution had permitted such an event.

From time to time the country has been pressured to develop a larger army. Secretary of State John Foster Dulles urged this course upon Japan during the Korean War in the early 1950s, and there have been other requests made at various times. The United States relied upon Japanese participation in the Gulf War of early 1991, but this was mostly in the form of financial assistance for the war effort. More recently, some small Japanese military units have served in the peace-keeping forces of the UN in Cambodia. In general, Japan has tried to hold down its military expenditures below a level representing 1 percent of the gross national product, but it is not certain that this guideline will continue to be followed. What the future holds for the security agreement binding the United States and Japan remains to be seen, but in neither country can major policymakers imagine working without the cooperation and assistance of the other.

Japan's foreign policy is developed and administered by its Ministry of Foreign Affairs, but there are also roles for the Defense Agency and for the Ministry of Finance; and MITI, according to all accounts, also has a voice in this vital area, as one might expect. It is quite accurate to say that Japan regards its security needs in an economic and political context as much as, or perhaps even more than, a military perspective. In part, this is based upon the nation's vulnerabilities; it must import raw goods for processing and it must export finished goods if the great prosperity generally enjoyed by the nation is to continue into the future.

It was this sensitivity to the international flow of goods that motivated Japan's entry into World War II and into the various acts of military aggression it carried out. Japan's security seemed threatened, in the 1930s and 1940s, by the trade embargo tactics then being fostered by the United States, Britain, and other western nations. This sensitivity should be borne in mind by anyone measuring the history and motives of the country.

The Future

Japan and the United States are entering a period fraught with difficulties. Their relationship, good at most times in the recent past, now appears threatened by trade issues, though not so much by security issues. The only security issue that appears to be of great moment is the one of Japanese financial participation in military actions launched by the United States in broad concert with other members of the international community, such as the Gulf War. There are also some relatively minor differences on environmental issues. The issue of overseas aid has long since disappeared because Japan participates heavily in foreign aid efforts, and frankly uses these to a great extent in the development of overseas markets.

The focus on trade issues will continue into the foreseeable future, however, because both nations feel misunderstood by the other and the differences now seem to extend even to questions of good faith. Carried out against a backdrop of a slow- or no-growth world economy, sharp economic conflicts may escalate in the years immediately preceding and following the turn of the next century.

These two great partners now have new governments facing each other across the Pacific. Whether this can make any difference remains to be seen, but the bureaucracies and policy establishments on both sides seem well entrenched. Whether these can be overcome is an open question.

Further Reading

Banno, Junji. *The Establishment of the Japanese Constitutional System.* New York: Routledge, 1992. Though this work concentrates on the last decade of the nineteenth century, it is instructive on the development of constitutional government within the Meiji framework.

Calder, Kent E. *Crisis and Compensation: Public Policy and Political Stability in Japan, 1949–1986.* Princeton: Princeton University Press, 1988. Calder created the thesis of Japan as a politically compensating system, which is relied upon in this chapter.

Curtis, Gerald L. *The Japanese Way of Politics.* New York: Columbia University Press, 1988. An authoritative political science text on the Japanese system.

Hayes, Louis. *Introduction to Japanese Politics.* New York: Paragon House, 1990. Charts the dynamics of Japanese institutions and political processes in an approach quite satisfactory for the student who is new to the subject.

Ishinomori, Shotaro. *Japan, Inc.* Berkeley: University of California Press, 1988. Presents Japanese concerns about U.S. trade relations and the international economy in a comic book form used in Japan for domestic consumption; informative.

Morita, Akio. *Japan That Can Say No: As Excerpted from the Congressional Record.* Washington D.C.: Jefferson Educational Foundation, 1990. Strident approach to trade and other issues, which caused some resentments upon its publication.

Neff, Robert. "How the Nikkei Was Rescued." *Business Week*, April 19, 1993, 44–45. Describes Japan's economic stimulus approach to its hoped-for revival of the economy.

Prestowitz, Clyde V., Jr. *Trading Places: How We Are Giving Our Future to Japan, and How to Reclaim It.* New York: Basic Books, 1988. Acclaimed and controversial examination of trade issues as set out by a former Bush administration trade official.

Reischauer, Edwin O. *Japan: The Story of a Nation.* New York: Knopf, 1981. A history written by one of the most knowledgeable Americans ever to encounter Japan, a former ambassador known, among other things, for his mastery of the Japanese language.

Shimizu, Yoshihiko, Hiroaki Takita, and Umesawa Masakuni. "Keiretsu: What They Are Doing, Where Are They Heading?" *Tokyo Business Today,*

September 1990, 26–36. A useful introduction to the operations of the Japanese industrial system.

Tyson, Laura D'Andrea. *Who's Bashing Whom? Trade Conflict in High-Technology Industries*. Washington, D.C.: Institute for International Economics, 1992. This is of more than passing interest since Tyson is President Clinton's chair of the Council of Economic Advisers. A firmer stance toward Japan on trade is advanced through an approach called "cautious activism."

Chapter 5

China and India: The Giants of Asia

No nation of Asia can ignore China or India, the world's two most populous countries. Neither can the rest of the world, for that matter, for China and India are the homes of two out of five of its citizens. It is naturally the case that nations of this size are important traders, which they have always been, but they are also politically important, militarily powerful, and culturally influential.

These two giants have evolved along very separate paths during their modern period of nationhood, which extends back to World War II. China has been unified because of the victory of revolutionary Communist forces in 1949; India, however, was split into two and later three nations as a result of the compromises forged by its British and national political leadership in 1947.

China's Recent History

> . . . we can hardly urge China to be more like
> us. Instead, we must scrutinize the adequacy of
> our basic assumptions about the Chinese scene.
> —John K. Fairbank,
> *China: A New History,* p. 432

China has been a unified nation on at least two occasions prior to the twentieth century, but the consolidations of power achieved by the republican leaders Sun Yat-Sen and, later, Chiang Kai-Shek in the early decades of this century were the first to occur in a very long time. The 1920s, however, saw a split take place in the Nationalist movement between Chiang and the Communists, who were led by Mao

Zedong. Chiang held the upper hand militarily at this time, forcing Mao and his followers into a desperate "Long March" into the mountains and remote areas of the country for their survival. Two or three veterans of this "Long March," which took place in 1934 and 1935, are still in the top echelons of government leadership today; and it is generally supposed that they and many of their elderly cohorts remain attached, sentimentally and ideologically, to the goals and purposes of their Marxist revolution.

The civil war resulting from the Nationalist-Communist clash was suspended, more or less, during the years of World War II so that both sides could concentrate their fire upon the Japanese, who occupied much of the country. The end of the war and withdrawal of the Japanese brought a resumption of hostilities, which saw the Communists driving Chiang's forces south and, finally, to the humiliation of taking refuge on the island of Taiwan. (The government there still refers to itself as the Republic of China.) Taiwan's superior economic performance since 1949 has now become almost legendary; China, on the other hand, experienced slow and limited growth during most of the post-revolutionary years.

Ideology and a measure of military adventurism took priority positions. The Chinese leadership, under the influence of the strong revolutionary commitment of Party Chairman Mao, sought to establish what is fairly termed an almost pure form of Marxist-Leninist dogma. Mao believed, for example, that the Soviet and other examples of revolution had failed to provide for their permanence by keeping the flame of ideology and commitment alive. These other revolutions had become bureaucratized, corrupted, and out of touch with the cause. A variety of techniques were therefore developed to insure permanence. One of these was the spirit of "self-criticism," which was rendered in verbal exercises in virtually every rural commune, urban apartment house, factory, or school. This required most, if not all, individuals to examine themselves to see where they had fallen by the wayside in terms of their revolutionary zeal and their commitment to the principles of Chairman Mao. A kind of "confession is good for the soul" idea dominated such sessions, and, generally speaking, no punishments were meted out for these various transgressions and shortcomings.

From time to time Mao would set out such decrees as a provision requiring middle-class and professional types, whether they be bureaucrats, professors, or whatever, to work in rice fields or factories. This kind of close touch with the ordinary people of the country and their work was argued to be salutary in reinforcing the commitment of such people. There were, of course, more authoritarian measures taken as well in order to insure conformity to the principles of the revolution.

Perhaps the zenith (or low point, depending on one's point of view) of this revolutionary spirit came in the mid-1960s with the Cultural Revolution. During this time, the chairman, and especially his more youthful followers, sought to purge the country of Western, bourgeois, and capitalist influences. This brought about a variety of demotions from desirable or privileged positions, humiliations, imprisonments, and some terrible and crude punishments, including death, and a very broadscale attempt to remove the slightest hint of Western decadence from the society. The fears and reprisals wrought by the Cultural Revolution proved to be dysfunctional for the society and perhaps especially for the economy. There were riots, various other forms of civil unrest, and disruption of everything from railroad operations to university life. And, as often happens in the course of events in dictatorships established by revolutions, ideology took a sharp turn against many of the important perpetrators of the Cultural Revolution (except for Chairman Mao). Purges were set up against those who had committed excesses during the Cultural Revolution, and these resulted in demotions, humiliations, imprisonments, and deaths. The "gang of four" leaders considered most responsible for the Cultural Revolution, including Mao's wife, were later tried and executed. A de-emphasis upon ideology was therefore in effect well before the death of Mao in 1976, and many true believers lost their faith in the chairman and in Marxism-Leninism.

The major reason China is feared by other Asian nations, however, has less to do with ideology than the regime's habits of undertaking military ventures from time to time. It provided direct and major help with its troops during the Korean War of 1950–53, supporting the Marxist government of the North against the South and its main ally, the United States. It has sponsored insurgent and sometimes successful groups in countries as varied as Burma, Laos, Cambodia, Malaysia, and Indonesia. Tibet, which must be regarded as a separate nation despite its proximity to China, was invaded and taken over in 1959, and its people have been subjected to untold brutalities and cultural genocide. Taiwan and Hong Kong have been threatened from time to time, and India's border areas were invaded by China in 1962. Border wars have been carried out against the Marxist-Leninist regimes of the Soviet Union and Vietnam. And perhaps only intelligence analysts have any idea of the purposes behind recent Chinese missile installations off the south coast of Burma. China is a major arms supplier to the rest of the world; its missile systems have been sold to Iran and a variety of other powers viewed by the United States and other nations with suspicion; and, quite significantly, China, one of the world's nuclear powers, has never deigned to sign the Nuclear Nonproliferation Treaty. All of this means that any nation in the Asia-Pacific region must be aware of China and its purposes and must cast a wary eye toward its leaders and policymakers. American diplomats who work in various Asian countries often report, informally at least, that China is the greatest fear of most nations in the region. The lessons of history are informative as well, since regimes established by revolution—France in 1789 or the Soviet Union in 1917 are good examples—are often zealous about spreading their ideologies across their neighbors' lands.

The Economic Transformations and Human Rights Setbacks of the Deng Xiaoping Era

Long March veteran Deng Xiaoping has served as party chair and therefore chief policymaker for most of the years since the demise of Chairman Mao. His rise to the top has not been altogether smooth, for he has known demotion and disgrace. His general image has been that he is a "moderate" voice within the hierarchy. It is believed, all the same, that the present chairman, who is well into his eighties, retains a great deal of ideological sentiment and commitment to revolutionary principles. One of the most common scenarios involving the future of China, in fact, rests upon an overly simplistic premise of a de-emphasis—or perhaps an end—of Communist dogma in favor of broad-scale capitalist development. Such a speculation carries no assurance from those who offer it and, as will be shown, there are some solid reasons for doubting such assumptions.

What gives this scenario some cogency is that economic reform is now a very strong current. The 1980s first saw capitalist and entrepreneurial development in the areas adjacent to Hong Kong. This then spread to the rest of the south of China, then up along the coastal areas (including such important urban centers as Shanghai), and, even more recently, into the central areas of the country, including the cities and industrial areas of the Yangtze River valley, such as Wuhan. This has caused some observers to claim that rather than China taking over Hong Kong, which it is scheduled to do in 1997 when the treaty with Britain expires, it is Hong Kong that is taking over China. In most cases, however, though certainly not all, this areal growth of capitalism has had the support of governmental decrees.

The most casual observer traveling in China today can witness the stark and abrupt economic turnaround that is taking place. Factories set up by the government to produce cement, steel, or other products—many of them quite inefficiently—are being sold to foreign investors, who are eager and are being welcomed with open arms. New housing developments, especially in the South, betray a wealth not known during the years of Chairman Mao (or even later.) The demand for consumer goods, from automobiles to electronic equipment to lipstick, is very heavy as well as enthusiastic. Citizens of the People's Republic of China, as it is called because of its Communist beginnings, now take holiday excursions to Europe and other far-flung locations. And the annual growth rate of the economy has been exceeding 12 percent in recent years, a level that almost all observers agree cannot be sustained. An overview of the country is shown in Figure 5.1.

The recent economic development of China is characterized by some unique features of industrial organization. In some cases, state-run industries, not all of which are inefficient, are upgrading their

Fig. 5.1
China

Gross national product per capita	$435
Gross domestic product growth, 1993	12.7%
Gross domestic product growth anticipated, 1995	10-11%
Annual population growth rate	1.2%
Infant mortality per 1,000 births	31
Literacy	73.3%
People per doctor	724
People per telephone	65.4
Population	1.1941 billion
National capital	Beijing
Major trading partners	U.S.A., Japan

Sources: United Nations, World Bank, and various publications

products for acceptability in the export market. In at least one case, a state-run firm has expanded its operations to the point that it has bought out a foreign firm. In other cases, something resembling un-trammeled entrepreneurship has been taking place, in which perhaps Hong Kong, Taiwanese, or other interests have been able to establish a factory, a hotel, or, in one case, a toll road under appropriate governmental grants and regulation. In the vast majority of cases, however, the newly developed prosperity of China seems to rely heavily upon regional or urban corporations that operate a variety of firms and industries. These units use their own capital resources and, as might be expected, they often tie these to the assets of a foreign investment consortium of one kind or another. This regional or munici-pal model of industrial organization—and of these two, the latter appears to be more important—is proving to be an efficient wedding of government and industry with spectacular results. The uniqueness of this industrial model, along with the case of the unique keiretsu model of Japan, may indicate that resolution of problems of industrial organization are culturally based.

On the subject of models it is also instructive to look at the possibili-ties for application of the W. Arthur Lewis paradigm (see chapter 2) to the situation we find in China. It is not difficult to surmise that international investment, whether it comes from Asian or Western sources or whatever, has been attracted by the combination of low wages and adequate levels of nutrition. Hard data and the views of observers of contemporary China confirm that these factors are in existence. There may be a question of political stability raised by those who are sympathetic to the many victims of the regime's violations of human rights, but it must be admitted that, in the main, the ruling group appears to be a stable force that is quite capable of governing in the foreseeable future. And this is the case despite the advanced age of some of the party and government leadership. The Lewis model seems to operate in another dimension of China's economic develop-ment, however, and this is pointed out here even though the author risks the charge of trying to place every peg into a classification. This dimension is internal. For some years, such centers as Shanghai and Guangzhou have been experiencing rapid economic growth and have achieved levels of considerable prosperity by national standards. These are important coastal cities, which are blessed both by long commercial traditions and by edicts of the regime that have permitted a large-scale revival of capitalism. Now these centers, as well as similar cities and regions scattered across the south and east of

China, are considered less desirable spots for the location of factories, especially those of the low-tech variety. These prosperous cities are seen as high-tech, service, and office headquarters locales. Wages in the hinterland are lower, often considerably lower, than in a place like Shanghai, and nutrition levels throughout China may be sometimes rather low but they are nearly always adequate. Investment patterns therefore do seem to be following the path outlined by Lewis both within the country and in terms of the whole of China as a site of financial opportunities for international investors.

It is an almost miraculous transformation that has taken place, and it is already causing important economic and financial adjustments in many places in Asia and around the world. China is now the United States' second largest debtor; that is, the U. S. balance of payments deficit is greater vis-à-vis China than it is with any nation except Japan. China's growing middle class ensures a continued pent-up consumer demand for a variety of products over the next years and decades, and most indications about the nature of this market are more hopeful from the standpoint of the United States than is the case with Japan. Recently an order for more than fourteen thousand U.S. automobiles was placed with Detroit by Chinese interests; there have also been orders for Boeing planes, for computer and high-tech products, and for grain shipments, and there may be more deals of this kind in the future. There have been trade disputes of various kinds but, all in all, it is a bright and promising economic picture, and the potential of the world's largest national market must surely whet the appetites of American and international business interests.

One should not be carried away by the dynamic changes that are occurring in economic and political structures of China, however, because development is not synonymous with modernization. The latter implies an evolving, perhaps even a mature, set of institutions and norms to be at work; and this is not invariably the case in China. An improving economy, even one that is apparently as dynamic as that of China, may or may not contribute to the democratization and modernization many people hope to see.

Government regulation of the new economic boom is treated in a curious way by the administrators, workers, consumers, and other people who are the objects of such directives. A great many decrees are still handed down that are based upon Marxist ideology, and industries and the people who work in them are expected to abide by these. It seems to be the case, all the same, that many directives are ignored and that sometimes elaborate mechanisms are set up to get around them.

The government seems to recognize that economic development will require a solid infrastructure base, and it is therefore embarking upon ambitious building schemes to provide the roads, hydroelectric power, telephone systems, and other needs of its factories, service centers, and workers. Even these kinds of projects have attracted some levels of foreign investment. The enthusiasm of such investors appears to be far from sated, and a great variety of foreign interests are well represented in the new economy; the United States is one of the major players in this group.

This U.S. presence is in evidence despite the intensity of criticism directed at the Beijing regime in 1989 and the years that have followed. A large reservoir of support for reform of the political system was built up within the country during the 1980s, and there is little doubt that much of this was animated in the wake of economic reforms. The reforms themselves were probably possible because of a very broad-scale disillusionment with the idea of a state-run economy after the excesses of the Cultural Revolution.

Much of what we see in Asian political systems today, however, tells us that economic and political reform do not necessarily go together, whether a regime's despotism is based upon Marxist or other authoritarian principles. Certainly this is the case in China. The movements among workers, students, intellectuals, and others for democratic reform culminated in protests in May and June of 1989 in Tiananmen Square, the very center of the capital city of Beijing and the locale, among other national treasures, of the body of Chairman Mao. The government's lack of a militant response to the democracy protests—it first sent in bands of unarmed troops—encouraged the students and their supporters to the point that they were ill prepared for the bald and vicious put-down of their protests on June 4. Several hundred protesters were killed and more than one thousand were injured, according to most estimates of the situation. The government claimed that the military bore the brunt of the injuries and deaths, but there is no hard evidence of this claim. Tiananmen Square, despite its great importance as the center of the universe of the People's Republic (and perhaps of Chinese culture itself), has now become a word that is synonymous with political repression. The position of the United States has been ambiguous on this matter at best; for while they condemned the repression, the Bush and Clinton administrations continued to award "most favored nation" trading status to the regime because of the obvious economic benefits to be obtained. It is not certain that this status will be maintained in the future, since the Clinton administration has a commitment to human rights policy whenever the "most favored nation" arrangement comes up for renewal. Whatever status China may have, however, its economic growth continues to set a furious pace.

Chinese Political Culture

It is difficult under the best of circumstances to summarize the most important and lasting values of Chinese political culture. We are dealing with an old and great country; indeed, this is unquestionably one of the world's great civilizations. It is rather obvious to fasten upon such influences as Confucianism, Buddhism, the role of the family and especially of the extended family in political, economic, and other types of socialization, and the authoritarianism that is attached to the father (or sometimes grandfather) figure.

Confucianism is strongly associated with the work ethic for which Chinese culture is so well known, and it also stands for such values as order, meeting the expectations others may have of you, security, honor, respect, and a general downgrading of privacy. To a certain degree it is supportive of conformity within the boundaries set by society, family, and—though this is less tangible—perhaps the government as well. Buddhism calls the individual to a higher plane of reasoning, to a certain nobility and virtue of thought, to self-improvement in moral terms, and to an attempt to understand, or partially understand, some of the meanings of life. The combination of Confucian, Buddhist, and other traditional influences gives us one of the world's unique and lasting cultures, and it is not always the case, of course, that daily lives are governed by anything resembling a strict adherence to the entire retinue of these values. Philosophy and theology appear to be selective forces in the daily lives of the Chinese.

The China known to the world today, however, has also experienced heavy overlays of other kinds of values, most of which are Western in origin. Marxism-Leninism is derived from the work of Western theorists, even though Chairman Mao managed to adapt it to Chinese needs. His emphasis, for example, upon peasants as the vanguard of revolution is a variant of considerable importance, since Marxist-Leninist thinkers had traditionally given the urban proletariat this key role. And the unique emphases upon self-criticism and the need to establish a permanent revolution represent other important variants.

Prior to the revolution, China was subjected to a variety of other Western ideas brought by commercial and imperial interests as well as the ubiquitous missionaries. Not all of these contributions to China yielded the expected results, however; for the Communists and, for that matter, their Nationalist opponents as well, reacted against Western imperialism and "guidance" for the country, which, ultimately, amounted to a rejection of Western values and ways.

It has been pointed out by some Asian scholars that the Confucian-Buddhist philosophical matrix should be seen as a framework that is receptive to socialist ideas and values. Buddhism in particular places an emphasis upon such concepts as sharing, self-effacement, self-denial, and cooperation with one's friends, neighbors, or associates. In a not very convincing way, it has been shown that Buddhist societies in Southeast Asia, to cite an analogous example, have generally been receptive to socialist political forces of one kind or another. All of these examples, however—Burma, Cambodia, Laos, and Vietnam—involve systems in which the political order is coercively enforced.

Whether Chinese political culture today is a product of its many long-held traditions or whether, on the other hand, it has been largely molded by its revolutionary experience, is a topic of considerable interest and intellectual debate. There is a body of writers who in recent years have held that the institutional focus upon revolutionary Marxist values has made Chinese traditions much less important than they once were, though few would claim that these have been eradicated altogether. And values have a way of springing back: Confucius was regarded as unacceptable at one time by the Communist regime, but he has undergone some revival in recent years. It could be argued by those who emphasize the nation's traditional values that the economic changes of the past decade are a reflection of the permanence of such values and of the transitory character of regime beliefs.

It could be said to the contrary, however, that the maintenance of state and collective roles in these economic developments only underscore the importance of revolutionary articles of faith. Either argument can be made, then, but it is important to recognize that there is undoubtedly an impact of each of these influences upon the other. This cross-fertilization of ideas is sometimes missed by analysts, sometimes acknowledged, but it invariably faces the problem of discerning just how this interaction occurs.

One of the good reasons why anthropologists like to study primitive or "pure" societies is that they are then sometimes able to avoid this problem of sorting out cultural influences. For political or social scientists seeking to analyze a modern society like China, however, there is no easy answer or approach. It therefore appears to be most prudent to say that China today represents a combination of traditional and revolutionary influences, and that it is probably impossible to sort these out in a very systematic way.

An example of the clash between traditional and regime China is found in the government's enforcement of population policy. This is a major goal of the regime, and it is often faced with disappointments in seeking it. The original target of holding the total number of people in the country down to 1.2 billion by the end of the century, to cite one instance, was revised in 1992 to acceptance of a probable 1.294 billion. The law presently requires a limit of one child per couple, and there are severe economic punishments for violating this guideline. This has led to conformity with a law that goes against the grain of Chinese tradition, but it has also meant that violations of policy occur, and these violations involve some truly egregious conduct. The cultural predisposition for male children has occasionally meant that female fetuses will be aborted for gender preference reasons, and a population imbalance is likely to be the result of such actions. Whether the policy in question involves population, or business practices, or economic policy, however, there is little question that regime decrees are bent and modified by the people to develop a better fit with the political culture.

Foreign and Trade Relations and National Security Policy

It is clear that China has become a formidable trading nation, and this is a unique accomplishment since this has never been the case with any other Communist nation. It is apparent that the new formulas of state, regional, and city guidance of profit-making corporations have so far managed to fit well within Chinese social and governmental frameworks. The large trade surplus balances established with the United States and other developed countries are a strong testimonial to the arrival of a new and significant player on the international economic scene.

How does this new and important economic role fit with the political aims of the regime? At first impression one might think that the market orientation and freewheeling entrepreneurship now being fostered are evidence of a softening of the government's long-held ideological zeal. Making money is often viewed as an antidote for political problems of many kinds; and this may be the case with the regime in China. Further examination, however, makes this seem unlikely. It is true, of course, that concessions have been made in order to conform to realities of the international marketplace. This implies that China must be outward-looking in its perspective; it must deal with the rest of the world and is therefore willing to subject itself to foreign influences. This is a break with attitudes of past eras and with the xenophobia so evident during the Cultural Revolution. In certain respects, however, the new economic order wrought by the entrepreneurship of the 1980s can be seen as a way of strengthening the hand of the regime and of furthering its ideological and even military goals. Economic power is always a given for a nation that seeks to embark upon any course toward international influence, whether this course is peaceful or otherwise.

In the case of this regime, there is a great deal of evidence that the course is otherwise. The roles of arms supplier to the world (something the United States is hardly in a position to criticize) and go-it-alone member of the nuclear club cannot be reassuring to Asian or other members of the world community. And, most unfortunately, there is some evidence that China is using its new prosperity, in part at least, to purchase and build up an arms cache that will be a significant threat to neighboring countries. The perception of these activities can alone provide China with some leverage against these countries, for they are not likely to want to provoke this giant power. Its interest in ASEAN, the emerging trade bloc in Southeast Asia, is, for example, not likely to be directly rebuffed. This leads us to a conclusion that may be surprising to some: that the openness of China on trade and economic issues, sometimes heralded as a signal of flexibility and—who knows?—eventual democratization, is paradoxically a servant of traditional motives and designs. Until there is real movement in the area of human rights, it should be assumed that this is the case. For those who are not convinced, the year 1997, when the fate of Hong Kong is to be decided, will provide a test.

The linking of Hong Kong to China will also provide this great giant with a test of unity and will. The nation has been divided through more of its history, after all, than it has been unified; and the attitudes taken toward Hong Kong, which must maintain some separateness of identity in order to continue in its place in the world, will have a marked effect upon the South in provinces like Fujian and Guangdong. These are likely to demand a continuance of the arrangements they have worked out so well with the British Crown Colony, though it is possible that other regions will demand a more thorough integration. The problem, therefore, will be one of continuing and maintaining national unity in the face of such stresses.

The history of U.S.-China relations shows that insularity is not wholly a Chinese trait. After the fall of the Nationalist government in 1949, the United States continued to insist, for a considerable (and some would say insufferable) length of time that we would not diplomatically nor otherwise recognize the mainland regime. We therefore participated with Taiwan in promoting the myth that this island was the home of the government of China. It was politically unpopular, and extremely difficult, to advocate a more realistic course. Even the loyalty of such advocates was questioned. The Taiwan lobby, moreover, was quite powerful and effective during these years. The year 1972 finally brought the U.S. "opening" to China when President Richard Nixon made his famous trip to Beijing; this visit had an ironic nature about it, since Nixon had himself made a career out of his adamant opposition to recognition of Beijing and had often questioned not only the wisdom of such a move, but the loyalty of those who had taken a contrary position.

With its circumstances of growth, prosperity, and an important trade position on one hand and a disregard for human rights and an intimidating foreign policy stance on the other, the necessary policy approaches to China appear clear enough. The United States must continue to be aware of the great potential opportunities for commerce and exchange that will benefit both societies, but these advantages cannot be realized if the price is a reward to the regime for its generally inhumane approach to the international community and, most especially, to its own citizens. These two sets of issues are linked, sometimes in easily demonstrated ways. It is good, for example, to purchase products from a country if these are considered desirable and the price is right; fair competitive practices and common sense urge such a course. When a product has a good price but has been produced by prison labor, as is sometimes the case, and these prisoners are victims of political repression or are simply treated inhumanely, it cannot be justified as an ordinary entry in a free market. And international human rights agencies and organizations tell us that this is true of many of the goods offered by China. This also tells us that China's "most favored nation" status with the United States, which gives it certain trade advantages, must be seriously reviewed at any time it comes up for renewal. In 1994, however, President Bill Clinton decided to give the regime more time to meet human rights requirements.

The point is often made that if we do not trade with China, then some other country surely will. In most cases, however, developing our policy is not an "either-or" proposition. Gradations of trade activity and response can be set in accordance with tangible results in the human rights and foreign policy arenas.

India's Recent History

> It has appeared as if the nation ha[s] taken leave of its reason.
> —The *Times of India,* May 23, 1991

This statement of despair, written in response to a host of events in the recent history of the country, is a far from unique example of the hopelessness expressed from time to time in this great subcontinent by its media, its leaders, or its citizens. But India has survived, and has survived as a democracy, from the 1947 beginnings of its rocky road to independence, economic turmoil and hope, and self-esteem.

India's hope for a unified future as a nation was dashed at the time of independence, when the Muslim minority and the assenting British established the separate state of Pakistan. Tumultuous sectarian violence between the Hindu majority and the Muslims was the reason for this partition. And though a case can certainly be made for the nationalist aspirations of the minority, who were not in a position to trust the Hindus, it is also true that this violence continues both within and between the two nations. It can therefore be said that the purpose of partition was defeated in any event.

Sectarian and ethnic violence is a curse that never appears to abate for long. In December 1992, Hindu fundamentalists destroyed a 430-year-old mosque in the city of Ayodhya in the state of Uttar Pradesh. It was claimed that a Hindu temple originally occupied the site. Clashes ignited by this incident resulted in the loss of thousands of lives across India, Pakistan, and Bangladesh as Hindus and Muslims burned homes and businesses, beat one another, and also spawned official—in other words, police—violence. The latter included unprovoked acts against Muslim neighborhoods and communities.

The religious differences that divide India include the well-publicized Sikh aspirations for a separate state of Punjab, which would take in Pakistani as well as Indian territory. Violence has accompanied these demands as well, and it was in fact some of her Sikh bodyguards who assassinated Prime Minister Indira Gandhi in 1984. She had recently ordered troops to carry out an assault against the Golden Temple in Amritsar, the holiest of places as far as the Sikhs are concerned.

The divisions of India are not solely religious. Ethnic, caste, and economic distinctions also run deep fault lines under the nine hundred million people who make up the world's second most populous nation. Indira Gandhi's son, Rajiv, who served as prime minister and, after his defeat in 1989 as the leader of the Congress (I) party, was assassinated in December 1991, while on a visit to the southern state of Tamil Nadu. It has been confirmed that this was the work of Tamil "tigers," a terrorist organization that hopes to establish a separate Tamil state in the nearby island nation of Sri Lanka. There is also talk from time to time about Tamil separatism in South India itself, but this has never materialized into a broadscale effort of the type found in Sri Lanka. It is the case, all the same, that important separatist and nationalist movements are found in Assam and other states, as well as the Punjab, and some of these use terrorist tactics.

These severe and perhaps irreconcilable differences are affected by an overlay of poverty that is as severe as any known anywhere in the world. India is a poor and developing nation with low income levels and intense problems of administration, a lack of resources (except, of course, human resources), a lack of hard currency, and resistance from the international investment and banking communities. Even the growth rates of the economy, which are reasonably high, are misleading because population growth and inflation combine to kill off most of these gains. The only significant gain India has probably made in the post-independence era is its ability, now fading fast, to feed itself because of the "green revolution" experienced in Third World agriculture. An overview of the nation is shown in figure 5.2.

India must therefore be seen as unstable by much of the world and, of course, by its own citizens as well. How, then, has it managed to go from crisis to crisis for all of these years of independence? The violence, hatreds, and lack of economic progress are enough to overwhelm most any nation seeking its place in the world. One of the specialists who has made India his life's work, Professor Myron Weiner, has pointed to an Indian paradox—its very high and excessive levels of violence on the one hand and, on the other, its quite adamant insistence upon a democratic form of governance. No Third World

Fig. 5.2
India

Gross national product per capita	$310
Gross domestic product growth, 1993	4.2%
Gross domestic product growth anticipated, 1995	6.0% +
Annual population growth rate	2.1%
Infant mortality per 1,000 births	79
Literacy	52.1%
People per doctor	2,272
People per telephone	111
Population	903.9 million
National capital	New Delhi
Major trading partners	U.S.A., Japan

Sources: United Nations, World Bank, and various
publications

nation can claim a greater fealty to democracy; for even though it was temporarily suspended by Indira Gandhi's 1977–1979 Emergency, it is clear that she and the nation felt that democratic forms of governance are the only ones that are legitimate.

It is, of course, an imperfect democracy. Every election is accompanied by violence, ballot box-stuffing, and other egregious behaviors. Not all of the forces or parties in India seem committed to democracy, and these especially appear to fail one of the premier tests of any such system—namely, tolerance for minorities and their rights.

The democratic commitment seems to remain despite all of these problems, and there are some obvious reasons for this. First, the institutions bequeathed to the system by the British are ostensibly—though certainly not invariably—democratic. Parliamentary government, a bureaucracy that supposedly listens to the people and their complaints (one would wish for a better word than "supposedly" here, but that is the best that can be done), a federal system that may make some allowances for regional (though not caste, class, or religious) differences, party systems that provide some choices of policies, ideology, and leaders, and a court system that observes some (if not always all) rights of the accused—all of these are institutions that contain the promise, if not always the practice, of democratic governance.

Second, the military, which always is a force to be considered in the Third World, seems to subsume its interests under the civilian political leadership. Not all of the reasons for this are entirely clear, but it does appear to be a strong tendency. The military has never taken full advantage of situations when opportunities—and there have been many of them—have arisen for the implementation of its authority. Socialization, tradition, and other factors may account for this.

Next, it should be pointed out that Indian politics are based upon very extensive networks of support. At village or neighborhood levels, ideology and policy issues sometimes appear to be less important than established—and often changing—patterns of recruitment, favors, patronage, and working relationships. Identity with local or neighborhood leaders can be an important voting criterion; and, quite naturally, such patterns and loyalties are affected by the honeycomb of interests that work their way through all levels of Indian society, such as caste or class. The implications of these factors involve a broad level of participation in politics that is not always limited merely to the act of voting. The Indian public, by and large, seems to take an interest in politics and, depending upon time, place, and other circumstances, can be quite enthusiastic about candidates or parties. Ultimately, this provides strength for democracy because of the actions and expectations of this public.

Last, there may be a cultural reason that helps to explain this democratic commitment. This is a hazy area in which to make such a claim, perhaps, but it has been observed that while India is a country in which collective values are often espoused—practically every politician considers himself or herself a socialist of some sort—it is at the same time an individualistic society as well, full of small-scale entrepreneurs, farmers, and others who depend upon a great deal of self-reliance to carry them through the rigors of life. This rugged independence manages to ignore the bureaucracy, the politicians, and even the law on those occasions when this appears necessary, desirable, or both; and it is in most senses a democratic spirit that guides this individualistic independence.

This set of attitudes is found on the city streets and in the villages, and it is related to the hopes of Mohandas Gandhi, often considered the father of Indian independence, who led nonviolent protests against British rule. Gandhi believed that villages and urban neighborhoods could develop economic self-sufficiency through such activities as

spinning and weaving cloth, encouraging the development and employment of local tradespersons, and small-scale farming. This dream
appears to be losing its cogency as India moves into modernization
and industrialization. Perhaps it was never a practical or long-term
approach. This may be a source of sorrow to some who have adhered
to the Gandhian tradition; but an even greater regret is the loss of
commitment to nonviolence, and the loss of the memory of Gandhi
himself, which seems to have taken over the nation. Today's Indian
young people are found in long lines in front of theaters showing
violent, "Rambo"-type movies.

Nehru's Vision and India's Drift:
The Fate of a Democracy in Disorder

The first prime minister of India, Jawaharlal Nehru, took office in
1947 with a specific vision of his nation's hopes. A socialist with a
British education, he believed that a great deal of the Gandhian idea of
village and neighborhood organization of the economy could be applied, for he was a strong supporter of Indian self-sufficiency; but he
also believed in a modern industrial framework as well. He thought the
Soviet Union provided a good example of quick industrialization,
though he apparently had no enthusiasm for the brutal methods of
Stalinism. He believed in democracy, and he thought of his party, the
Congress party, as the operative vehicle for national aspirations since
it had been the political instrument of the cause of independence. He
believed the party should be an all-embracing mechanism to the
greatest extent possible, for it had a pluralistic structure that seemed
to take in the major castes, classes, regions, and economic interest
groups of India. He believed that socialism is both efficient and just,
and that such a system would more fairly distribute the fruits of the
prosperity, which the nation, in time, would surely come to enjoy.

India must be modernized, Nehru thought, and he had faith in the
processes of reason—as opposed to passion, tradition, or religion—
which, after all, are the mark of modernity. It is fair to say that he was
not a religious man; indeed, he looked upon religion as India's great
hindrance. He believed that the caste system must be done away with,
and quickly; on this point he underestimated quite badly the powers of
religion, tradition, and social life. He was of course a nationalist and
anticolonial, and biographies tell us that he imbued his daughter, Indira
Gandhi, with these values, and that she carried these forward with her

into the office of prime minister. Nehru was by all accounts close to the national hero, Mohandas Gandhi, though he never fully adopted his pacifism.

He could be quite ruthless. He used armed force to kick the Portuguese out of their enclave of Goa, on India's southeast coast; this could be justified, of course, in the name of anticolonialism. He also used armed force and the simple fact that the ruling maharajah of Jammu and Kashmir was a Hindu to prevent that state's affiliation with Pakistan. It could be reasonably argued that Jammu and Kashmir, with their large Muslim majority, should be joined with the Muslim state of Pakistan; but Nehru would have none of it. He fought wars to retain Kashmir and he defied UN resolutions in favor of a vote of its people to determine which nation they would join.

Nehru enjoyed prerogatives, as well as a certain deference, during his seventeen years as prime minister, which undoubtedly accompanied his role as hero of the independence movement. No prime minister who has since held the office has had this kind of power at his or her disposal (though Indira Gandhi, some would argue, came close to this). Some of this deference, however, was undoubtedly tied to a belief that this was a man who had a definite, long-range, and workable vision for the future of the country.

An important portion of that vision was Nehru's concept of India's role on the world stage. It is generally conceded that Nehru, perhaps with the limited help of advisers, came up with "neutralism," the idea that there was no need to be aligned with the Soviet Union nor with the United States in their great power struggle. This was later changed to the idea of "nonalignment," but that is merely a question of semantics. At the core of this idea was a positive, rather than passive, role in world leadership. Nehru believed that his "neutralism" could provide an example for other nations to follow; and in this case he was quite right, for many did do precisely that. This approach was supposed to carry important moral weight with it. Though critics would demur on this point, the idea did possess some power. Neutral or nonaligned states were supposedly eschewing the power politics of the world in favor of something far more positive; namely, the development of the world's poor nations in order to rid their peoples of the plagues of starvation, disease, homelessness, and hopelessness. Few can deny that such a message has some merit in it.

In addition, this approach to world politics contained an advantage for nonaligned nations. They could ask for help from the West or the East or both, and to a very limited extent—much more limited than most observers seem to suppose—they could leverage this support for aid because of the prospect that the other side would also be giving aid. To a great extent, the nations who adopted this stance owed any success to the path-finding approach established by Nehru and by the government of India.

India itself benefited from this course, as one might expect; indeed, one who travels across almost any region of the country will find a Soviet-inaugurated project here, a European Community agricultural or industrial project there, a U.S. project here or there (though many or most of these are privately launched, rather than governmental), and many others as well—British, Australian, United Nations, charitable groups, and religious groups, usually but not always Christian. On one hand it is clear that many of these are good for India. On the other, the traveler might observe that many people seem to have ideas and prescriptions for India, which was just the case in colonial days. In some ways India seems to have changed over the years; but in other ways, perhaps not.

One of the perennial presences in India is the Congress party, now called Congress (I). The additional initial is a legacy of Indira Gandhi, whose tumultuous fifteen years as prime minister, which ended with her assassination in 1984, formally factionalized the party. Congress is not the dominant force of the Nehru, or post-independence, years, but it still enjoys a status as the party of governance, which the country invariably seems to turn to; it has ruled India for very much the majority of the time since 1947. It seems to be less successful today at the state level where, quite often, a state-based party of one kind or another provides strong competition. These state parties regularly eschew participation in federal elections, a situation that can create fluid loyalties. Some persons, leaders, or local political machines may support one party federally and another at the state level. State parties also are frequently tied to an ethnic or language group; this is the case in the Punjab, Assam, and Tamil Nadu, for example. The Communist parties—there are two of these—seem to enjoy the greatest level of support in the states of Kerala and West Bengal; in the latter, their base is in poverty-stricken Calcutta. One of the worldwide trends involving Communist parties is a decline in support since the demise of the Soviet Union and other Communist states; but this is not the case in India. Probably the most important new current in party politics is the Bharitiya Janata Party, or BJP, the Hindu nationalist party. As this is written it possesses the status of the official opposition, since it has more representation in the national parliament than any other opposition party. Many observers have thought its star would rise because it seems able to play upon a variety of grievances, including affirmative action laws, and because it appears consonant with a kind of Hindu revival that is both socially and politically important. It also benefits from the stance of support for religion, a unique position amidst all of the secular parties of the nation. Recent state elections, all the same, have given the party significant setbacks, reflecting a tendency of many or most voters to support secularist traditions. Since it has never held power at the national level, the BJP can effectively direct some of its appeals against the corruption that typically has accompanied Congress governments. And even the most casual observer will note that the BJP is a disciplined party in which the leadership has an advantage of respect and authority. The Congress Party, by comparison, is invariably involved with factionalism, dissenting groups, and an organizational character that can only be called chaotic.

Political campaigns are raucous affairs. The violence of these has already been noted; but they are also loud, quite enthusiastic affairs (at least on the surface), and they are surely media-oriented. Accusation and hyperbole are the order of the day. A significant portion of the electorate is illiterate and probably unsophisticated, but there is also a wariness about politicians that can be felt in the villages and urban neighborhoods. Crowds are bought; that is, politicians or their intimates actually pay groups of people to show up to demonstrate their "support" for a candidate. Loudspeakers and music are often employed in the villages or perhaps in a park or open space in one of the cities.

Film and television play special roles in the country's political campaigns. Candidates make films and present them at village meetings or other rallies. India is a film-going nation by any measure, standard, or comparison that can be devised, and so this is a popular medium indeed with which to develop a campaign. Candidates are known to make films at rallies, focus on a variety of individual supporters, and then show the film later with the candidate and the chosen subjects in obvious "starring" roles; this device is exceptional for ingratiating politicians with voters. And candidates themselves are often involved with the film industry in a variety of ways—as stars (as in the case of the premier of the Tamil Nadu state), as producers, or as persons situated in some other capacity in this very popular industry.

Political rallies can often be centers of very animated mass behavior. Emotions run high and violence can ensue, and this is specially the case if the topic—such as affirmative action law or the situation in Kashmir—is one that touches upon ethnic or religious differences found in the country. And peace can seldom be found to prevail in the country, because there is nearly always an election to be run somewhere, at either the national or state levels. State elections are operated at staggered intervals and do not work in concert as they do in the United States, for example, where many or most of them are held simultaneously. In addition, there often seem to be some extraordinary factors at work that can create further instability; an example of this can be shown by the fact that four state governments dominated recently by the BJP were placed under federal control on the grounds that this is necessary for security reasons in the aftermath of sectarian riots.

Despite the overall commitment to democratic norms and practices, it can be said that human rights problems abound in India. The religious riots that occurred after the destruction of the mosque at Ayodhya, for example, also produced examples of police authorities, almost invariably Hindus, beating Muslims or even sacking their homes. Less sensationally but more widespread, the problem of child and poor labor bondage is acute. Children, and sometimes their parents, become indebted to sweatshop operators, often found in such trades as garments or shoes, who then work them for long hours in exchange for little or no pay. Somehow the employer never manages to find that the debts of these bondage victims are wiped off the books. This activity is illegal, but enforcement is the problem. The position of women, especially in village life, is in substantial need of improvement. Dowries are misused so that a practice of actual bride purchase, and sometimes enslavement, is set into motion. And in the worst instances, wife burning and other cruelties are carried out. Amnesty International, the civil liberties watch organization, is far from giving India a clean bill of health in its judgments.

India's Political Culture

Generalizations about India, just as with China, are made even by specialists with some fears. The diversity of India is daunting enough, whether the subject is region, society, economy, religion, caste, class, language, or the matter of urban and rural contrasts. It could be claimed that India is made up of many nations, and it is certain that each of these diverse elements can manage to win the attention of politicians.

The division between North and South is one of the most obvious and important of the sets of social, historical, linguistic, and political differences found in the Republic. The North has been subjected, more often and more intensely than the South, to invasions from the East and West, both military and cultural. Lasting legacies from these invasions include a more pronounced Muslim presence in the North, a greater mixture of diverse ethnic and religious groups, and influences upon dress, art, architecture, and cultural values. South India is held out by many as the home of the "true" culture of India, a place in which foreign intervention into the life of the nation has been minimized to a much greater extent. The South, also called Dravidian India, contains peoples who, for the most part, have therefore less to do over recent centuries with peoples who have come from other lands. Their languages, cultures, and ways of life seem more traditional; and this image is buttressed by a weaker emphasis upon industrialization and modernization. These are generalizations, of course; and one can point to less-developed areas in the North, such as the state of Rajasthan, or to the technological center of the South, Bangalore, to make exceptions to these.

The states of India also provide a dimension of regional difference, since their boundaries come close to coinciding with ethnic and language demarcations. In some cases, like Assam and the Punjab, these involve broad and dynamic nationalistic aspirations; in others, such as Tamil Nadu or West Bengal, the idea of a nation as such may be less intense—if such matters can be measured—but there are forms of assertiveness and resentment that can be sensed. In the cases of the two latter states, there are resentments against making Hindi the national language and the language not only of the bureaucracy, but of anyone who seeks to enter into it. (Hindi is probably spoken by more Indians than any language, but it is not the tongue of a national majority.) There are also a variety of sometimes subtle, sometimes obvious differences in religion, political choices, and cultural values.

Religious differences have been a major fractionizer running under, and sometimes threatening, Indian society. The massacres and riots between Hindus and Muslims have received worldwide attention, but there are also significant differences within each of these groups. There are also deep divisions, however, between the Sikhs and the rest of the country, which have recently led to violence, and there can be frictions with smaller groups as well, whether these be Christians, Buddhists, Jains, or Zoroastrians.

The most unique social differences found in India, though, are based upon caste. The caste system is a part of the creed of Hinduism that is not always well understood in the West. It provides a social and occupational role to each individual so that everyone understands his or her rung on the ladder and knows what society may expect of him or her as a result of this placement. It is tied to the Hindu belief in reincarnation, and an individual can apparently better her or his lot in the next life by setting a good example in the present one. The highest caste, the Brahmins, are the source of recruitment for Hindu priests, and all Brahmins are vegetarians. The lowest caste, the Untouchables, must distance themselves from other castes and can sometimes communicate only by the use of indirect and approved customary methods. The four major caste groups found in most parts of India are further subdivided into various categories, and the caste system is not a uniform system throughout all of India. In the southern state of Kerala, for example, the caste system appears to be far more complex than that which is operative in most other states. Following Nehru's vision, the national government has not really tried to abolish caste, as he would have liked, but it does seek to soften its harshest effects through affirmative action laws that give lower castes (and sometimes middle castes) certain advantages in seeking government or other employment.

Some Indians claim that an end to the caste system is only a matter of time; and some of these will even set a limit of only two more generations. But the caste system has endured far longer than its critics and opponents have, and it will therefore be necessary to wait and see if the demise of caste is in the offing. So far, there seems to be little sign of this. True, some modern and urban types have chosen to ignore caste in their marriage patterns, their work life, and so forth, but this group clearly is in the minority.

Caste, it goes without saying, helps to establish the nation's class system, and to a great extent, this even affects the lives of non-Hindus. This is because it is quite impossible to avoid the implications of the caste system anywhere in India. If, however, we are to describe class differences in economic terms, it is clear that India lives with these as well. Though it is a nation known for its masses of people who live in poverty and perhaps for its relatively small numbers of rich people, the modern economy has evolved to the point at which there is now a middle-class market of 175 million people. This market is larger than the entire market of customers in many nations.

Western cultures have made some mark on India, especially in terms of the values associated with economic development and modernization. Though it is a republic that does not recognize the British monarchy, India has maintained an active role in Commonwealth meetings and deliberations and has provided leadership on issues like apartheid in South Africa. There has also been a strong retention of the nongovernmental links established by the Commonwealth connection, such as education, cultural exchange, and some economic connections. The argument over whether most Indians value modernization as opposed to tradition is an old and somewhat tedious one, but it seems clear that most of the people prefer the advantages of modernization while still holding on to their heritage. The overall impression one will probably obtain if she or he visits India is that the years of British rule amounted to little more than a gloss on the much older and more complex social and aesthetic structures of the country. The idea that the British could affect India very much more than this was patently absurd from the beginnings of the colonial period; and it was a relief to all concerned, the British included, when the Union Jack was removed in favor of the Indian flag over the Red Fort in Delhi in 1947. Perhaps the strongest evidence of this mere patina of British influence is found in the style of colonization that prevailed, an indirect rule that left many of the governing mechanisms in local hands.

The Economy, Foreign and Trade Relations, and National Security Policy

Nehru's nonaligned vision of India applied to the domestic economy as well as to the nation's foreign policy stance. He liked the Soviet emphasis upon state ownership of heavy industries and equality of resources distribution, but he preferred the easier-going ways of democracy for the political system. This meant that the nation would have a mixed economy made up of state ownership, regulation, and entrepreneurship, with the latter most in evidence at the small firm level. There have been of course some large-scale private entrepreneurs in such fields as the manufacture of trucks, garments, and home appliances. But the emphasis upon a socialist economic life for India brought with it a big emphasis upon Eastern bloc trade and upon filling up the country with Soviet economic and technical advisers of various kinds. These contacts and the neutral stance taken in foreign policy caused the United States to stay at arm's length from India, trading and providing aid in sporadic and sometimes minimal ways.

Economic arrangements can affect security strategies, and this has certainly been the case with the United States and India. The United States turned to Pakistan, a smaller but more cooperative power, and linked it to two treaties—the Central Treaty Organization, or CENTO, and the Southeast Asia Treaty Organization, or SEATO—in which the United States is the dominant member. (Pakistan now has neither of these obligations.) In addition, Pakistan became a favored aid recipient; in recent years, though no longer, it has held a position among the top five aid donees for U.S. largesse. To a great extent, this is because Pakistan provided moral, material, and logistic support for anti-Communist rebel forces in neighboring Afghanistan. This tilt toward Pakistan, a neighbor that has frequently waged war against it, has further cooled India's attitudes toward the United States.

At a people-to-people level, relationships between Americans and Indians have nearly always been amicable on both sides; but on a government-to-government level, the United States and India have not managed to get along very well through most of the Cold War era.

Only now, with the end of the leverage of Third World countries based upon nonalignment, is this relationship finally warming up; conversely, the U.S.-Pakistan alliance seems to be breaking down under the pressures of Pakistan's noncompliance with the Nuclear Nonproliferation Treaty and with U.S. requests to refrain from building atomic weaponry. These are offenses that historically have been committed only on the Indian side.

A major reason for this warming up is that the United States has probably always preferred to get along well with India. It is frankly much bigger and more important than Pakistan. But differences remain. These have now moved most markedly into the area of international trade. The United States seems to believe, officially at least, that India is an unfair trading partner for a variety of reasons. It allegedly dumps products on the market at prices below cost; it does not permit sufficient access to its own market; and it does not observe international patent and copyright protections. It has been impossible, for example, to obtain Coca-Cola in India until very recently because of a dispute between the company and the government of whether the latter should have access to the "Coke" product formula. On the other hand, it is quite easy for one who knows what he or she is doing to buy well-established international computer software products very cheaply in shops in India. These are major sore points for the U.S. Commerce Department, and India has been placed on its list of major fair trade violators several times in recent years—on more occasions, for example, than Japan.

During the term in office of Prime Minister Rajiv Gandhi (1984–1989), the son of Indira and grandson of Nehru, a loosening up of economic arrangements took place. Rajiv reduced some of the regulatory apparatus that plagued foreign investors, either through changes in laws or administrative practices, and he looked into the possibilities for selling off some state-run industries, though he did little of this. He also opened up some of India's trade administration—customs, product requirements, and so forth—while making it clear that foreign investment was more welcome than in the past.

It is fair to say that a trickle of foreign investment was brought in, and that some has been occurring since; but the trend has not been one of straightforward progress. And India is probably quite right about safeguarding its own interests, a view that requires moving slowly in this area. The economy has sometimes had good growth rates in recent years, though it is difficult to assess whether increased foreign investment has had a lot to do with this; but this growth comes close to being outpaced by the twin evils of inflation and an overabundance of people.

The population problem is serious. The average couple in India reproduces at a rate of five children per family. Population measures taken in the past have been far too severe to win the confidence of the people; these have included forced sterilization and the tracking down of poor, pregnant women by authorities. This overkill approach, taken during the days of Indira Gandhi's power, resulted in hindering rather than furthering the causes of family planning and birth control.

The population problem of India is evident on every hand. Anyone who goes through the streets of Madras in a very early morning hour, for example, will notice clusters of youths gathered around water pumps. They fill their stainless steel vessels with water from these pumps; but why do they do this in the wee hours before dawn? Because there simply will not be any water to pump at some point later in the day. The tanks are filled shortly after midnight by water trucks that have come from the South after a visit to a riverside area. These trucks fill the highways from the South with their quenching loads. At one time not very long ago, however—certainly less than two decades ago—there was no need for such trucks. Now, however, the population of Madras is so great that water must be brought daily to the city, and this problem is only expected to get worse before it can in any way get better. This is but one striking example of the changes in peoples' lives dictated by population pressures. The major one, most would agree, is the reduction in living standards forced upon most people by this pressure. India's economic growth is obviously jeopardized by this handicap.

U.S. policies in recent years could have been more helpful, at least indirectly. The Reagan and Bush administrations enforced the Buckley Act against India and other nations by refusing to fund any aid programs, UN, other public, or private, which included assistance on abortion or birth control matters, including the dissemination of information. President Bill Clinton rescinded this order during his first month in office.

Another policy matter that affects the Indian economy is the insistence in recent years, particularly during the period of Rajiv Gandhi's leadership, upon building up a large military machine. As a result India has become a major Asian power and indeed is the dominant military presence in the South Asian region. Troops have been dispatched to such nearby countries as Sri Lanka and the Maldives; sophisticated weapons systems have been purchased; and India has adopted what it feels is the appropriate belligerent stance toward Pakistan, Nepal, and other nations. The military buildup has been so extensive that Japan has noted it and has filed its objections. China undoubtedly also looks askance at a neighbor that seems, in some ways, to be imitating its policies. The overall effect is destabilizing in a region that is a powder keg.

Further Reading

China

Dryer, June T. *The Chinese Political System: Tradition and Modernization.* New York: Paragon House, 1993. A new text written by a well-regarded China scholar.

Fairbank, John K. *China: A New History.* Cambridge: Harvard University Press, 1992. Cultural insights and a consistency of treatments of various topics makes this one of the best books of its genre.

————. *The Great Chinese Revolution: 1800–1985.* New York: Harper and Row, 1986. A detailed account of nineteenth-century growth and change and the two attempts of China to create a modern society.

Hinton, William. *Fanshen: A Documentary of Revolution in a Chinese Village.* New York: Vintage Books, 1966.

———. *Iron Oxen: A Documentary of a Revolution in Chinese Farming.* New York: Monthly Review Press, 1970. Hinton provides a deep and sympathetic look into the system of Mainland China at the village level, including a thorough examination of such institutions as Maoist self-criticism.

Macchiarola, Frank J., and Robert B. Oxnam, eds. *The China Challenge: American Politics in East Asia.* New York: Academy of Political Science, 1991. Excellent collection of papers from a recent conference devoted to Chinese political economy and foreign policy.

Newman, Robert P. *Owen Lattimore and the "Loss" of China.* Berkeley: University of California Press, 1992. Documents the hysteria in the United States in the early 1950s, which led to a national incapacity to deal realistically with China.

Ningkun, Wu. *A Single Tear: A Family's Persecution, Love and Endurance in Communist China.* Boston: Atlantic Monthly Press, 1993. Gripping personal narrative of an intellectual who still believes in China and its future in spite of enormous suffering and personal sacrifice.

Pye, Lucian W. *The Spirit of Chinese Politics*, new ed. Cambridge: Harvard University Press, 1992. One of the preeminent Asia scholars examines Chinese culture; controversial and thought provoking.

Wasserstrom, Jeffrey, and Elizabeth Perry, eds. *Popular Protest and Political Culture in Modern China.* Boulder: Westview Press, 1992. One of several works that examine the 1989 student protests and their aftermath.

India

Ashe, Geoffrey. *Gandhi.* New York: Stein and Day, 1968. Hundreds of books describe the life and work of Gandhi, so this is one of many efforts.

Brecher, Michael. *Nehru: A Political Biography,* abridged ed. Boston: Beacon Press, 1962. There are many works on Nehru, but this one is a good introduction because it is both concise and readable.

Houseman, Gerald L. "India and the U. S. Press." *Indian Journal of Political Science* 32 (July/September, 1991): 396–405. Considers mutual perspectives of the two countries in the aftermath of the assassination of Rajiv Gandhi.

Jayakar, Pupal. *Indira Gandhi: An Intimate Biography.* New York: Pantheon, 1993. Heralded new biography that describes a key period in recent Indian history.

Kohli, Atul. *Democracy and Discontent: India's Growing Crisis of Governability.* New York: Cambridge University Press, 1990. Covers most of the major problems facing India today and places them within the context of this overall problem of governability; very insightful.

Kohli Atul, ed. *India's Democracy: An Analysis of Changing State-Society Relations.* Princeton: Princeton University Press, 1990. Sometimes uneven as with all collections; but these essays and articles describe and assess groups, institutions, and issues within an overall framework of some continuity and consistency.

Naipaul, V. S. *India: A Million Mutinies Now*. New York: Viking, 1991.

——. *India: A Wounded Civilization*. New York: Knopf, 1977. Examinations of India through the eyes of a great literary talent and cultural examiner; his two books carry contrasting assessments that reveal changes in India or in the author or perhaps both.

Rudolph, Lloyd L., and Susanne Hoeber Rudolph. *In Pursuit of Lakshmi: The Political Economy of the Indian State*. Chicago: University of Chicago Press, 1987. Authoritative analysis that, despite its title, examines the politics and culture as ably as it covers the economy.

Tully, Mark. *India: Forty Years of Independence*. New York: George Braziller, 1988. This is probably a good history with which to begin a study of India; more in-depth works can be taken up after achieving the basic kind of understanding provided here.

Chapter 6

The Asian ''Tigers''—The Strong New Economies of Hong Kong, Singapore, South Korea, Taiwan, and Malaysia—and the Hopefuls Who Want To Join Them

An abrupt change in the established wisdom about Asia, and about development theory in general, has been caused by the strong perform-ance of five economies over the past decade—Hong Kong, Singapore, South Korea, and Taiwan, which have each acquired the label of new Asian ''tiger'' because of their swift and strong growth. The fifth is Malaysia, which has also turned in a very impressive performance but still has some way to go to match the living standards of the other four. These nations have witnessed a rise in almost every area by which their economies and living standards can be measured, and they have all established themselves as serious and worthwhile trading partners in the international marketplace. And, not incidentally, their success has demonstrated the potential of other nations, Asian and otherwise, who aspire to participate fully in the world economy. It is believed, for example, that Indonesia, Thailand, and, perhaps, the Philippines have some hope of eventually following suit.

The fast growth rates and other signs of progress in the five newly advanced countries, first noticed by scholars and journalists in the mid-1980s, may at first impression suggest that these nations found one magic formula that they all followed. But the facts of governmental administration and economic organization, as well as elements of sheer political style, seem to show that this is not the case.

129

It is true that these countries contain cultural influences such as the work ethic and orderliness associated with Confucianism. It is also certain that a number of economic conditions were brought to bear upon these countries at about the same time, if not simultaneously. The Lewis model (see Chapter 2) is a good reference to these conditions, for all of these countries have long passed the point of maximum investment opportunity for low-tech ventures; in other words, they have established not only adequate or better nutrition levels, but they now have labor costs that exceed other potential arenas of interest, such as Indonesia and Thailand. The workforces of these five nations have acquired skills that seem to keep them in investment range for sophisticated or high-tech industries, but which remove them from consideration as laborers in low-tech industries.

Generally speaking, the five countries also meet a minimum or better standard of political stability, a further requirement for enticing the interest of investors. The one exception to this on our list might be Hong Kong, but the special factors there will be explained.

The importance of cultural and economic factors in the development of these nations is undeniable, but there have also been notable political changes as well. In all cases these countries can be held to fall short of generally accepted standards for a democracy even today; but today is in all cases an improvement upon the past.

Hong Kong of course is a colony, which by definition means that it is not self-governing; so one of the basics of a democratic society is missing. The people of Hong Kong and the British government have, all the same, sought to establish a measure of democratic representation within the political system in recent years. The motivation for this is the assumption of rule by China in 1997. With some democratic representation in place, it is hoped, China will be somewhat less likely to be as repressive as it might otherwise be; elected representatives, after all, possess a measure of legitimacy that is difficult for a regime like China's to match. The Beijing government, so far, has shown disdain for these arrangements, and it would unquestionably prefer to take over a traditionally run and completely undemocratic political system.

The city-state of Singapore is only a quarter-century old. It split off from Malaysia in 1965 by mutual agreement. Various reasons are given for this split, but it is hard to avoid the conclusion that Chinese-majority Singapore preferred to run its own affairs without the interference of Kuala Lumpur. For its part, Malaysia, which is politically most controlled by its Malay majority, undoubtedly preferred the removal of this large number, literally millions, of Chinese from its politics. (To say that the two nations can ignore one another, however, would be too great a stretch for the imagination or for hardheaded analysis.) Singapore has had only one grouping, the Peoples Action Party (PAP), in charge of its government since its founding, and it has only known two prime ministers. The first of these, Lee Kwan Yew, served for twenty-five years and continues to hold the positions of senior minister and PAP leader. Opposition parties exist, but they have never won more than four of the eighty seats in the national parliament, and their leaders have experienced acute problems at times in the past, including incarceration.

South Korea has also been no great home for democratic government. In certain respects, this is more ironic than in the other cases listed here, since U.S. and UN forces fought a bloody three-year war from 1950 to 1953 in order to repel Communist forces from the North and China and to ensure self-rule. More than fifty thousand Americans died in this conflict. Most of the time since this war, the country has been under the authority of what can only be termed a military dictatorship. Among these leaders, Syngman Rhee and Park Chung Hee must be called embarrassments to the United States, which worked very hard to keep their regimes propped up. Student rebellions and other protests that have been carried out over the years have led to the toppling of such leaders, though often at a considerable cost in lives and injuries. The tradition of student rebellions continues to be strong and the labor movement has joined these legions of protest, but the past decade has seen a more serious commitment to elected government with a viable opposition. The current president, Kim Young Sam, is the first nonmilitary leader to rule the nation since 1956. He impressively won a three-way election race in 1993, which is too recent an installation for determining his lasting power. A discernible trend toward democratization is in evidence, however, despite its tentative qualities.

Such a trend now has appeared in Taiwan as well in recent years. This island country really initiated its modern history with the arrival of Chiang Kai-Shek and his battered and fleeing Nationalist remnants in 1949. The humiliation of defeat on the mainland was in turn met by a further humiliation of nonacceptance by the native Taiwanese (Formosan) people, who did not necessarily identify their fate with the Nationalists. This was the starting period for the long and drawn-out charade that this is indeed the government of China and, as the previous chapter points out, the United States was for many years a major supporter of this propaganda line. The Chiang Kai-Shek regime, first run by the vaunted general himself and later by his son, was ruthless and repressive, and many of its critics claimed that it was a police state to an extent almost as complete as that of the mainland regime. A gradual loosening seems to have appeared in the years since 1987, which, as in South Korea, marked the end of martial law; and for the first time it is possible to form opposition groups and seek election to the national parliament. The most recent election, in fact, saw a near-toppling of the government.

Among these shadings of regimes and practices, Malaysia may also be considered to be moving toward a system that is really democratic. It has functioning opposition parties and groups, though these have never won power at the federal level. On a few occasions they have won power at the state and local levels, however; and they hold many more seats in the national parliament than has typically been the case in countries like Singapore or Taiwan. The ruling party, the United Malays National Organization (UMNO) also contains constituent elements such as the Malaysian Chinese Association (MCA) and the Malaysian Indian Congress (MIC), which have some impact upon national policy making as well as upon UMNO's political machinery. There is even a rather well-organized civil liberties group built around the critical magazine *Aliran*. Unfortunately, the government's fealty to democratic practices and procedures has not been constant. A recent year, 1987, saw the imposition of national emergency measures, including the closing down of a newspaper and the arrests of members of the national parliament. And there is undeniably a tie between such practices and ethnic divisions, which can be a source of friction in Malaysia. The inclusion of Malaysia in this category of Asian "tigers" is qualified by its lower living standards and the worry that its infrastructure—roads, telephone system, water systems, and so forth—may not hold up under the pressure of further industrial and economic development.

Hong Kong—Is There a Life after 1997?

Possibly the greatest upheaval facing Asia and the Pacific Rim in the next years could take place in Hong Kong. The year 1997 ends the treaty between Britain and China under which Hong Kong and the New Territories have held the status of Crown Colony for a hundred years. (The New Territories are a mainland area adjacent to Hong

Kong and other islands.) At that time the area will formally come under control of China once again. And most observers presently agree that the politics of the colony now reflect the reality of this takeover.

Like Shanghai, Guangzhou, and other ports of China, Hong Kong has been under control of a European power. The only difference is that the British, French, and others have long since lost their positions of control in the other coastal cities. In a certain sense, Hong Kong must be seen as an anachronism of the colonial era.

Hong Kong has really made its mark since 1949 when Communist forces took over mainland China. A cold and harsh swim, a short boat ride, or similar means have been used by millions of Chinese to leave the mainland and establish a new home in the Crown Colony. The population growth of Hong Kong and the New Territories has therefore proved to be nothing short of phenomenal: from a level well below two million in 1949 to well over six million today. A statistical overview is provided by Figure 6.1.

Anyone who takes even a brief look at Hong Kong will notice that it is what can only be called "the tallest city in the world." Short buildings in the colony are certainly the exceptions to the rule—the authorities have deliberately kept some old colonial administration

Fig. 6.1
Hong Kong

Gross national product per capita	$18,500
Gross domestic product growth, 1993	5.5%
Gross domestic product growth anticipated, 1995	5.0%
Annual population growth rate	1.8%
Infant mortality per 1,000 births	5
Literacy	88.1%
People per doctor	866
People per telephone	1.5
Population	6.1 million
National capital	Victoria
Major trading partners	U.S.A., Germany, Japan

Sources: United Nations, World Bank, and various publications

buildings intact, for example—while apartment blocs of forty or more stories are common. And this kind of construction does not stop on Hong Kong Island or its outlying areas such as Repulse Bay; Kowloon, across the harbor, is equally tall, as are the settlements and industrial parks found farther up in the New Territories, within very close proximity of the border with China. These tall buildings, one after another, jammed against each other in what is perhaps the most land-scarce political unit in the world, make a statement that says, very decisively, that the people in them do not want to live in China.

But they must, anyway. The British lease on the colony is to expire, and what is to happen then? In the previous chapter, it was suggested that maybe Hong Kong is closer to taking over China than vice versa. This was said tongue in cheek, however, and only for the purpose of suggesting the dynamism of the capitalistic processes set into motion—often by Hong Kong or Taiwanese interests—within the boundaries permitted by the mainland's Marxist rulers. The only answer that can be given to the question of what will happen to Hong Kong, then, is that it will depend upon what the 1997 rulers of China think and do. They may see that it is to their advantage to allow Hong Kong to keep doing its capitalistic thing; in other words, it will be seen—if it is not now recognized—that the roles performed by Hong Kong in the world benefit China far too much for any interference with the functioning of the economy to be practical. It is the base of operations for many of the profitable enterprises now found in China. It is the banker, trader, broker, and sometimes the money-launderer for China's links with the world. It is a consumer of Chinese products, especially foodstuffs, but also of a wide variety of Chinese services. And it is a supplier of many of the goods valued on the mainland, whether these are produced in Hong Kong or elsewhere.

It could also be the case that Hong Kong will be subjected to a variety of ideological strictures and even human rights violations, so that the third year prior to the end of the century is looked upon as the beginning of very dark days. There are also a variety of other responses the regime might make in which shadings or gradations of this or that tendency will appear while others do not. Even the most optimistic observers concede, however, that Hong Kong will lose many of its market-spawned efficiencies and will pick up some dead-handed bu-reaucracies that are bound to change the character, and certainly the economy, of the place.

The future must therefore be regarded as uncertain; but the re-sponses of Hong Kong show both confidence and its lack. Investment, construction, and other patterns of endeavor do not, in the main, seem to belie any impending sense of doom, though there can be fits and starts. The two years after the Tiananmen Square repression and deaths set Hong Kong on edge, and there were slowdowns in the economy caused by a lack of investor interest and a rather large amount of emigration. Key and valued employees of many firms left for Canada, the United States, Britain, and other climes (though Thatcherite Britain, it must be said, hardly put out the welcome mat for Chinese emigrés). Sometimes bizarre ideas and policies take hold: the small Central American state of Belize, for example, offered Hong Kong residents its passports at a price of $25,000 (U.S.) each, and a letter to the editor of the *South China Morning Post* earnestly suggested that the people of Hong Kong could all be taken to the Falkland Islands, off the Argentine coast, to make new homes for themselves there.

The years since the post-Tiananmen period have largely seen a revival of Hong Kong's economy and a posting of very impressive levels of growth. This suggests a measure of confidence for the future that one might hope is not misplaced.

The role of Britain in helping to protect this future must be considered ambiguous at best and altogether expedient at worst. It is true that in 1992 and 1993 the appointed governor, Chris Patten, sternly demanded Chinese respect not only for the human rights of Hong Kong people after 1997, but also agreement that newly instituted procedures for electing representatives to a council will be maintained. His leverage on the Beijing government for this is necessarily limited, but Patten has felt that exposure of the Chinese regime and its policies to world public opinion and to Hong Kong residents would be beneficial. Prime Minister Margaret Thatcher and her successor, John Major, however, have made no policy moves or statements that would suggest that Hong Kong citizens can harbor any hopes of migrating to Britain should this become necessary. An apocryphal story has one of these leading Tories asking another person, "What would happen if five million Hong Kong Chinese moved to Britain?" And the person answered, "We would probably see a steep rise in economic growth."

The mainland regime carries out an intensive surveillance of Hong Kong's government policies and administration. It objected to the recent establishment of elections for some of the legislative positions. It freely offers advice on budgetary questions and can be adamant about its views on these. Beijing does not like a new airport project, for example, because it believes that this helps to drain the Hong Kong treasury in this period just prior to the Chinese takeover and may incur financial obligations with which it does not want to be saddled. Most ominously, Chinese pressure against British officialdom has sometimes been so great that the latter has discouraged criticism of Beijing. This has an effect, of course, of implementing suppression of free speech even before authority changes hands.

The great success of Hong Kong's economy over recent years has relied extensively upon its role as a port and the many services implied by the status of a relatively free state—at least in economic if not in political terms—sitting in an advantageous locale on the rim of the world's largest country. Some analysts hail the success of the economy as a result of the colony's unique positions, both in political status and in geography; while others hold that Hong Kong's regulations-free approach to economic management is the major factor. There is little doubt that there has also been some benefit from its position on the Lewis model curve, which at one time would have brought in a variety of investment initiatives. Hong Kong no longer is the relatively cheap labor market it once was—its per capita income now easily exceeds Britain's—but it can continue to make the most of its natural and political advantages.

Culturally, Hong Kong's roots are close to the same ones found on the mainland (see Chapter 3). Its security in the future will clearly be in the hands of China, for good or ill, and no analyst, Chinese, British, or American, seems to dispute this.

The prosperous Portuguese colony of Macau, located across the mouth of the Pearl River delta from Hong Kong, has a lease that is to last two years longer. China can legally take it over in 1999. Macau is a tiny enclave that does not even fill out the peninsula upon which it sits. It is difficult to travel more than two and a half miles in the same direction and remain within its borders. Its size is slightly supplemented by three small islands attached to it. Macau was once a part of a chain of Portuguese ports that included Malacca on the Malay Peninsula and Goa in India. Today it is known for its gambling halls, horse races, nightclubs, and other entertainments. It is dependent upon Hong Kong, since access to the outside world relies mostly on its airport. The fate of Macau's 450,000 people, many of them former residents of China, will hinge upon the attitudes and policies of the Chinese leadership at the time of the lease expiration; to a great extent, of course, this is already the case.

Singapore—A Model for Asia? Or Perhaps the World?

The elegantly manicured city-state of Singapore is a delight for many tourists or traveling business people. Its orderly traffic so untypical of Southeast Asia, its clean streets, and its profusion of malls, restaurants, and hotels make it a magnet for visitors from the West or elsewhere. The usual problems associated with the urban scene—crime, unemployment, homelessness, and some types of environmental pollution—are nonexistent or at least well under control. The standard of living is very high indeed, whether comparisons are made with other parts of Asia or with the whole list of nations in the world. As in the case of Hong Kong, the measurement of living standards shows a level above that of Britain, which once ruled the city (see Fig. 6.2).

If imitation is a form of flattery, Singapore should feel quite good about itself. The sultan of Oman has said that his desert kingdom should be like Singapore, and he has set out decrees following this pattern. The nearby states of Malaysia and Thailand have both been at work on their national identity card programs, and the system they seek to emulate is Singapore's. And a variety of books, articles, and

Fig. 6.2
Singapore

Gross national product per capita	$17,400
Gross domestic product growth, 1993	11.0%
Gross domestic product growth anticipated, 1995	9.0%
Annual population growth rate	2.0%
Infant mortality per 1,000 births	5
Literacy	91.6%
People per doctor	711
People per telephone	2
Population	3.1 million
National capital	Singapore
Major trading partners	U.S.A., Japan

Sources: United Nations, World Bank, and various publications

conference papers state that Singapore is a paradigm for the future of Asia if not for the world. In response, Singapore offers seminars, conferences, and publications for the benefit of would-be imitators.

Working against this consensus are two international human rights organizations who have noticed the shortcomings of Singapore in this vital area of concern; in addition, occasional press reports, such as a recent description of a law banning chewing gum from the country, help to give the city-state a quirky reputation. Singapore is known, for example, for its heavy fines for littering, failing to flush a public toilet, or smoking in an unauthorized location, for its absolute limit on the number of automobiles permitted in the country, and for its red light cameras at certain traffic locations. Perhaps the best known phenomenon of Singapore society, however, is its proposal for an efficient and complete electronic identity card system, which some analysts equate with Big Brother statism.

Adding to this image is the heavy socialization and propaganda effort carried out by the government in television messages. It urges couples to marry and procreate at a young age; it stresses the growth of families; and it calls for strong support of the military as it seeks to provide protection for the little state. Most importantly, these television commercials identify and promote the nation as a multicultural land in which all groups—Chinese, Malay, Indian, or whatever—can participate fully in the rewards of being Singaporean without fear of bias or discrimination.

Singapore is sensitive to its multicultural heritage. It has to be, because it experienced race riots prior to its establishment as an independent country in 1965 and, just as compelling, it continues to feel the tensions generated within society by the various ethnic groups. An example of response to this is the rule that limits the number of members of ethnic groups in each housing bloc or neighborhood. Since this rule sets out proportions based on population numbers, however, it means that every locale will have a Chinese majority. The Chinese population represents approximately 76 percent of Singapore, and the remainder is made up of Malays, the original inhabitants of the area, and Indians, who were brought in by the British to work in the rubber and palm oil plantations of the Malay Peninsula. Singapore is the only country in Southeast Asia in which the Chinese segment of the population controls its own political destiny; this is hardly the case in such nearby countries as Malaysia, Indonesia, or Thailand. It hardly needs to be said that they intend to hold on to this position of power.

Lee Kwan Yew and the government like to remind people that as recently as the 1970s, Singapore was a poor Third World nation. Many of its citizens lived in kampongs, poor villages on the outskirts of the central city, and they did not enjoy modern housing or sanitation standards. The government took a receptive stance toward international investors and sought to encourage the kind of atmosphere businesses are most likely to appreciate. At the same time, the dynamics of the Lewis model were at work, bringing investment to the scene of low labor costs coupled with adequate nutrition. Singapore made the most of these advantages, providing political stability, a comparatively well-educated workforce, and to some degree, a rather heavy-handed role in the lives of its citizens.

Singapore made itself the shopping mecca of Southeast Asia, the headquarters city for Asian operations of many firms, a center for tourism, and an innovator in economic and business policies. It has few if any natural resources, but it has made up for this with a sharply competitive approach. It has no oil, for example, but it is a major oil refiner in its part of the world. It does not have enough water for its people, so it purchases water from Malaysia, uses it, and also processes it for resale to Malaysia. It has a small population in comparison with most countries, but it has developed a formidable and modern military machine, all the same; and it is a major weapons exporter as well.

The results so far are the envy of many nations. An annual growth rate of GNP or GDP of 5 percent is considered low by recent historic standards. The trade balance with the United States, the European Community, and other partners is strongly on the plus side. The inexorable nature of the Lewis model works against Singapore, of course, because it has become a relatively high-wage nation that is well past the curve as a center for optimal low-wage investment opportunities. Whether its planners have heard of Lewis or not, they appear to be aware of these trends and are carrying out policies to make the best of Singapore's situation. They are using the city-state as a corporate headquarters and highly skilled center for industries whose manufacturing facilities are located in nearby low-cost labor markets such as Indonesia, Thailand, and, still to some extent, Malaysia. Indonesia's Batam Island, located just a short boat ride away from Singapore, has become an industrial park for many of this small country's investors.

As is the case with so many Asian nations, the U.S. balance of payments problem with Singapore is serious if it is looked at in per capita terms—that is, if it is viewed in the context of the size of the

Singapore population. It is not a serious problem, perhaps, if it is seen in absolute terms or in comparison with the overall trade deficit problems of the United States.

Although it is technically a nonaligned nation, Singapore sees itself as coming to the rescue of the U.S. fleet after its forced withdrawal from the Philippines. The city-state may therefore take on some, though hardly all, of the importance that has historically been attached to those facilities. But it may well serve, over the objections of Malaysia and other nearby states, in a vital supporting role for the continued presence of U.S. naval forces in the region.

South Korea—The Beginning of a New Era?

The possible trend toward a permanently democratic system in South Korea means that this nation may be entering a new political era. If this is the case, a democratic life for the Republic may enhance economic progress as well, though there seems to be no evidence that these two necessarily go together. Korea is presently looking for an economic turnaround, all the same, because the early 1990s recession has taken a heavy toll on employment, growth, and living standards. The term "recession" must be put into its proper context here. South Korea has known such a good performance in recent years that double-digit growth figures are not unusual; now, however, growth rates have dipped to the 5 percent range, which is good by international—but not Korean—standards. And even though we can say that economic progress and democracy may not work in tandem, it does appear that recession breeds political discontents. And Korea has experienced many of these.

Korea's position on a peninsula located between the two great Asian powers of China and Japan has caused a great deal of back and forth movement over the centuries as first one and then the other of these powers sought to assert its will upon the country. Until the Meiji era in Japan, which was inaugurated in 1867, it could not be said which of these important powers received the most attention from Korea. Japan forcibly settled this issue, it seems, by taking over Korea in 1910 and, in effect, making it a colony. This loss of national independence lasted until 1945, when the end of World War II saw the great powers divide the peninsula, north and south, into the two Koreas that exist today. The long period of Japanese hegemony, which included some coopta-tion of Korean professional and elite groups, a settlement of some

Koreans in Japan, and close commercial ties between the two countries, built a solid base for the bilateral economic relationship that now exists. South Korea is the recipient of Japanese investment more than any Asian nation; and the trade, banking, finance, and corporate ties between the two countries have never been stronger. A variety of these basically binational firms producing electronic products cooperatively innovate, produce, and market their wares while the well-known Hyundai automobile, manufactured in Korea, uses Mitsubishi engines; Hyundai, for that matter, is partially owned by Mitsubishi.

The United States has played a continuously important economic role in Korea since the end of World War II. The large-scale war effort of 1950–53 by itself demonstrates this; but the United States has been heavily involved with Korea both before and after this war. It has provided extensive military aid and billions in economic aid; the latter has often been in the form of grants rather than loans, so that the commitment to Korea ranks very high among the priorities of the United States during this past half century. There has been more aid for South Korea than for any Asia-Pacific Rim nation. And because South Korea was willing to commit its troops, more than three hundred thousand at one point, to fighting in the Vietnam War, the grateful United States essentially picked up all of the costs of this effort. In addition, Korea was rewarded for its Vietnam War efforts with extensive aid, contracts, trading concessions, and other favors. The United States continues, with Japan, to be one of the two great trading partners of South Korea; and military aid continues to be an important consideration both in terms of financial assistance and in the commitment of troops stationed in Korea.

Such a boon to the economy has played an important supportive role in the country's development. Korea's own efforts must be accorded the most significant place in national development, however, and it is generally agreed that growth acceleration first occurred under the authoritarian Park Chung Hee regime in the 1960s. (Once again we see that growth and development are not necessarily accompanied by a free political system.) This regime inherited an economy of many problems including slow or no growth. A multicentered system of policy inputs was established that involved government, the private sector, and suggestions from various elite groups. The government has not eschewed a heavy hand in policy making as it has sought to make the nation's exports and production processes more competitive. It has developed specific and rather tightly controlled guidelines for such policy areas as taxation, industrial development, public and private

finance and monetary policy (Korea has a strong central bank), population, agriculture, health, education, and an almost negligible number
of social welfare initiatives. Most significant among these policies has
been a stark and often brutal repression of labor unions. This brutality,
which has even included shootings of workers, makes any talk of the
"competitiveness" of such industries highly questionable.

It is nonetheless true that South Korea has demonstrated a very
strong economic performance since 1963, when living standards were
approximately the same as in India. A heavy emphasis upon education,
urbanization, and, to a lesser extent, infrastructure has yielded spectacular results. The capital city of Seoul has grown to become the
world's fourth-largest city (see the statistical overview in Fig. 6.3).

As in the case of Japan, the nation's elite does not care to leave
matters to the raw world of chance represented by the free marketplace
if this can be avoided. This means there must be commitment to the
appropriate planning, organization, subsidies, and, in a few cases,
outright protectionism.

Connected with this very high degree of integration of private and
public policy making are the strong interlocks of political, military,
and industrial elite families who seem to run the country. There are
few countries, especially in the category of those with dynamic and

Fig. 6.3
South Korea

Gross national product per capita	$7,250
Gross domestic product growth, 1993	5.5%
Gross domestic product growth anticipated, 1995	7.0% +
Annual population growth rate	0.9%
Infant mortality per 1,000 births	8
Literacy	96.0%
People per doctor	1,370
People per telephone	2.3
Population	44.4 million
National capital	Seoul
Major trading partners	U.S.A., Japan

Sources: United Nations, World Bank, and various
publications

modern economies, which have a more tightly organized elite. A *Wall Street Journal* article of August 21, 1992, is accompanied by a chart that depicts these interlocks, and this excerpt from the article demonstrates the situation well within a brief space:

> Members of the founding family of Samsung, for example, are connected by marriage to the rival Lucky-Goldstar Group, as well as Hanjin, Doosan, and Korea Explosives Groups. The marriage network is so vast that a group of reporters recently published a 448-page book on the relationships, complete with charts, that has become a best-seller.

This tight control of government, society, and the economy at the top is enhanced by a traditionally rigid class system that goes beyond even the traditions of Japan or China. This system has generated a tremendous inequality in wage levels and in access to the nation's resources, such as land. The adoption of some Confucian principles and attitudes, it has been remarked, has been quite literal as well as forceful in Korea.

This does not mean that Korea's elite is invariably able to generate a consensus on important matters. Tactical approaches to student protests have been the subject of debate. Recently, a major conflict between the leaders of the Hyundai conglomerate and the government has received extensive publicity. Economic planning and goals are known to cause differences. In addition, it is altogether probable that the security threat represented by North Korea is such an important consideration that it causes a variety of responses to be advocated as circumstances unfold.

Dissatisfaction among the public at large often manifests itself in student rebellions, which are usually cheered from the sidelines by other antigovernment Koreans. Violent clashes in 1993, for example, were based upon student demands that political leaders be tried for their role in suppressing student demonstrations and allegedly causing deaths in 1980. The newly legalized but weak labor movement contributes to these protests. Some of the student demands call for greater attempts to be made for unification with the North. In any event, it is clear that South Korea must deal with intense problems of inequality and income redistribution if it is going to continue to progress. There is a widespread feeling that the hard work of employees and students is not being properly rewarded. The dynamics illustrated by the Lewis model show that redistribution will be more difficult to achieve as low-skilled jobs, and possibly some high-skilled ones as well, are lost in the competitive economic race with other Asian and world neighbors.

Koreans, incidentally, are one of the largest student groups in the United States, and they are known for their reluctance or refusal to return to their country. This has not caused many problems for the U.S.-South Korea relationship; what has caused trouble from time to time, however, has been the activities of the Korea lobby in Washington, D.C. Scandals have been brought about through Korean payoffs and favors for members of Congress.

The darkest cloud hanging over the future of this nation continues to be the hostility and potential aggression from the North. The buildup of nuclear potential and the withdrawal from the Nonproliferation Treaty in 1993 by the Kim Il Sung regime has made everyone in Northeast Asia nervous. But South Korea is obviously the most directly threatened of any nation. The two sides hold occasional meetings devoted to the topic of reunification, but no progress is made, nor is likely to be made, at these sessions. The grim and fortress-like character of the border provides a reminder to the entire country that the threats and dangers for its future are constant; and the fact of this threat strengthens the hand of the South Korean government should it decide upon any policies aimed at suppression of dissent.

Despite this ominous situation, the future role of the United States in Korea is conjectural. It is definitely to the advantage of the United States to have a continued presence in the Asia-Pacific Rim area, but this does not necessarily extend to supplying ground troops to defend the Korean peninsula. The appropriate response to North Korea's nuclear rumblings will have to be international and diplomatic if it is to be effective at all; but the response to the threat posed by conventional armaments now most appropriately appears to be the task of South Korea. The presence of U.S. troops may provide some marginal deterrence to a conventional initiative, but the evidence seems to show that the South can defend itself. The South is also able to afford the costs of defense, which it could not do in 1950 when it was attacked. Even with the recession occurring at the time this is written, South Korea's financial ability to shoulder its own defense is not in doubt. The United States, on the other hand, continues to face trade and payments deficits in Korea and, more broadly, throughout the Asia-Pacific region. It therefore appears prudent for the United States to withdraw from the peninsula while remaining close to the scene with regional forces.

Taiwan—Prosperous Island Fortress

Taiwan is not China. Most readers would certainly agree with this simple, flat statement; but in a historically recent period of time, the years from 1949 to 1972, it was the official policy of the United States that this was indeed the case. An apocryphal claim holds that many of the observers and politicians who accompanied President Richard Nixon on one of his first trips to Beijing, people like William F. Buckley, Jr., the editor of the conservative *National Review,* asked about where they were upon their arrival in the capital because this might be China, they said, but it certainly "did not look like Taipei" (see Fig. 6.4).

This island nation has historically been a province of China, though the early decades of this century saw Japan ruling it. It still refers to itself as the Republic of China, which is the name of the former mainland regime headed by Chiang Kai-Shek. Chiang took the remnants of his forces to Taiwan in 1949, facing the fact that it was the last refuge for his government.

The unreality of American government policies and attitudes during this period is amazing to behold in retrospect. Central to policy making was denial of diplomatic recognition to the Communist regime on the mainland and opposition to replacement of the Nationalists by the Communists as one of the five permanent members of the UN Security Council. Beyond the policies, however, and most certainly just as momentous in their effects, were the attitudes that were developed by the American public and in government circles at the time. The

Fig. 6.4
Taiwan

Gross national product per capita	$10,215
Gross domestic product growth, 1993	5.5%
Gross domestic product growth anticipated, 1995	6.0 % +
Annual population growth rate	1.2%
Infant mortality per 1,000 births	5
Literacy	92.4%
People per doctor	910
People per telephone	2.4
Population	21.0 million
National capital	Taipei
Major trading partners	U.S.A., Japan

Sources: United Nations, World Bank, and various publications

question of "Who lost China?" was often posed in national debates, as though China could be lost by a country that had it in the first place. The resulting poisonous atmosphere, which was fueled by what can only be called an anti-Communist hysteria, resulted in the loss of key government personnel and advisers expert in the policies, cultures, and ways of China. Some critics allege that the loss of this expertise because of the "red-baiting" of that epoch was instrumental in the fateful and highly unsuccessful involvement of the United States in Vietnam, though such a claim must of course be conjectural.

The China lobby in the United States, which should have been more accurately called the Taiwan lobby, managed to wield enormous influence. It had strong financial resources, as one might expect, as do many lobby groups. It was also able to trade well on the emotions of anti-Communism and the "loss" of China, and it could rely upon an able network of economic interests, the Pentagon, Chinese-Americans, who were largely hostile to Beijing, and missionaries and others who had had direct contact and experience with China. The strength of this lobby and the national atmosphere had its bizarre side: John F. Kennedy, for example, took a position in his 1960 campaign for the presidency in favor of defending not only Taiwan but even two tiny fortress islands, Quemoy and Matsu, located just off the coast of China and held by the Nationalists. Thus an indefensible policy position was taken and was viewed as politically defensible, since Kennedy thought it was important to show that he, like his opponent Richard Nixon, was "tough" on the matter of Communist aggression.

The year 1972 brought momentous changes to Taiwan, as well as China and the United States, with the "opening up" policy taken by President Nixon and his influential secretary of state, Henry Kissinger. This led to diplomatic recognition of the Beijing government, its seating on the UN Security Council in place of the Nationalists, and a long string of diplomatic switches made by nations who had held, with the United States, that Taiwan was China. The nature of the Taiwan-China relationship at this time precluded diplomatic relations with both, so nations were required to choose up sides. Neither entity would abide a "two-Chinas" policy.

These were grim days for Taiwan. Despite repeated reassurances from President Nixon and the U.S. government, the island nation saw its future in doubt. The requirements of diplomacy meant that Taiwan had few embassies left within its borders. (South Korea is one of the few governments that have held firm over the years.) Trade missions were sometimes established in their stead. The only leader the Nationalists had ever known, Chiang Kai-Shek, stepped down in favor of his son, Chiang Ching-Kuo, but the apparatus of authoritarian rule remained in place. International civil liberties watch organizations and U.S. critics of the Taiwan regime have held that the island's government is in many ways as repressive as the mainland state it abhors. Even with its many faults, however, it is unlikely that Taiwan today matches Beijing's scale of repression.

This period of political reversals, however, also marks the beginning of a renewed determination to progress economically. Unlike South Korea, where the economy and its growth sometimes appear to be almost micromanaged, Taiwan's leadership determined that a free-swinging and largely unregulated market economy model would prove best for the nation's development. This has proved to be the case. The island republic has established some of the best growth records of the past two decades, even though it now is moving rapidly into a position in which its wage levels are not competitive. The products of skilled workers and high-tech industries have been receiving the most emphasis in recent years, and this trend can be expected to continue.

If Taiwan has had such startling results with a free enterprise model that is about as close to Adam Smith's classic strictures as one can find in Asia, can it be said that this is the way other nations should go? The first answer to such a question is that other Asian states have decided upon different courses—a whole range of courses, in fact—which seem well-suited to each individual case. The second answer is that Taiwan carries out some practices and has had some costs that must be considered. On the matter of practices, it is clear that Taiwan is the world's leading bastion of noncompliance with patent and copyright agreements. Consumer products, software, books, or whatever seem to be produced in an atmosphere of abandon, for no writer, composer, creator, or inventor is going to be recompensed by this system. How much longer Taiwan can grow and continue to ignore these international protections remains a question; the new GATT Treaty is expected to dent or end such activities, but Taiwan is not a GATT signatory. Another cost of phenomenal growth is environmental. Taiwan has been adjudged by any number of organizations and observers as the worst place on earth for air, water, and quality of life matters related to ecological sensitivity.

Political evolution since about 1986 has shown more promise. Opposition parties and candidates have developed, and these are now in a position to make strong runs against the government and its slate of entries. The ruling KMT (Kuomintang) party saw its percentage of the total national vote drop to an unimpressive 53 percent in national elections held in December 1992. The leading opposition party, the Democratic Progressives, saw their legislative strength move from 18 seats to 50 in a 161-member assembly. (Other opposition groups won 9 seats.) The years of KMT hegemony are perhaps coming to a close in one of these future years, as the DPP and perhaps other groups gain strength. Not surprisingly, one of these groups is a Green party, which can obviously make its case in so polluted an environment; but the DPP has also heartily embraced the environmental cause.

In the meantime, political scientists and other observers are debating how to characterize the Taiwan regime. Terms like "soft authoritarianism" or "semi-democracy" or "hybrid democracy" are being thrown about, and all of these have some descriptive validity. Democratization of Taiwan, though it may still be far off, is now in sight; and this has already had an effect on policy issues and choices. The KMT orthodoxy that there is only one China, namely Taiwan, is being openly questioned by those who see the future of the island tied to the mainland regime in various ways.

One of those ways, clearly, is in matters of trade and investment. Taiwan business people have been very active, perhaps the most active of any national group outside Hong Kong, in seeking out opportunities in China. Much of this activity is discouraged or forbidden, but it has been burgeoning so rapidly and with such enthusiasm that the Taipei leadership is rather alarmed. It is pointed out that China continues to be a security threat to the island and that it has purchased new attack aircraft as recently as the latter half of 1992 for the purpose of patrolling the Formosan Straits, the narrow body of water located between Taiwan and the mainland. The entrepreneurial class seems immune to such warnings, all the same, and even the most conservative estimates place the figure for Taiwan investment in the mainland at $3 billion plus. This commitment can be expected to increase.

But it cannot be stated with any certainty just what the future of Taiwan will bring. The mainland and Taipei both continue to insist that they are the real China, and as long as these positions are held in place, little progress toward reconciliation can be expected. The Taipei government can and should be expected to come to terms with the Taiwanese people whose political, social, and economic lives were disrupted by the 1949 arrival of the Nationalists. Since this group represents the majority of the island's populace, such consensus building only makes sense.

Malaysia—Moving Up the Development Curve

> Professor: Why are you so happy all the time?
> Student: I suppose it is because I live in a good
> country with a good future. I believe there will
> be a good job waiting for me when I am finished
> with my education.
>
> —Conversation in Malaysia, 1989

Scholars, journalists, business people, government officials, and tourists alike claim that Malaysia is one of the most pleasant nations they have ever visited. It has retained much of the charm one might typically expect of an Asian nation, yet it has progressed to a point of considerable modernization and prosperity (see Fig. 6.5). It offers traditions but also comforts. And, in many ways, this fits with Malaysia's position as a nation that has moved well beyond the poverty of Third World status. It is still aiming at development and the prosperity of a country that has seen a high degree of modernization, but it still has some way to go before it can match the numbers of a nation like Singapore or South Korea.

Statistics on Malaysia show that it may not really be considered a

Fig. 6.5
Malaysia

Gross national product per capita	$3,230
Gross domestic product growth, 1993	8.6%
Gross domestic product growth anticipated, 1995	9.1%
Annual population growth rate	2.6%
Infant mortality per 1,000 births	14
Literacy	78.5%
People per doctor	2,656
People per telephone	8.8
Population	19.4 million
National capital	Kuala Lumpur
Major trading partners	Japan, Singapore

Sources: United Nations, World Bank, and various
publications

"tiger" yet—that is, one of the newly industrialized economies on the scale of the other four found in this chapter—but it seems to be on its way. And it is clearly ahead of any potential rivals who are further down the list on development, modernization, and, most importantly, the standard of living. Its economic growth has been hard-won through a combination of government planning and entrepreneurship, and it therefore can hardly be seen to be an accident.

In the dynamic region of Southeast Asia, Malaysia often stands out as the economic growth champion. It has posted growth rates as high as 8.75 percent in recent years, and such figures coming out of the country are often given the most conservative cast. The government has had to damp down the growth rate with monetary measures from time to time, in fact, because of fears of inflation. Investors, whether they are based in America, Europe, or Japan—and the latter has surely become the most important group of these—can only be pleased with the overall performance of Malaysia. The Malaysia Fund, for example, which is listed on the New York Stock Exchange, has grown by as much as 141 percent in a single year. Profitable new industries, including consumer electronic items, oil, automobiles, computers, food and beverages, and services of various kinds have been established in the past decade and a half. And Malaysia is the world's largest producer of air conditioners and microchips. Large new industrial parks, especially those located around Penang in the north of the country and Shah Alam, a suburb of the capital of Kuala Lumpur, in the center, continue to sprout new manufacturing plants, offices, and warehouses. And a role of some significance in the economy is still carried out by the traditional, but much less profitable, primary industries such as rubber, tin, and palm oil. Forestry products are very important exports as well, though their harvesting is a cause of much national and international controversy.

Malaysia, all the same, is not an economy that gives much to the arguments of those who stand for a more or less unbridled form of capitalism. Government ownership of firms is not uncommon, though this has had mixed results, but government planning in Malaysia is often carried out on a very long-term basis. The year 1990 marked the end of the twenty-year-old New Economic Policy (NEP), a multifaceted set of initiatives aimed at modernization, development, and prosperity for the peoples of Malaysia and, not at all incidentally, better chances in business, government, education, housing, employment, and other fields for the nation's Malay majority. A new twenty-year plan has now been put into effect as a replacement for the NEP.

The NEP and allied statutes and directives have been a source of considerable criticism from the non-Malay minorities of the country, particularly the Chinese. They involve affirmative action in hiring for the benefit of the Malays, requirements such as a minimum number of Malay representatives on corporate executive boards, and government contracting provisions that can benefit Malays or, on occasion, leaders of ethnic groups, whether Chinese or Indian, who are affiliated with the coalition of the governing party, the United Malays National Organization (UMNO). Perhaps the most clear-cut case of policy on behalf of Malays, however, is found in education, particularly higher education. Supporters of the now-expired NEP make the claim, which can be backed with hard data, that Malays, though they represent a majority of the population, have not shared equally in the new-found prosperity of the country. A new long-range plan has been devised to replace the NEP and, with some changes, it will continue to give a favored position to the Malay community. Whether these policies are really fair or not is a difficult call for an outsider to make; it does appear certain that some characterizations of the NEP policies made in the United States (for example, by Thomas Sowell) are both inaccurate and bereft of cultural understanding.

Resentments against such policies, on the other hand, are undeniable; what is more, they must be considered politically significant since people of Chinese origin make up approximately 38 percent of the population, and Indians, though they are a smaller group, represent some 7 or 8 percent. In this background of ethnic differences is the haunting memory of May 1969 when race riots led to deaths, injuries, and a permanent scar on the body politic.

Assessing these horrible events and their causes, a young Malay leader of the time, Mahathir bin-Mohammed, wrote a book setting out the thesis of economic discrimination against Malays in what they have always considered their own country. It was hardly surprising, then, that when Mahathir came to power he implemented the NEP with the support of UMNO. Many of his backers will also point out, however, that they believe Mahathir has been sensitive to the needs and demands of other ethnic groups and that his priority has always been communal peace. He and his government, so far at least, have accomplished this; and the economic miracle that is Malaysia today has undoubtedly helped to quench the fires of resentment. Surely these continue to linger, but the nation's prosperity, as long as it lasts, will keep these fires banked. Mahathir, meanwhile, enjoys the confidence the people seem to have placed in him during his many years at the helm and as he looks forward to retirement. It is often pointed out that he is one national leader who can freely walk among the people without a bodyguard.

Malaysia's political culture is probably like no other found in the world. It brings together the values of three ethnic groups who continue to live and work separately at times, but who have influenced one another as well. Intermarriage between these groups seems to be rare, but other facets of life, such as the workplace or the market, bring these groups together so that they are more or less used to each other. The Chinese have a reputation, earned or not, for entrepreneurial skill and a hardworking approach to life that accords with Confucian values. The Indians, brought here by the British to work the tin mines and rubber and palm oil plantations, are probably at the bottom of the social ladder, but they are represented in the professions—medicine, law, and education, for examples—in fairly large numbers. The Malay majority holds the political reins of the nation and tends to dominate such areas as government employment and the state-run industries.

In their formative years, Malays are exposed to the value of "halus" behavior, a term not easily translated that relates to consideration, gentleness, and kindness. The "halus" pattern seems to be most instilled in those who live the village life, but it is easily discerned in urban Malays as well. This friendly and often smiling approach to strangers, acquaintances, and family alike provides a distinctive character to Malay culture. It may also lead to a false idea that Malays are not hardworking or ambitious, but the tangible results of effort seen in Malaysia show how misleading this can be.

Attachment to the Muslim religion also gives the Malay population a strong defining characteristic. A small minority of the Indians in the country are Muslim as well, but the force behind Islam as a national faith is largely Malay. Islam came to the Malay Peninsula early in the fifteenth century, brought there by Arab traders, and its contemporary impact on the nation is considerable. It is possible, though not proven, that Malays are more attached to Islam as a symbol of identity than, say, Indonesians are, because Malays feel the necessity to assert themselves against the large concentrations of other ethnic groups in the country. (Nearby Indonesia, by contrast, is an 88 percent Muslim nation.) Examples abound of what Americans might call conflict between religion and the state, or perhaps between groups of followers and nonadherents. In the state of Selangor, the legislature recently established the age of puberty in line with Muslim belief, much to the dismay of the minority party, the Democratic Action Party (DAP), and its mostly Chinese backers. In northern and largely rural Kelantan, where the governing party is PAS, a much more strictly Muslim group, measures have been passed requiring women of all ethnic groups or religious faiths to dress in the modest manner required of very religious Muslims. The sultan of Kelantan, who has had a number of disputes with Mahathir and the federal government, and the state premier threatened to place all non-Muslims under sharia (religious) law even in matters of criminal punishments. The prime minister, however, has pointedly insisted that criminal law is under all circumstances a federal matter.

Defense and security issues bring into play the relationship of Malaysia to the United States, Japan, India, Indonesia, Singapore, and other powers. The prosperity of the country has permitted it to make weapons purchases and to modernize its conventional forces. Malaysia expresses concern from time to time about Singapore's formidable military establishment, but few would expect any major troubles on this front. More pointedly, however, Malaysia has objected to the willingness of Singapore to permit the U.S. Navy to use its dock and refueling facilities. (This offer was made by the city-state to make up for the U.S. loss of its big Philippine bases.) Malaysia feels that it is inappropriate to accommodate the Americans in this way, particularly since both Singapore and Malaysia are supposed to be nonaligned states. Objections to these operations appear at the moment to be the only security issue of any moment between the United States and Malaysia, though there are some big differences on trade questions.

International human rights organizations have registered concern over treatment of some political prisoners and some problems of press censorship. Some executions by hanging of drug offenders have drawn considerable international attention so that Malaysia's strict enforcement of these measures is well known. Less well known is the law that calls for the same treatment for gun possession, which is also enforced.

Malaysia is assertive in setting out an international leadership position despite its relatively small size. It aggressively seeks to serve as the site of international conferences, meets, and occasions of all kinds from sporting events to Commonwealth gatherings, and its leadership has spoken out on a wide range of international issues. These include apartheid in South Africa, Israeli-Arab relations, the slaughter of Muslims in Bosnia, and, most vehemently, the establishment of a new and large trading bloc, the East Asian Economic Caucus, which is to be led by Japan and which, in its original form as proposed by Mahathis, is to exclude the United States, Canada, Australia, and all

Western nations. The official U.S. position on EAEC is one of support; unofficially it is probably opposed.

The rise of the new "tigers" of Asia, perhaps more than any economic factor present in the Pacific Rim countries, has given a continuity and a binding quality not only to the Lewis theory which guides much of this analysis. It has also shaken the general suppositions of development theory. Most importantly, it has changed the politics, lives, and expectations of the peoples of these countries as well as other countries of the Pacific Rim.

A brief mention should be made here of Brunei, a tiny oil kingdom located on the island of Borneo, which it shares with Indonesia and two provinces that make up what is called East Malaysia. Although it has only a small population of 220,000, this tiny nation plays a significant role in OPEC, the Organization of Petroleum-Exporting Countries, and in ASEAN, the Association of Southeast Asian Nations. The Sultan of Brunei is the richest person in the world with a fortune estimated to be at least $38 billion U.S.; and although he enjoyed secular pleasures to a considerable degree as a young man, he now insists upon a strong Muslim code of conduct for himself and the citizens of Brunei. It may be recalled that the Sultan was generous to the Reagan Administration when it sought funds to support the "contras" in Nicaragua against the will of Congress and existing law.

Hoping for a Brighter Tomorrow: Indonesia, the Philippines, and Thailand

The success of the four Asian "tigers" and Malaysia and the persuasive logic of the W. Arthur Lewis development model may be seen as reasons for the current hopefulness found in Indonesia, the Philippines, and Thailand. These countries have low labor costs, adequate nutrition levels, and are seen as relatively stable in their politics. Thailand does experience a military coup from time to time, but it has so far reverted each time to civilian rule afterwards. The Philippines has civil insurrection that has been carried out for the past forty years or longer. Indonesia, which is a formidable military power in its region, has been considered stable since 1965, but there are signs of instability. The largest cloud on its horizon is the advancing age of President Suharto, who has ruled the archipelago for twenty-eight years and has failed to name a likely successor.

The largest of these nations is Indonesia, which is the fourth largest country in the world in population size. It is the world's largest Islamic country, though it seems to get much less media attention than many smaller Muslim nations. Its disparate peoples are spread across thirteen thousand islands and speak two hundred languages and thousands of dialects. Islam is the major religion, with well over 80 percent of the population adhering to this faith; but Buddhism, Christianity, Hinduism, and animism each have an officially sanctioned status (see Fig. 6.6).

Indonesia's people are unevenly distributed across the archipelago. The island of Java, where the capital city of Jakarta is located, is the most densely settled place on earth; more than 110 million people live there. An additional 39 million live on large, oil-rich Sumatra. The disproportionate share of people in Java has led to ambitious government programs of transplantation. Workers, families, and industries are presently being set up, for example, on the sparsely populated half-island known as West Irian.

The political cultures of the nation are rich and varied. The Javanese cultures have produced great works of art and music; foremost among these is the well-known wayang kulit puppet play, which is presented in shadows on a screen. The complexity and variations of the wayang reveal some of the underpinnings of Javanese cultural values. The

Fig. 6.6
Indonesia

Gross national product per capita	$720
Gross domestic product growth, 1993	6.7%
Gross domestic product growth anticipated, 1995	6.0% +
Annual population growth rate	1.7%
Infant mortality per 1,000 births	66
Literacy	81.5%
People per doctor	11,641
People per telephone	107.7
Population	191.1 million
National capital	Jakarta
Major trading partners	Japan, U.S.A.

Sources: United Nations, World Bank, and various publications

great architecture of Java is perhaps best represented by Borobidhur, a mammoth Buddhist monument located near Yogjakarta. Indian temples and ruins are also found in great abundance, signifying the once-great importance of Hinduism on the island. The island of Bali, known for its beauty and its gentle ways, has kept its attachment to Hinduism through the centuries. Sumatra, the largest island, has a variety of cultures, including one known for its matriarchal patterns of tracing lineage and property ownership.

Dutch rule demonstrated the great prosperity possible through exploitation of the resources of what were first called the "Spice Islands" and, later, the "East Indies." (The term "Spice Islands" can be confusing because it was used in a broad and general sense during the age of exploration and because it still refers to a small area of Indonesia, the Moluccas.) The Dutch East Indies Company established its trading center at Batavia (now Jakarta) in 1619, and it immediately began to reap lavish profits. Dutch colonial rule represents one of the very worst examples of unscrupulous exploitation of a nation and its people; so it could hardly be a surprising development when Indonesia's leaders proclaimed their country's independence in 1945 at the end of World War II. The Netherlands sought to reestablish the control they had held for hundreds of years prior to the Japanese occupation of the war years, but this effort was fiercely resisted. Armed clashes lasted until 1949, when the Dutch finally realized the futility of their efforts.

Sukarno and the other leaders of the independence cause set out the principles of pancasila (a philosophy or creed) as the guidelines for the nation. These are (1) belief in one supreme God; (2) social justice; (3) sovereignty of the people; (4) unity of the state of Indonesia; and (5) a just and civilized humanitarianism. Pancasila democracy remains the centerpiece of the nation's aspirations and the topic of many political speeches. Pancasila is the title of many school and university courses, so it is well understood by the people.

Sukarno sought to balance a variety of conflicting interests as he led the new nation—business groups, Islam and its adherents and leadership, the military, and a large Communist movement. Many of the leaders of the first three groups worried about Sukarno's proximity to the Communists, particularly since they thought of them as agents of China and its aggressive interests. Sukarno was uniquely strong because of his position as hero of the independence movement but also weak because the state-guided economy went nowhere. In 1965, he was deposed and was allowed to live out his remaining years under house arrest in a splendid home in Bogor, which can still be seen.

This coup d'etat was not peaceful, however. The greatest slaughter of people in the history of Indonesia was carried out, and the most conservative estimate of the deaths is set at around 250,000. The occasion was a time to settle old scores against neighbors, creditors, or others who may or may not have been Communists. Members of the PKI (the Communist party) and the Chinese minority community were particular targets in this bloodletting. And U.S. involvement, still officially denied, appears to have been at least a peripherally important factor. Out of this rose General Suharto, who took the reins of state and has held them ever since. His international politics are nonaligned, at least officially; in fact, Indonesia took over the non-aligned movement leadership in 1992. But there can be little question that the United States is much more approving of Suharto's regime than it was of his predecessor.

All would agree that the economy has had better results under Suharto. Although growth was slow throughout the 1970s and most of the 1980s, recent years have seen some very solid gains. Health and living standards have greatly improved, at least on the main islands. Nearly all of Java's housing was considered substandard just ten years ago; today only 15 percent fits this description. Real wages have moved up, though only slightly, and jobs are now slightly more plentiful even though huge surplus labor pools remain. Low-tech industries from the United States, Europe, and other parts of Asia find Indonesia an attractive site for production of such items as garments, toys, or shoes. A strong movement toward deregulation of industries and, most significantly, of foreign investors took hold in the mid-1980s, and these efforts are continuing. Another major accomplishment of recent years is a relative reduction of dependence upon petroleum as the major earner of foreign exchange. In the past there was almost a total dependence upon this one product; today it accounts for less than half of the hard currency flowing into Indonesia.

Serious problems abound, all the same. Most of the outer islands have received a lesser share of the newfound prosperity evident in Java or Sumatra. The balance of payments remains in a serious debt position, and the worldwide recession of the early 1990s has reduced the ability of the country to earn foreign exchange. This recession has visited Indonesia and has exacerbated perennial problems of unemployment and economic dislocation. There is also some pressure exerted against Indonesia by international environmental groups concerned about the heavy amount of cutting of forests. Corruption is so rife in the banking system that most of the state-controlled banks are heavily burdened with bad loans made to politically important persons, groups, and businesses.

The political abilities of the regime are also sometimes questioned. There is a general impression that the base of support is eroding, and that this dissatisfaction is found in the mass public and in all elite groups, even the military. The task of balancing elite interests is probably still the major concern of the governing elite, just as it was in Sukarno's days. The only major difference is that Communists no longer play a role in these balancing endeavors.

Three major dissenting groups are now seen as sources of instability. One of these is Islamic fundamentalists, who are not considered a major force. A second is students and intellectuals who are devoted to the human rights cause. They protest press closedowns and the stifling of free debate, and their leaders and activists have met with beatings, imprisonment, and expulsions from universities. But the largest and most potent dissenters are labor unionists. A large and illegal union movement has become powerful and capable of shutting down factories and services. The city of Jakarta alone saw more than two hundred strikes in 1993. Other important centers—Surabaya, Semarang, and especially Medan—have been scenes of considerable strife and even violence. The army has been called upon to deal with these dissident groups, and its response can be brutal.

The failure of Suharto to name a successor is a growing worry and a possible future source of even more instability. This concern is somewhat intensified by recent evidence of an increasing share of power taken by the military in this coalition of governing elite groups. Rebellions here and there across the three-thousand-mile-long island chain raise the specter of secessions. These are unlikely, however, for the government has been quick and forceful—perhaps too forceful—in putting these down in such places as Aceh, in northernmost Sumatra, and the island of Timor, which was once divided between Indonesian and Portuguese authorities. International human rights groups and the UN have severely criticized these activities, and President Bill Clinton pointedly brought up the matter of Timor in a 1993 Tokyo meeting with Suharto.

American policy toward Indonesia has been one of encouragement of modernization and development. In important ways the United States has had an impact upon Indonesia through its influence in international organizations, such as the World Bank. The responsive stance taken by the Suharto government has probably pleased U.S. policy makers and economic interests. As mentioned above, Indonesia plays a leading role in a number of regional and international groupings, including OPEC, the Organization of Petroleum-Exporting Countries; the non-aligned movement; and ASEAN, the Association of Southeast Asian Nations.

Most significant is the fact that Indonesia is one of the great military powers of Asia and is number one in this category in Southeast Asia. Its size and importance also mean that it will continue to influence the economies and cultures of its part of the world, but this influence cannot hold if the nation's instability becomes any greater.

There is little doubt that the Philippines are still paying for the long years of the disastrous, corrupt, and undemocratic regime of Ferdinand Marcos, who headed the government from his election in 1965 until he was deposed by force in 1986. Marcos was initially a popular leader, the first president of his country to win reelection. But deep and unprecedented levels of personal and official corruption displayed his contempt for any checks and balances in government, and his repression went as far as the cancellation of elections and the ordered assassination of a political rival, Benigno Aquino. Marcos instituted martial law in 1972, and this remained in force until 1986.

The broad scale of corruption was matched by an intolerably inept style of economic management. This has led to a close surveillance of the Philippines by the International Monetary Fund, the World Bank, commercial banks and other interests who now constrict the nation's economic and policy choices to a narrow range of measures devoted to debt repayment and recovery.

Corazon Aquino, widow of the slain rival of Marcos, took power in a free election in 1986 after Marcos was deposed and forced to flee the country. (He and his rather infamous wife, Imelda, known for her personal collection of three thousand pairs of shoes, found refuge in Hawaii as a kind of "guest" of the U.S. government.) Aquino lifted martial law, offered amnesties and some minor political concessions to revolutionaries who had been active in the rural areas of the country for decades, began paying down some of the nation's debts, and sought to eliminate corruption. The latter goal was her most unsuccessful endeavor, but it is clear that the scale of corruption was reduced.

In 1992, Aquino was succeeded by Fidel Ramos, a military leader who had served the Marcos regime but also had a reputation for honesty and, most importantly, for being Aquino's choice. Neither Aquino nor Ramos, at least so far, can point to much economic growth or development during their years in office; but hopes for the Philippines continue to be voiced both in the country and in international financial circles.

Difficulties for the United States are found in great abundance in the Philippines. The legacy of colonial rule, which was begun in 1898 with intentions stated in racist and ethnocentric terms, has produced little affection for America; and this is true despite the pro-U.S. reputation of the country in international forums such as the UN. Colonial rule brought economic rule. Many of the plantations, factories, and other businesses in the Philippines are still controlled by Americans or, more likely, by American-based multinational corporations or wealthy Philippine interests. U.S. government leaders have shown no particular interest in whether the Philippines are well-governed as long as American interests, both economic and military, have been safeguarded. This was painfully obvious during the Marcos years: the president received warm praise from leaders such as Ronald Reagan and his vice-president, George Bush, at a time when brutal repression, corruption, and economic bungling were the order of the day. It was Reagan, however, who reversed himself when it appeared that Marcos was no longer a viable political ally; the United States therefore took a position in favor of Corazon Aquino's election in 1986.

The support of the United States for the Marcos regime is a fact that has not been lost upon Filipino citizens and voters. And there seems to be a direct connection between this dismay and the vote taken by the Philippine Senate against continuing the leases on the long-established U.S. bases at Clark Airfield and Subic Point. The loss of these bases has been exaggerated by some people into the end of a U.S. presence in Asia and the Western Pacific. Such a claim, however, is grossly misleading. U.S. naval and air forces are not in fact excluded from the Philippines; they simply do not have the very large dock, refueling, and other facilities they once had. These operations have been moved to the islands of Guam in the Pacific and Diego Garcia in the Indian Ocean, and the United States may be required to use facilities in other locations as well.

Clark and Subic Point did provide the Philippines with a continuous source of hard currency and very large payrolls; but long-term economic planning and growth should probably not rely upon military spending by a foreign power. Military circumstances and needs are subject to change, as the end of the Cold War has demonstrated.

In recent years the Philippine government has targeted growth at annual levels of four percent or more, but these have not been achieved. A statistical overview can be found in Figure 6.7. Performance of the economy has ranged from a minus figure to perhaps a 2-percent growth figure. This suggests that hopeful as the nation may be that it, too, will someday become an Asian "tiger," the realities of the moment are rather grim. The debts of the Marcos years must be reduced and international investors must be enticed. Neither of these events has occurred to the extent necessary to hope for better growth levels, according to analysts, and their views are backed by the international debt-funding agencies who presently hold the fate of the Philippines in their hands. A few political leaders have called for debt cancellation, but though they have some following, they are paid little heed. Corruption, though less serious than that of the Marcos years, appears endemic to the system. The nation also faces some severe infrastructure problems. Its transport and communications facilities are in need of upgrading. There are plans, just beginning to be realized, for new utilizations of the old U.S. bases. Most serious of all infrastructure problems has been the lack of electric power; but the country is no longer experiencing the long and debilitating power failures that have only hurt the economy.

Tourists and travel agents regard Thailand as a place of beautiful, even gaudy Buddhist temples and stupas, so that its image in the

Fig. 6.7
Philippines

Gross national product per capita	$850
Gross domestic product growth, 1993	3.8%
Gross domestic product growth anticipated, 1995	6.5% +
Annual population growth rate	2.3%
Infant mortality per 1,000 births	40
Literacy	93.5%
People per doctor	1,016
People per telephone	52.5
Population	65.6 million
National capital	Manila
Major trading partners	Japan, U.S.A.

Sources: United Nations, World Bank, and various publications

outside world makes it seem to be a land of mystery and dreams. It is assuredly the case that this is a nation which commits a large part of its resources to these beautiful religious monuments and meeting places, but there is obviously a great deal more to Thailand than this (see Fig. 6.8).

Socially and culturally, Thailand is an exceptional place. Its attachment to its monarchy and to Buddhism are basic characteristics of the political culture. The monarchy is probably more popular than most found around the world. It held absolute power until 1932. Now the monarchy is politically symbolic, and to that extent it is important, but the royal family has no discernibly great power. The family is a rather significant financial and economic presence in the country, however, because it is heavily involved in a variety of companies and projects. Buddhism, the national religion, is vested with a presence not only by the thousands of temples that delight the eye, but by a large priesthood, the sangka, which has developed its own niche in the body politic. Well over 90 percent of the population is considered Buddhist. Though it is a relatively homogenous society, Thais are not the only ethnic group found in the country; border areas abound with Thai-Lao peoples, Khmers, and others on the eastern perimeter and some of the many dissident peoples of Burma, such as the Karens, on the other. In

Fig. 6.8
Thailand

Gross national product per capita	$1,905
Gross domestic product growth, 1993	7.4%
Gross domestic product growth anticipated, 1995	8.5%
Annual population growth rate	1.5%
Infant mortality per 1,000 births	26
Literacy	93.0%
People per doctor	4,361
People per telephone	26.3
Population	59.5 million
National capital	Bangkok
Major trading partners	U.S.A., Japan

Sources: United Nations, World Bank, and various publications

the south, four small provinces are homes to a Malay minority. There are also the usual groupings of Chinese and Indians found in many Asian countries. The Constitution guarantees religious freedom for all of these groups, but only the Chinese minority has an important position in the economy.

The economy at the moment is setting a fast pace of growth and newfound prosperity. Like Indonesia, Thailand seems to be at the top of the curve of desirability for investment. It is relatively stable politically, though it has had some problems with the military very recently, and it has low wages and adequate nutrition levels. Thailand does pose a problem for our simplified version of the Lewis model of development, however, because it has been a site of low wages and adequate nutrition for a long time, much longer in fact than its current takeoff stage of entrepreneurship would indicate. The Lewis model, therefore, does not seem to square on all fours in this instance. Perhaps—and this is really just a guess—Thailand's perennial problems with its military have been a deterrent; but the best explanation without further research seems to be that the long period of war in the bordering states of Cambodia, Laos, and especially Vietnam were strong hindrances to investor interest and economic development. It has been a relatively short time ago, for example, when writers were posing such questions as whether Thailand would be another Vietnam. Its military did carry out operations, after all, against Communist insurgents in the Thai-Lao border areas.

There are other bad omens for Thailand's development hopes. The opium trade, which uses long-standing routes and contacts that cross borders into Burma and China, must be considered an unhealthy and undesirable part of the nation's economic activity; it breeds violence and crime. Thailand has also become known as a center for the AIDS virus, and this is due in part to the ubiquitous prostitution carried out in such centers as Bangkok, Changmai, and Pettaya. The country probably has more AIDS cases per capita than any society in Asia.

And, like all of the Asian nations seeking to enhance their development, Thailand has serious infrastructure problems. In its case, however, these seem more obvious to even the casual observer than they may seem elsewhere. The capital city of Bangkok has perhaps the worst air quality found in Southeast Asia. An unhealthy-looking haze is nearly always hanging over its office buildings and beautiful temples. Substandard housing, sometimes mere shacks built in various areas or along rail tracks, is on display, and this means severe problems of sanitation and health have not been addressed. Roads are clogged with cars, creating some of the world's worst traffic jams; and, in a recent year, car sales went up 19 percent, showing that conditions can only be expected to get worse. These sales also demonstrate that some prosperity is evident as well. The city is developing an extensive subway system, but this is seen as a catching-up measure that probably will not substantially improve air quality or perhaps even traffic jams. The nation's extensive river system is terribly polluted, and water quality is therefore a serious problem that has been neglected.

Most of Thailand suffers with the problems of poverty and inequity found throughout the Third World; and this is because the economy has developed along the lines of a two-tier system, namely Bangkok and the rest of the country. This, too, can be seen as an infrastructure problem of sorts; but the greatest effects are social and political. It means that migration to the capital city is encouraged at the expense of villages and rural areas; that income disparities are so great that averages used in reports on the country are misleading; and that inequality is a pattern enforced by urbanization and geographic and demographic realities as well as by class structure, employment status, and all of the factors we conventionally assign as causes.

Despite all of these problems—and many of them, such as the AIDS epidemic, must be considered severe—Thailand is attracting the interest of investors, particularly low-tech producers of such commodities as shoes, food products, toys, and garments. Its work-force is considered able and efficient, and there are large pools of unemployed workers, especially in areas outside of Bangkok. Invest-ment generated from within the country is substantial as well. There are complaints and criticisms, however, of Thai investment groups, who are said to be uncaring about the environments or resources of neighboring countries, such as Burma, Laos, and Vietnam, where gem mining and forest cutting are proceeding at a very fast clip.

Foreign policy and national security ties follow a path of great power accommodation that has been a long-standing tradition. This goes back to the nineteenth century, and even before, when a major price for continued independence from colonial domination was for Thailand to appear willing to go along with some imperial demands on such matters as trade or the refueling of ships. This tradition was also evident during World War II, when accommodations were made with the ruling occupier, Japan, which were unique in the region and which have been a source of criticism from neighboring states like Malaysia.

Thailand's great ally since the early 1950s has been the United States. This alliance was formalized in SEATO, the now-defunct

Southeast Asian Treaty Organization which came into being during U.S. Secretary of State John Foster Dulles's "pactomania" period. Thailand remained faithful to SEATO and the United States throughout the Vietnam War period; it served as host to American air bases and to military personnel on leave from Vietnam hostilities. American bases remain in the country today, and the forces of the United States and Thailand conduct joint training exercises such as the "invasion" of a Thai beach. So, even without the SEATO apparatus serving the purposes of coordination and administration, the United States and Thailand have been able to continue to work in close contact on mutual security problems. Indeed, it can be said that since Thailand has eschewed the status of being a nonaligned nation and has made its pro-U.S. stance well known, it should be considered the linchpin of U.S. security interests in the Southeast Asian region. This means it certainly will be important in any future considerations about a continued U.S. presence in Asia. As with most or all of the countries around the world which serve in some way as a U.S. client, Thailand enjoys certain aid and trade advantages.

The United States has not officially commented very much upon the subject of human rights abuses in Thailand, but international monitoring groups have. These problems may seem most obvious when the military asserts itself in the politics of the country and takes over the government, as it did in early 1991. Democratic elections have taken place to restore civilian rule, which has become increasingly prevalent in the nation's years of drive toward economic development. But abuses have occurred under civilian rule as well. These include the sale of children to foreign prostitution rings, mail-order bride systems, and other forms of exploitation. Not incidentally, Thailand completed the development of a national identity card system in 1990, a goal that can effectively raise problems for its citizens. It is not an electronic system of the kind devised in Singapore, but it does facilitate the use of governmental power for almost any purpose, legitimate or not.

Further Reading

Amsden, Alice H. *Asia's Next Giant: South Korea and Late Industrialization.* New York: Oxford University Press, 1989. The importance of Korean competitiveness is set within a somewhat novel but controversial thesis; a provocative set of ideas.

Ariff, Mohamed. *The Malaysian Economy: Pacific Connections.* New York:

Oxford University Press, 1991. Describes the international economic position of Malaysia and sets out policy suggestions.

Asiawatch Reports. *Silencing All Critics*. New York: Asiawatch, 1989. Brief
but very informative report on human rights violations in Singapore.

Bresnan, John. *Managing Indonesia: The Modern Political Economy*. New
York: Columbia University Press, 1993. Recaps all of the major economic
and political events in Indonesia in recent years with expert analysis.

Chan, Joseph Man. *Mass Media and Political Transition: The Hong Kong
Press in China's Orbit*. New York: Guilford Press, 1991. One can perhaps
better understand the pressures of present-day Hong Kong in the shadow of
China by looking at what has happened to the press in recent years.

Chan, Ming K., and David Clark, eds. *The Hong Kong Basic Law: A Blueprint
for Stability and Prosperity under Chinese Sovereignty?* Armonk: M. E.
Sharpe, 1991. The question of 1997 hangs heavily over this set of analyses
of the integration of Hong Kong with China; these are not reassuring treatments.

Chew, Ernest C. T., and Edwin Lee. *A History of Singapore*. New York:
Oxford University Press, 1991. Supplies insight not only into the city-state
and its development, but reaches into other areas of Southeast Asia and
Asia generally in its description.

Clark, Cal. *Taiwan's Development: Implications for Contending Political
Economy Paradigms*. Westport, Conn.: Greenwood Press, 1989. Practically
a tour de force in combining the advantages of incisive analysis with
employment of development models; also provides a good look at how
international forces affect development and the economy.

Crouch, Harold K. *The Army and Politics in Indonesia*, rev. ed. Ithaca, N.Y.:
Cornell University Press, 1988. An extensive guide to the politics of this
complex nation.

Jacobs, Norman. *The Korean Road to Modernization and Development*.
Urbana: University of Illinois Press, 1985. Not only valuable for its analyses
of Korea, this work makes manifest the important and sometimes lasting
differences between modernization and development.

MacIntyre, Andrew. *Business and Politics in Indonesia*. North Sydney, Australia: Asian Studies Association of Australia; Allen and Unwin, 1991. Two
studies which provide a look at the competition for power among the elite
forces of Indonesia.

Means, Gordon P. *Malaysian Politics: The Second Generation*. New York:
Oxford University Press, 1991. One of the better recent books on Malaysian
politics; shows the rapid development of economic forces and modernization
among other factors.

Minchin, James. *No Man Is an Island: A Study of Singapore's Lee Kwan Yew*.
New York: Allen and Unwin, 1987. Biography of one of the most complex
and able of Asia's leaders.

Robinson, David. *Thailand: Adjusting to Success*. Washington, D.C.: International Monetary Fund, 1991. Review of current economic and finance trends in the kingdom; offers suggestions for future growth.

Shapiro, Michael. *The Shadow of the Sun: A Korean Year of Love and Sorrow*. Boston: Atlantic Monthly Press, 1990. Light but readable treatment of Korea's history, politics, and society; specially good in discussing the student movements that have been so important in the modern politics of this nation.

Smith, Douglas C., ed. *The Confucian Continuum: Educational Modernization in Taiwan*. New York: Praeger, 1991. Studies which bring together the interactions of the dynamic forces of cultural values and modernization.

Stowe, Judith A. *Siam Becomes Thailand: A Story of Intrigue*. Honolulu: University of Hawaii Press, 1991. Recounts an important period in the history of modern Thailand.

Vogel, Ezra F. *Four Little Dragons: The Spread of Industrialization in East Asia*. Cambridge: Harvard University Press, 1991. Series of public lectures delivered at Harvard on the topic of development of the four new major models of economic development—Hong Kong, Singapore, South Korea, and Taiwan.

Chapter 7

The Less-Developed
Asia-Pacific Nations

Most Asians are poor despite the great gains made in recent years in some locations. And a majority of the Asian population, as well as vast portions of the Asian land mass, are found in the less-developed countries. China and India, though they are great powers and are the two largest nations in the world, must be classified as poor if their standard of living is assessed (see chapter 3); though their overpowering dimensions—military and cultural influences, for example—have required separate treatment. A case could be made for putting Indonesia and Pakistan in this category as well, since they are the world's fourth and seventh largest countries and are formidable military powers; but their inclusion at other places in this effort rests upon a combination of factors of analysis and convenience. The other seven nations considered here, however, are neither prosperous nor powerful. (Vietnam has been aggressive from time to time, but it hardly fits the definition of a great power even though it has humbled the United States.)

People of the less-developed nations of Asia may know about the relatively newfound prosperity of South Korea or perhaps Malaysia, but most of them know that such wealth is probably far off. In many cases such people are carrying out their lives in a rural habitat in ways much like their grandparents or other forebears did. There might be some radios in the village or even television, and some of the people may drink Coca-Cola from time to time. They may be among the millions who have migrated to Asia's cities, which have been experiencing phenomenal growth. Urbanization has been one of the great overall trends in the Third World for the past half century. The hope for a better life may not be very strong and the problems of day-to-day living might be all that people can absorb. For such citizens, political questions may appear moot or remote, and governmentally devised solutions to problems may seldom be contemplated. And even if a way of dealing with problems occurs to them, the political ability to cause the governance system to respond to needs is often minimal or nonexistent.

Inequity is probably the major element in the economic and political systems of these nations. The 1993 UN Human Development Report looks at this issue on a country-by-country and worldwide basis, and many of the greatest differences between the poor and the wealthy are found in Asia. Certain groups—landowners, the military, internationally and locally based business people, and political elites—seem to have a greater share of the nation's bounty and a greater voice in decision making. In some of these countries, the military is either continuously in charge, as in Burma, or the government often seems to revert to military rule, as in Pakistan. In others, notably Vietnam, the military is an important presence that must be given the attention and succor the ruling class can provide. A theme of corruption often seems to run through the systems of these poor nations, which can be seen as an opportunistic response to such problems as shortages of certain imported goods or of hard currency. In some cases, corruption is such a severe malady of the system that it saps the legitimate efforts made in the economic life of a country.

The less-developed countries of the Asia-Pacific region are treated here in classifications that lend them to analyses and comparisons. Four of these countries—Bangladesh, Pakistan, Nepal, and Sri Lanka—are South Asian nations; that is, they lie on the periphery of the great Indian subcontinent, and their politics and economic development are at least partially influenced by the trends and events in that great country. The remaining four—Burma, Cambodia, Laos, and Vietnam—are Southeast Asian lands that have failed to develop primarily because of political instability. Three of these represent portions of the former French Indo-China, which fell apart in 1954 before the United States made the fateful decision to move its military into this area. Burma, once under British rule, continues to live under a long-standing military regime committed to authoritarianism.

The Less-Developed Nations of South Asia:
Pakistan, Bangladesh, Sri Lanka, and Nepal

Pakistan, Bangladesh, Sri Lanka, and Nepal, together with the major regional power, India, are the principal members of the community of nations we collectively call South Asia. Two much smaller states, Bhutan and the Maldive Islands, are also a part of this region, but they receive scant attention in overviews of the area. A regional association of South Asian nations has been established, but it has not gotten off the ground because India boycotts its meetings due to organizational and procedural objections. Recent undertakings of the South Asia group show a new willingness to work together, however.

Despite cultural, religious, and governmental differences that are observable from one national setting to another, these four countries possess some common characteristics. All of them are poor. Population pressures are not only significant but burdensome. Development and modernization processes have generally evolved slowly. Regional, religious, and ethnic differences have been sources of violence and political instability in Pakistan, Bangladesh, and Sri Lanka. Civil wars of greater or lesser magnitude have occurred in all four of these nations. Inadequate nutrition levels are common in regions of Pakistan and throughout Bangladesh and Nepal. Disease can sometimes take on epidemic proportions in all four of these countries. And, ironically and tragically, purchases of armaments are a major budget item for all four governments. All four have officially declared themselves to be nonaligned nations, and all of them are now dealing with the problem of what this really means in the post-Soviet, post-Cold War world. (It is true that in the past Pakistan was allied with the United States in both the Central Treaty Organization [CENTO] and the Southeast Asia Treaty Organization [SEATO], but the practical benefits of these alignments have long since passed for Pakistan and, many would say, for the United States as well.)

Finally, it should be noted that events that occur in one of these countries will often affect those that are nearby. The activities of the Tamils in Sri Lanka represent a good example of this, since the violence of the group known as the Tamil "tigers" has had great effects upon both Sri Lanka and India, including assassinations of national leaders. The Hindu-Muslim turmoil wrought by the destruction of a mosque in the state of Uttar Pradesh in India in December 1992 resulted in violent clashes in Pakistan and Bangladesh. And, as one might expect, there is the matter of migrations of peoples. Although India must be regarded by all measures as a poor country, it nonetheless attracts illegal immigrants from Pakistan, Bangladesh, Nepal, and Bhutan. The people involved are usually economic refugees, but Hindus escaping violence in Kashmir also recently have been a major group on the move. One of these nations, Bangladesh, was formed out of a part of another, Pakistan. Prior to 1972, it was known as East Pakistan. From its founding in 1947 until 1972, Pakistan was split into two widely separated regions on either side of India. Both of these areas were to be the homes of the Muslim populations of the subcontinent. But various grievances and political ambitions came to the fore over the years, and these were encouraged by India. This secession is probably still a sore point for Pakistan, but it is a reality that has been accepted.

The major concerns of this bloc of nations, then, are the almost always miserable and disappointing economic facts of life and the great political instability that may be either a cause or a symptom of low living standards. If we employ W. Arthur Lewis's model of economic evolution, it can be seen that the day of arrival for these countries has not yet occurred. This does not mean, of course, that there is no investment at all in these nations. Comparatively small amounts of investment activity have taken place, but the scale so far is not significant enough to have any broad or perhaps even lasting effects.

Despite its economic and social problems and its almost endemic political instability, Pakistan can justly claim, for a variety of reasons, that it is one of the most important nations in the world (see Fig. 7.1). It is seventh, overall, in population rank, and it may soon become sixth. It is a significant military power even though it is clearly

Fig. 7.1
Pakistan

Gross national product per capita	$440
Gross domestic product growth, 1993	3.0%
Gross domestic product growth anticipated, 1995	2-3%
Annual population growth rate	2.9%
Infant mortality per 1,000 births	94
Literacy	35.0%
People per doctor	2,111
People per telephone	76.0
Population	125.8 million
National capital	Islamabad
Major trading partners	U.S.A., Japan

Sources: United Nations, World Bank, and various publications

overshadowed by its giant neighbor, India. And, next to Indonesia, it is the largest of the Islamic countries; moreover, it can probably claim that it provides more political leadership to the Muslim world than perhaps any country does.

Pakistan also has many factors working against it, however. It is a relatively arid and resource-poor land. It is locked in a psychological and sometimes violent struggle with its much bigger neighbor, India, over the question of Kashmir and sometimes other issues as well. It has had to shift its international affiliations and alliances from time to time because of changing needs and influences, and these have left the country somewhat disoriented in terms of its position in the world. It has internal frictions on the subject of religion; these are not so important in terms of basic beliefs, although there are important minorities such as the Sikhs in the Punjab, but in terms of what the general attitude and approach toward Islam must be. There are class differences and great contrasts in levels of wealth. There are ethnic differences and nationalisms; one of these is the Baluchi minority located in the southern province of Sind. There are also intense and occasionally violent social and economic rivalries between those who are native to the country and those whose families migrated from India at the time of partition in 1947; these are especially felt in the largest city and port, Karachi. The violence in this city has been so great in 1994 and 1995 that the city's services and normal life have been brought to a halt.

In a rather stark contrast to India, Pakistan's years of nationhood have seldom been marked by adherence to democratic governments or norms. The military has often held sway. Pakistan was placed under martial law, for example, for the years 1977–85. When elections were finally allowed to take place to restore civilian rule, the governing Pakistan Peoples' Party (PPP) and its leader, Benazir Bhutto, were only able to hold a coalition together for about a year. Her successor, Nawaz Sharif, who at first seemed astute in balancing elite interests, was deposed by the military in 1993. Bhutto then returned to power when the military set up an election. Many of the top leaders of government have come from the military ranks or, in almost all cases, have had some military support.

The instability of the country is further underscored by the assassinations, forcible removals, and other extraordinary tactics used by ruling elites upon one another. In the case of Benazir Bhutto, for example, there have been threats of arrest on corruption or other charges. Her father, who headed the government, was executed. Her husband has been jailed on a variety of charges of financial irregularities. Mohammed Zia al-Haq, who instituted martial law in the late 1970s and early 1980s, died in a mysterious plane crash, which has never been satisfactorily explained.

Corruption, as might be inferred, is a serious problem that has hindered development and modernization, and it is not always contained within Pakistan's borders. The worldwide scandal of the Pakistan-based Bank of Credit and Commerce International (BCCI), which broke during the years of the Bush administration, involved financiers, bank officials, and government officials in dozens of nations, including the United States.

Heavy pressures from fundamentalist Muslims, who sometimes take their cues from the thought and work of the late Ayatollah Khomeini of neighboring Iran, have been felt in the country since 1979, when Khomeini took over. These pressures show no sign of abating, and they have already had effects upon such matters as the arts, dress, education, and the rights of women.

The economy can only be badly bent by the nation's atmosphere of power intrigues, extra-constitutional political tactics, and violence; but policymakers are seeking to make some stride toward growth and prosperity. Some of the growth figures of recent years have not been bad, but they have been outpaced by inflation and mounting population figures. Pakistan is one of the fastest-growing places on earth, with annual rates above 2 percent and average family sizes including five or, more likely, six children. When this is factored against the country's resource base or even its recent respectable economic growth figures, it can be seen that progress is slight indeed. The major policy change of recent years has been a strong move toward privatization of state-owned industries. The state-run industries have largely been inefficient and unprofitable, and selling these off is considered wise. This conforms, incidentally, with a worldwide trend that seems to be found everywhere from Mexico to Britain to China. It is too early to assess results of this effort. A second change is a deemphasis upon regulation, whether this is in such areas as business practices or in matters such as the environment or labor relations. The country's stock market, which has attracted relatively little interest from international investors so far, has occasionally been accused of operating in shady ways.

Most of Pakistan's infrastructure—roads, communications facilities, and so forth—is weak and inadequate and will probably require infusions of hard currency in order to be built up in a way that is well directed at modernization. Unfortunately, hard currency infusions rely upon improvements in the balance of payments, and this is in substantial deficit at the moment. Thus, Pakistan, like most Third World countries, is caught in a vicious circle that works against hope of improvement because investment often awaits infrastructure, infrastructure awaits a financial commitment, and this commitment in turn depends upon investment.

Fortunately, Pakistan has proved that it is able to win aid commitments of substantial size from international agencies. The latter have been somewhat receptive in recent years to well-planned projects and demonstrated needs, and, earlier, the country was among the top five on America's favored list of aid recipients. This status, however, has gone by the boards because of Pakistan's insistence upon development of a nuclear capability and its failure to join the list of nations pledged to nuclear nonproliferation.

A major reason for insistence upon being a nuclear power is that India also insists upon this and has in fact had the bomb much longer than has Pakistan. A consequence is that the Indo-Pakistani border, especially in the front-line disputed state of Jammu and Kashmir, is a touchy and dangerous place. The two nations have fought three wars there in order to establish their relative claims to the area, and Pakistan continues to occupy approximately one-third of the territory (see chapter 3 for the discussion of this issue from the Indian side). Many Kashmiri Muslims, as might be expected, prefer to live in Pakistan rather than India; but in recent years, a movement has sprung up that calls for a totally independent Kashmir. Both India and Pakistan are capable of launching a nuclear attack, even if this is likely to be done in a more conventional way—using airplanes rather than missiles— than that which now seems to be envisioned by the nuclear superpowers. These capabilities combined with the confrontational atmosphere created by India and Pakistan make their borders some of the most worrisome potential flashpoints of any places in the world; and at the moment no immediate solution is in sight.

The policy and influence capabilities of the United States in this matter range from slight to nonexistent. The Pressler Amendment bars U.S. aid to Pakistan; and there is very little political leverage and there are apparently no persuasive powers available that can be utilized to cool down the well-aired differences voiced by the two sides. An approach to the problem through the offices of international agencies of one sort or another, most of them in the UN, is possibly the only course open to the United States at the present time. For the most part, there is going to have to be a great reliance upon the good judgment of the two sides, which is not necessarily a reassuring stance to take in this dangerous situation.

On occasion, an American or other Western press item will appear that sets out the thesis that Pakistan has been developing nuclear capability so that there can be an "Islamic bomb" that can be used to defend Muslim interests (or, in the more extreme of these treatments, can be used to forcibly impose the Muslim religion upon nonbelievers). The hard evidence for this idea, however, seems so far to be lacking. It is rarely the case that one nation likes to develop a weapon of this capability to be placed at the service of another nation, whether that country is made up of coreligionists or not. We can quite safely give short shift to this idea.

American policy options on nonnuclear issues involving Pakistan may be slightly broader. There is, after all, a background of a somewhat close relationship between the two countries for several decades. India's development of a neutral, or nonaligned, stance between the two great superpowers of the world, the Soviets and the United States, more or less ordained an interest of the latter in Pakistan. Even after Pakistan withdrew from formal treaty associations with the United States, it was given a strongly favored aid position, both economically and militarily, because of its great help in supplying anti-Soviet forces in Afghanistan. In short, it can be said that Pakistan was well regarded by U.S. policymakers because it accommodated the U.S. position on the Soviet presence in Afghanistan. Now, with that threat gone and with the sharp differences that have been drawn on the matter of nuclear weaponry, it will be harder for the United States to reestablish any rapport with this important nation. The only apparent avenue to influencing Pakistan at this point in time is in the vital area of development aid and this has been barred.

Bangladesh lacks many or most of the resources necessary for the processes of nation-building. Even its strongest asset, an alluvial soil that is very rich, has a downside because it is merely a concomitant of the flood-prone delta upon which most of the country is located. This area has not been prosperous in any recent historical period. When it was a part of India, it was considered one of the poorest regions, a land of tremendous population and few resources. When it became East Pakistan, it was seen as a politically less influential part of the country even though its numbers of people were the same, or even greater, than those of the West. When it became independent Bangladesh in 1972, it was welcomed into the world as one of its poorest nations, and it has remained so ever since. A family income of $1,000 a year would place its recipients solidly into the country's middle class.

The most cursory comparison of the numbers in Figure 7.2 will demonstrate some of the miseries extant in Bangladesh, whether one is looking at the literacy rate, income level, medical indicators, or the out of control growth of population. Undeniably, the greatest needs of the country are economic; but there are some deep environmental and social problems that assault Bangladesh as well.

Culturally, Bangladesh is a nation heavily influenced by the Muslim religion, although there is a significant Hindu minority. The people are mostly Bengalis, related by heritage, customs, and language to the people who inhabit the Indian state that borders the country, West Bengal.

The experiment with democracy is working out so far; but it is severely strained by the animosities developed between the two major parties, the Bangladesh National Party (BNP) and the Awami League (AL). The assassination of Sheikh Mujib, founder of the league, in 1975 is still a major issue because proceeding with a prosecution in the case requires repeal of the country's Indemnity Ordinance. The BNP government pledged that it would do this, but it reneged on this promise. At the moment, the entire Opposition has resigned the Parliament. Other pressures are also at work: any of the issues of the national newspaper, the *Bangladesh Times*, publishes quite a number

Fig. 7.2
Bangladesh

Gross national product per capita	$220
Gross domestic product growth, 1993	4.5%
Annual population growth rate	2.2
Infant mortality per 1,000 births	91
Literacy	35.3%
People per doctor	6,650
People per telephone	380
Population	120.7 million
National capital	Dhaka
Major trading partners	U.S.A., Japan

Sources: United Nations, World Bank, and various publications

of letters from sincere and militant followers of the late Iranian imam Ayatollah Khomeini, reflecting an allegiance to fundamentalist Islamic ideals.

Bangladesh has also had to brace itself heavily under the impact of thousands of Muslim refugees from the bordering country of Burma where they have been severely oppressed. The government has had to rely primarily upon UN and private relief agencies to accommodate these homeless and needy victims.

The greatest amount of news about Bangladesh that seems to reach the rest of the world, despite its many other problems, seems to occur when one of the nation's many disastrous floods inundates the plains of the delta. The floods of 1989 and 1990 were particularly bad, causing thousands of deaths and extensive property damage. The capital city of Dhaka was hit hard by this disaster. As a result, the United Nations has planned and financed a flood action plan to help prevent such a disaster in the future; but this plan is primarily aimed at helping Dhaka only and, in any event, does not seem to be well worked out in its details. There is a good chance that disastrous floods will recur.

The outlook for the moment, then, cannot be said to be very bright for Bangladesh. Poverty, overpopulation, the lack of development initiatives and of support for these in the international community, a fractious politics, and the potential for further natural disasters all hold the nation down. Critics, both domestic and foreign, claim that the government imposes too many regulations to make investment attractive. Whether this is the case or not, however, the United States, the world's richer nations, and international aid agencies must continue to carry out the task of helping this country, and perhaps for the very reason that it is one of the world's poorest nations.

If Bangladesh has a strength, it is its rather firm commitment to democracy. It is rough-style democracy, to be sure, as in the cases of India and Sri Lanka; but seventy-eight parties contested the 1991 national elections, all the same, and international observers—as well as some international accolades—confirm that democratic procedures and practices are much in evidence.

Like many Asian nations, Sri Lanka is divided along ethnic and religious lines; and in its case, this division has been the source of violence and deaths and, at times, a strong measure of governmental oppression. Declaration of an emergency and suspension of civil liberties and the ordinary processes of democratic government have often been the norm in recent years. This instability was even more obvious with the assassination of President Ranasinghe Premedasa in April 1993.

Perceptions of the tragic communal war in Sri Lanka naturally vary according to which side views the conflict. From the standpoint of the Sinhalese majority, the Tamil minority is not really a minority at all. It may be only 12 or 15 percent of the nation's 17.5 million people, but there are 46 million more Tamils living in the nearby Indian state of Tamil Nadu. To the Tamils of Sri Lanka, on the other hand, their minority status condemns them to an oppressive life that is visited upon them by the Sinhalese majority; and the fact that many of their ethnic brethren and sisters live in India is probably seen as irrelevant. This cannot be a totally irrelevant matter, however, since Tamil Nadu has served as a training and logistics base for the guerrilla force known as the Tamil "tigers."

The societal divisions go further than ethnicity, for the Sinhalese are Buddhists and the Tamils are Hindus. The economic and political position of the latter also exacerbates the problem, since it is often charged that Tamils do not receive equal treatment. Economic data on the position of the Tamils are not available, but many of them seem to be middle class members and shopkeepers. Their political position, however, probably does leave much to be desired.

As a concession to the Tamil community, the government undertook a reorganization in 1987 that brought about a supposed devolution of powers to eight regional councils. The idea was to provide Tamils with majority governments in those areas, primarily the Jaffna Peninsula in the north, where they are in fact a majority of the population. At almost the same time, Sri Lanka got rid of its British-model parliamentary system in favor of a Fifth Republic France-inspired system, which has a very strong presidency. Thus, a devolution of power in favor of regional councils was matched—critics would say ruined—by the installation of a very decidedly centralizing tendency. As a result, the president has great power over policy direction; he or she can veto any legislative act, for example, and it is then killed no matter what the legislative sentiment may happen to be at the time. Even more important, the president has extensive and broad discretion on such matters as issuance of emergency decrees and security measures.

There has been an occasional respite in hostilities, but no one can see an imminent end to the civil war now engulfing this beautiful island nation. Perhaps the Tamil demand for a separate state in the northern part of the island will have to be met, or partially met, before this is possible. It is not true, however, that the Tamil "tigers" are supported by the entire Tamil population. There is both a weariness and a wariness felt by many of these people, and time may in fact be working against the revolutionaries.

The difficulties with Tamil nationalism have had a marked impact upon Sri Lanka's relations with India. India once seemed to give tacit support to the Tamil cause by looking the other way as the "tigers" used Tamil Nadu as a training ground and base for launching attacks against the island. But Prime Minister Rajiv Gandhi turned this policy around, sending troops to Sri Lanka in aid of the government against the "tigers." This policy had a certain unpopularity in India, and there is little doubt that this led to Rajiv's assassination on a visit to Tamil Nadu in December 1990.

The calamitous civil strife undoubtedly holds back economic development. Investor interest and tourism are both badly affected by the hostilities, since common sense gives these people an almost invariable preference for more peaceful places. The assassination of President Premedasa in April 1993 only underscores the seriousness of the present situation and the government's inability to control it. India, in the meantime, has withdrawn its troops from the country for a variety of military, economic, and especially political reasons. The UN and a variety of human rights organizations have condemned some of the overzealous measures taken by the government as it seeks to track down and eliminate the Tamil insurrectionists; and though there is never an excuse for human rights violations, it is clear that the war atmosphere contributes to these problems.

Two hopeful factors seem to remain. The first, and it is a decided advantage, is that Sri Lanka, like India, has never abandoned its democratic form of government through all of its years of chaos and strife. This does not mean that democracy is practiced by a standard that is generally acceptable, but it does mean that societal and governmental forces are rather strongly committed to a democratic ideal. The second factor is that whenever the violent problems of the country appear to be receding or, occasionally, even quelled, the interest of investors and tourists seems to perk up almost immediately. This is because Sri Lanka is, after all, an attractive and enticing country. Although its living standards are modest by any measure, it is one of the few Third World countries that has been more or less consistently able to maintain a modicum of a welfare state; and its ratings in various indexes of living standards are, overall, quite good for a Third World country (see Fig. 7.3). If peace can ever be made a reality, the prospects for Sri Lanka's development would brighten quickly.

Fig. 7.3
Sri Lanka

Gross national product per capita	$550
Gross domestic product growth, 1993	6.9%
Annual population growth rate	1.0%
Infant mortality per 1,000 births	15
Literacy	88.5%
People per doctor	6,162
People per telephone	88.1
Population	17.8 million
National capital	Colombo
Major trading partners	U.S.A., Japan

Sources: United Nations, World Bank, and various publications

This strife-torn situation, as the experience of the Indian military seems to show, does not lend itself to foreign initiatives or intervention very well. The United States, it can be assumed, is quite powerless in this matter, and would probably only make conditions worse if any kind of intervention, even the most peaceful use of its good offices, was hinted.

Nepal is perhaps the most impoverished of all of Asia's countries. It has few resources, a poor but growing population, and relatively little foreign investment. It is landlocked between Tibet and India, and it has an isolated location among the peaks of the Himalayas. The only parts of the country that have had any noticeable development have been the small and relatively accessible valley areas adjacent to India.

Reports on the economy are not encouraging. Growth rates, which are in the first instance slow for Asia, anyway, are exceeded by population pressures and inflation. Students who have come to the United States recently from Nepal say that living standards, in their opinion, are actually going down. And no solution seems to be in sight, although the withdrawal of pressures from India, which was bottling up the country with a trade embargo for a while, has eased matters. Tourism probably has some potential for expansion, and this would bring in more badly needed hard currency.

The embargo highlights the problem of vulnerability faced by a small nation that lies between two great powers, India and Chinese-occupied

Tibet. The dispute with India was basically concerned with fuel prices. On many other matters, however, Nepal is susceptible to pressures from China and, perhaps even more, from India, whether the issue is one of foreign relations or a matter that is a specially domestic concern to Nepal. This means that the country's foreign policy is always devised with the idea of treading lightly so as not to invoke the anger of either giant. A simple matter such as taking in Tibetan refugees—and Nepal has done this—must be weighed carefully.

Politically, this little nation now seems to be stabilizing in the aftermath of serious ruptures in the system, which occurred in 1989 and 1990. Civil disorders and riots were the response to the royal family's refusal to give up absolute power. A new constitution, adopted in 1990, set up parliamentary government, which now shares authority with the king. Important problems continue to plague the system since the lines of authority between royalty and parliament are still not always clear. Some observers are alarmed, however, because a Communist government has been elected to power. Such governments nowadays, however, seem to encourage investment as much as anyone else does—one can look to China, Vietnam, or the Indian state of Bengal as good examples.

In addition, there are intense social problems of health, education, and infrastructure needs. And there are special problems of refugee settlement and treatment and a concern about the recent "ethnic cleansing" that has been carried out against long-resident Nepalis in the neighboring state of Bhutan.

A review of the statistics on Nepal in Figure 7.4 will show that the major problem of the country is economic. A nation with a low level of development and few resources faces difficulties at every turn: a low literacy rate, important gaps in treatment of diseases and in provision of sanitation, and many shortcomings in such areas as education, communications, and transport facilities. For the near future, at least, Nepal is going to rely heavily upon help from the wealthier nations and from UN and other aid sources. And this is the case even though the developed nations, faced with their own stringencies, are expecting to cut or eliminate this support.

The small Himalayan kingdom of Bhutan hardly plays any role of importance in Asian affairs. It is a country of ornate Buddhist temples and spectacular mountain scenery. Its population of 1.7 million is largely poor and illiterate, and an indeterminate number of these people become illegal immigrants in India. Bhutan was once ruled by Tibet and then, later, by Britain; today its independence is in some

Fig. 7.4
Nepal

Gross national product per capita	$180
Gross domestic product growth, 1993	2.9%
Annual population growth rate	2.3%
Infant mortality per 1,000 births	88
Literacy	26.0%
People per doctor	16,830
People per telephone	174
Population	20.8 million
National capital	Katmandu
Major trading partners	U.S.A., Japan

Sources: United Nations, World Bank, and various publications

ways nominal since, even less than Nepal, it is hardly able to carry out policies that do not have India's blessing. Very little of the land is arable, and malnutrition is therefore a serious problem. The kingdom has often taken a negative stance on having outsiders in the country at all; it is only in recent years that organized tour groups and mountain-climbing excursionists have been allowed to visit. The Bhutanese majority, which comprises some 70 percent of the population, has typically been less well off than the Nepalese minority, which largely practices Hinduism. In recent years, ethnic strife and government decrees have worked against the Nepalese, forcing migration into India or to Nepal. For the present, then, Bhutan seems as much on the periphery of world affairs as it is on the edge of the great Himalayan mountain chain.

The Less-developed Countries of Southeast Asia:
Burma, Cambodia, Laos, and Vietnam

The four poorest nations of Southeast Asia—Burma, Cambodia, Laos, and Vietnam—have had quite similar fates in their political and economic development since 1945. All four have emerged from a type of colonial rule that was particularly despotic and shortsighted. Burma's history demonstrates one of the worst examples of British colonial administration; and the policies of the French in what they called Indo-China, which includes Cambodia, Laos, and Vietnam, have been well chronicled; to some extent, the latter transgressions against humanity are better known because of all of the debates and publicity surrounding the Vietnam War and its aftermath. The well-known Academy Award-winning film *Indochine,* a 1992 production, added to the general public's knowledge of these depredations.

Even more important, these areas have suffered through almost continuous states of war since the end of World War II. Burma's government has always been intact during this period, but it has been fighting at least thirty-three separate wars against minority and dissident groups, most of them located in border regions. The three former French colonies first carried out a war against France, which ended successfully in 1954. Then the United States stepped in, and it carried out the longest war effort in its history before being humiliated in 1975. But the end of Western military initiatives did not bring peace. Vietnam hurled its troops into Cambodia to join the civil war there and has pressured Laos as well. And Cambodia's Pol Pot had his troops slaughter more than one million of their own country's people in one of the greatest examples of genocide in the history of the world. Cambodia remains unstable and the threat of a renewal of civil war is constant.

Not to be overlooked as a cause of poverty is the "command economy" approach taken by these four countries. The Indo-China states—Cambodia, Laos, and Vietnam—all adopted Soviet-style approaches of mandating prices, wages, and production goals, and the results have been similar to those of the Soviet and East European experiences. Waste, inefficiency, poverty, and a lack of growth have characterized these economies until very recently, when Vietnam began to encourage foreign investment while also undertaking some privatization and deregulation. Burma has continued to follow the "command economy" mold, even though the government has often fought Communist insurgents. Its preference for insularity, its repressive military rule, its corruption, and its more or less complete governmental control of the economy has met with the results we might expect. Only recently has Burma relented, however slightly, on the matter of private foreign investment.

As in nearly all of Pacific Asia today, however, economic change is strongly anticipated in these countries, especially in the case of Vietnam. Vietnam and, for that matter, the other three nations as well, are considered candidates for the ASEAN trading bloc during the next few years (see chapter 8). The problems of these economies, all the same, are great indeed.

Burma, which has been called Myanmar by its military regime since 1989, gained its independence in 1948 and, unlike most former colonies of Britain, chose not to become a member of the Commonwealth. The most recognized leader of the independence movement was Aung San, who was parliamentary leader of the governing party; he and six cabinet ministers were assassinated shortly before independence was obtained. The first elected government to come into existence was therefore headed by U Nu of the Anti-Fascist Peoples Freedom League (AFPFL). U Nu's group had weak support among certain elites, including the military and the bureaucracy and was the target of both ideological and ethnic opponents. Communists took up the revolutionary cause in the hinterlands while members of the Karen minority took up arms against the Rangoon regime upon the death of Aung San. Wars and rebellions have been going on ever since, and today it is estimated that the central government is fighting more than thirty actions against one group or another. In 1962, a military coup led by Ne Win took over the government and this group has remained in power for the past three decades.

As one might expect, military rule has not been a boon for Burma, and even the regime has had to admit for the past several years that the economy is mired in low growth levels, corruption, inefficiency, and a heavy dose of political repression. Today Burma is one of the poorest countries in the world, and its populace seems to be caught up in a despondent mood, which can hardly be a basis for a bright economic or political future (see Fig. 7.5).

Mass demonstrations against government rule seemed to spontaneously break out in 1988. In a grand gesture in July of that year, Ne Win resigned his party post and called for a national referendum to establish a new multiparty government. But he rejected this stance and installed an unpopular and repressive figure, General Sein Lwin, as leader of the nation and its governing party. This provoked greater and more widespread demonstrations and bloodshed, resulting in the installation of Dr. Maung Maung, one of the regime's few civilian leaders. A now confident opposition demanded the establishment of an interim civilian government before national elections were to take place, but they overplayed their hand. A general strike was called in August 1988 and a paralysis of governmental and other services resulted. But this prompted a military coup led by Saw Maung, a man not known for compromise nor for democratic instincts.

Fig. 7.5
Burma

Gross national product per capita	$890
Gross domestic product growth, 1993	5.8%
Annual population growth rate	2.1%
Infant mortality per 1,000 births	81
Literacy	81.0%
People per doctor	12,500
People per telephone	416
Population	45.5 million
National capital	Rangoon
Major trading partners	China, Japan

Sources: United Nations, World Bank, and various publications

The repression that followed resulted in the deaths of thousands of demonstrators and an intensive isolation of Burma carried out by Western governments and international human rights organizations. Aung San Suu Kyi, daughter of Aung San, had played a key role in the opposition to the government. Her democratic group in fact swept the national elections of 1990, but she was not allowed to take power; instead, she was placed under house arrest and has remained in this status ever since. She was awarded the Nobel Peace Prize in 1991.

The State Law and Order Committee (SLORC), headed until recently by Saw Maung, closed down the nation's universities for more than three years. They were reopened in 1992, but the military presence on the campus of Rangoon University and other institutions, the boot camp-like indoctrination and discipline, and the repressive atmosphere make university learning a sham.

More than fifteen thousand political prisoners have been identified by Amnesty International, and a UN report claims that the regime is the object of more than a thousand allegations of abduction, forced labor, murder, rape, torture, and arbitrary arrest. In the meantime, wars have continued to be prosecuted against minorities such as the Karens, the Kachins, and the indigenous Muslim population. At the moment, however, these wars have been put on hold as tense negotiations have been taken up with these minority groups. Some of the minority groups continue to control portions of the countryside and even some small cities. Tensions are great in the border areas because Muslims have escaped to Bangladesh on the western side and Karens, probably the leading ethnic opposition group, generally operate from Thailand as well as the border areas within Burma that they control. The harsh treatment of minorities by the regime seems to require, at some time in the future when reform and democracy are really possible, that some kind of federal setup will be necessary in order to provide for national stability. In addition, such an arrangement seems only to make sense in a nation of more than one hundred languages and sizable minority groups.

A few points about the political culture should be set out, because this has been well-researched, notably by Lucian Pye and by other scholars as well. The Burmese family atmosphere seems to connote an active, busy, noisy, and crowded way of life. Burmese are consequently brought up to feel that nearly all activities should take place in a group setting; this seems in keeping with the Asian emphasis upon consensus building. Elders are given positions of priority, and cooperation and interdependence of families and their members are encouraged.

One of the prominent and culturally related terms used in the country is "ahn-eh-deh." This is the expression of one's uneasiness when others are required to take some trouble for this person's well-being. But since "ahn-eh-deh" is found in all spheres of activity—political, economic, or social—it has the effect of smothering interpersonal relationships. The spirit of democracy seems weak within Burmese culture, and this fits with the spirit of "ahn-eh-deh," but Burmese people nonetheless demand the freedom and opportunities they associate with democracy. This sets up inherent conflicts; Maung Maung Gyi, a Burmese scholar, argues that from the earliest history to today, Burmese in superior positions have been haughty, aloof, and cruel while those in inferior positions are invariably timid, passive, and sycophantic.

The result, it is said, is an enduring politics of intimidation and fear. Gyi holds that the Burmese thought pattern accepts the idea that government is repressive and evil, that misery is a natural state of affairs, and that common people should not concern themselves with what their rulers do. At the same time, there is a strong tendency to see the government as omnipotent, omnipresent, and omnicompetent. Anyone outside of government is therefore of no particular significance. Opposition has therefore been seen, historically, as foolish, hopeless, and something that is an object of scorn more than of sympathy.

There will unquestionably be further inquiries into the nature of Burmese culture and politics, but these insights appear useful for the moment. They give clues to the workings of Burmese society specifically and they imply that a great deal of work needs to be done to understand all political cultures.

The state-run economy continues to be centered upon nationalized industries that were first established in 1963. Foreign debt and trade deficits are substantial, and inflation has been a horrific problem in recent years. The government blames the small private merchants for this state of affairs. Japan, the United States, and the European economies have shunned Burma as an aid recipient, although Japanese interests are now carrying out a few probes into investment. This has caused the regime to look to other Southeast Asia governments for closer trade and diplomatic ties. One result of this policy is the broadscale exploitation of the nation's natural resources by Thai and other interests.

Leaders of the ASEAN (Association of Southeast Asian Nations) bloc generally believe that a policy of what they call "constructive engagement" will persuade Rangoon to change its policies. (At odds with this at times is Malaysia's Mahathir, who resents the horrible treatment of the Muslim community.) The ASEAN officials have stated that they will resist Western attempts to impose human rights standards on Burma because such a precedent might be applied to other Asian countries. Membership in the association appears a likely development in the near future. China and Singapore, among other nations, have supplied the weapons used by the regime to suppress democracy and dissent. For now, at least, the outlook for Burma and its people is both grim and unstable.

Cambodia has probably suffered more human misery than any Asian country over the past half century. In the late 1970s, it was the scene of horrible slaughter as one million or more of its people died at the hands of their government. This traumatic period has unquestionably affected all political matters and events that have taken place since then. Most unfortunately, the convoluted and often hate-filled politics of the country continue to show that there can be no real assurance that a repetition of this horror can be avoided in the future.

The nation's evolution might have been different. For a lengthy period of time between independence from France in 1953 and American military intervention in 1970, Cambodia was held together by a fragile coalition headed by Prince Norodom Sihanouk. Sihanouk has always been a skillful builder, negotiator, and soother of complaints. He has also been regarded as an important symbol of the nation and its hopes. All of the major groupings and interests in the country— Communist, royalist, Buddhist, pro-Western, pro-Vietnam, or whatever—were more or less restrained by Sihanouk's balancing and coaxing efforts in the 1953–70 period. And today, long after his initial fall from power, Sihanouk is still regarded as important to any coalitional efforts. Perhaps his greatest recent triumph is the victory of the opposition party, the royalist party, in UN-sponsored elections held in early 1993.

The invasion of Cambodia, ordered by President Richard M. Nixon in 1970, was motivated initially by the belief that a Viet Cong headquarters could be found there. This center was supposedly directing the war effort against U.S forces then operating in South Vietnam. It was never found. But the new presence of the United States in Cambodia had an effect of smashing the carefully ordered coalition Sihanouk had put together. A coup took place, and the pro-American government of Lon Nol took power. The prince, who was well-liked by the political left, took refuge in China.

Lon Nol's regime, however, did not enjoy even the fragile kind of support Sihanouk had managed to construct. In 1975, the murderous Pol Pot and his Khmer Rouge regime, supported by Sihanouk, took power. Pol Pot also had the tacit and rather incredible support of both China and the United States. Neither of these powers cared for the Soviet- and Vietnam-connected forces opposing Pol Pot. (A book review article by Philip C. Brown in the April/June 1993 issue of the *Bulletin of Concerned Asian Scholars* goes over some of the key literature and documentation of this period.) Whatever shortcomings the Vietnamese-dominated faction or, for that matter, any other faction may have had, there could not have been any path taken more mistaken than this one. A severe ideologue, Pol Pot unleashed wanton slaughter on his people for their failure to live up to his expectations. A rather quiet and certainly beautiful land of temples and forests became a nation of killing fields. Massive forced movements of people took place, resulting in deaths, injuries, and disease. One incredible decree required everyone to move out of Phnom Penh, the capital city. It should not be surprising that both Cambodians and foreign observers look askance at the idea of Pol Pot and his Khmer Rouge forces ever participating in government in the future in any way.

The Khmer Rouge were ousted from power in 1978 by a Vietnam-backed regime, and the country has experienced considerable turmoil and uncertainty since then. Tangled factionalism and the threat of revived civil war have kept Cambodia on edge through all of these years. Thousands of the country's citizens have had to live in refugee camps located both within its borders and in neighboring Thailand. Economic growth, needless to say, has been on the back burner while the nation's political future remains in doubt. Most threatening of all is the chance that Pol Pot and the Khmer Rouge might come to power again, a prospect that strikes fear and loathing into all reasonable persons.

The Khmer Rouge undeniably remain a force in Cambodia, all the same, and they control some provinces absolutely. And it was recognition of their base of power that led international negotiators from the UN, from other Asian nations, and from within the country itself to include the Khmer Rouge in deliberations about the future of the nation. In recent years, a UN peacekeeping force has patrolled the country and kept the rival factions apart in an attempt to set up something resembling a democratic government.

The tortured negotiations between the Khmer Rouge, the Vietnamese-backed government forces, and the Sihanouk royalists finally resulted in UN-supervised elections in 1993. Although these elections could not be conducted in all parts of the country, the overall tallies were considered a fair result. The royalists managed to do better than anyone else, but the sitting government has apparently decided to join with them in a coalition arrangement; and both of these groups decided to bring the Khmer Rouge into the power sharing as well. This arrangement did not last long. The Khmer Rouge have continued to prosecute military actions and their leaders have now been ordered out of the capital city of Phnom Penh.

For the moment it must be admitted by all observers that the future of this lovely land remains tenuous, just as its much-looted and desecrated national monument of Angkor Wat, one of the great sights of Asia, also remains in doubt. A statistical overview of Cambodia is found in Figure 7.6.

Laos is a landlocked country that, lying adjacent to Vietnam, has shared many of the fates of that much larger nation. An ancient kingdom, it was under colonial rule until the French forces were finally defeated in 1954. It had carried out a strong and highly successful guerrilla war effort against France for many years prior to its independence. The independence forces, totally dominated by the Communist-aligned Pathet Lao (meaning the "Lao nation"), controlled most of

Fig. 7.6
Cambodia

Gross national product per capita	$200
Gross domestic product growth, 1993	5.7%
Annual population growth rate	2.2%
Infant mortality per 1,000 births	111
Literacy	35.0%
People per doctor	16,365
People per telephone	1,212
Population	9.0 million
National capital	Phnom Penh
Major trading partners	N/A

Sources: United Nations, World Bank, and various
publications

the northern half of this small country even before the French quit
the scene.

It did not control the southern half, however, and the Pathet Lao
was forced to carry out a tough and not-always-successful civil war
against the government centered in the capital city of Vientiane. (The
ancient and royal capital of the kingdom is a different city, Luang
Prabang.) A cease-fire took effect in 1961, and a delicate coalition
government was installed in 1962. This government had three important factions—the Pathet Lao, a neutralist party, and a pro-U.S. group.

This setup was doomed to failure, and by 1965 it had collapsed. Civil
war broke out again; and the warfare was more intense this time
because of larger and more advanced stocks of weaponry and, assuredly, because the war in neighboring Vietnam was heating up. The
Vietnam War, in fact, had severe effects upon Laos, which was invaded
by American and South Vietnamese forces. In addition, according to
later-revealed U.S. government documents, secret air attacks were
launched against the country. A major reason for this military interest
in Laos was that it served as the locale for a significant portion of the
Ho Chi Minh trail, which was used to supply Viet Cong forces in
the South. These forces were fighting against the South Vietnamese
government and the United States in an alliance with the North
Vietnamese government.

As was true in Vietnam, the Communist forces grew ever stronger as the conflict wore on; the neutralists, royalists, and pro-U.S. forces finally had no stomach for a long war. The decisive victory of the Pathet Lao, not surprisingly, coincided with the abandonment of Vietnam by the U.S. military in 1975.

The Pathet Lao regime instituted a command economy like the Soviet and Vietnam models in which prices, production, and all economic factors were determined by decree. A few food markets continued to operate without supervision, but these were the exception. A close relationship with the Soviet Union developed, which amounted to dependence upon that country; when the USSR collapsed in 1990, Laos was left in a bad position for trade, aid, and other economic needs. It has had to look elsewhere for the development of commercial and investment patterns. Following a worldwide trend, the government embarked upon some measures of privatization and deregulation.

The economic future remains murky, however. Thailand, which has had strained relations with Laos because of border incursions originating in the latter, has been the source of fairly heavy investment in forestry products. This has meant, as is the case in so much of Asia and the world, that large stands of timber have been cut to satisfy short-term economic interests. Handicrafts and art objects as well as illicit drugs have provided some export revenue; Buddhist treasures from Laos are specially prized by collectors and travelers. The more optimistic Laotians believe that the strong interest in Vietnam now exhibited by Japanese and other foreign investors will eventually have a fallout effect on their country as well. It is a very long road to prosperity and decent living standards because wars and the command economy have taken their toll (see Fig. 7.7).

Obviously, the United States can have little or no effect on Laos. The history of hostility toward the Pathet Lao means that this government is not likely to listen to much that the United States might have to say. Unlike the case of Vietnam, however, the United States recently decided to remove the embargo against Laotian goods and trade and, also unlike the case of Vietnam, the United States and Laos have established diplomatic relations.

Culturally, Laos, like Cambodia and Vietnam, can be said to be a once traditional and hierarchic Buddhist society that has increasingly felt the shock of modernity smashing up against its ancient ways. The Pathet Lao abolished the monarchy and has urged, ever so slightly, a secularist course for the nation. But a large population of monks is evident to any casual visitor, and the temples remain in place. And

Fig. 7.7
Laos

Gross national product per capita	$230
Gross domestic product growth, 1993	4.0%
Annual population growth rate	2.9%
Infant mortality per 1,000 births	96
Literacy	83.9%
People per doctor	4,380
People per telephone	510
Population	4.6 million
National capital	Vientiane
Major trading partners	Former USSR, Vietnam

Sources: United Nations, World Bank, and various publications

these scenes seem to contribute to the image of Laos as one of the quietest, most peaceful countries on earth, even though it presently is locked into conditions of poverty and slow or no growth.

Vietnam is by far the largest of the three nations once referred to as Indo-China. The combined populations of Laos and Cambodia are perhaps one-sixth or one-seventh of the Vietnam total. Historically, culturally, and militarily, Vietnam has often been the dominant nation in the region. At the present time it is a very hot investment and trade center; it is generating an enormous amount of interest in Japan, Europe, the United States, and other places. Some of this enthusiasm is premature, for the bureaucracy and the Communist party are still forces to be reckoned with. The very low pay levels, sometimes averaging $17 U.S. per month in the North, combined with adequate nutrition levels and a fair amount of political stability, do make this a primary target for low-tech manufacturing. It is ideal as a center for creating export markets if we are to accept the validity of the W. Arthur Lewis model and the hard evidence that today shows exceptional investor interest and excitement. This trend is helped by a more relaxed attitude of the Communist government toward investment enterprises.

To most Americans, however, the mere mention of this country brings to mind our longest and most unsuccessful war; not an ordinary war by any means, if such a phenomenon exists, but a war that split U.S. society, culture, and politics with deep and perhaps permanent fault lines. Vietnam brings pain to the minds and hearts of many or most Americans. Some feel the pain of actual war wounds or of a family loss. Some feel the pain of defeat and disgust and what they may see as the disloyalty or naivete of some of their fellow citizens. And some regard the Vietnam War as the event that woke them up to the sad realities of politics and shattered their belief in America as a nation that is steadfastly idealistic. This last group is likely to regard the Vietnam War as a squandering of resources, both human and material, in a hopeless effort.

All of this has an effect on U.S. policies toward Vietnam today. There remains an important concern in the United States about American troops who have been missing in action or who may still be prisoners of war. Vietnam has been helpful in providing some information about these persons, but there is still a substantial number of Americans who believe that it has not been as forthcoming as it should be. In the cases of those who have lost a loved one, the continuance of this hope is understandable. The facts, however, point to a very unlikely continued presence of American prisoners of war in Vietnam or Laos. The passage of time and the absence of any practical policy reasons for keeping such prisoners, as well as a genuine lack of evidence, works against such hopes.

The Clinton administration lifted a long-standing U.S. embargo on trade with Vietnam in 1994. The embargo was based upon the supposition that the latter has not been sufficiently cooperative on the matter of prisoners of war. This policy of trade restriction, though not necessarily a hindrance to some multinational types of corporations, had a tendency to work against U.S. investment initiatives in Vietnam. And this has occurred at a time when Japan, European interests, Taiwan, South Korea, Singapore, and other nations and groups are almost feverishly involved with Vietnam.

The very physical appearance of Vietnam today demonstrates the rapid changes the nation is undergoing. The shops and streets of Ho Chi Minh City (formerly Saigon) have generally been amenable to the sale and distribution of all sorts of wares long after the Americans have left; but even the more austere precincts of Hanoi, the national capital, are alive with commercial activity. The signs and logos of Sony, Hitachi, and other well-known consumer brands are seen on the streets and in the shops; and perhaps more importantly, a variety of U.S.-based corporations have set up offices in the country. Caterpillar and

IBM are two examples of this. Dunkin' Donuts became, in 1994, the first international food franchise to locate in Vietnam.

Like Cambodia and Laos, Vietnam was ruled by the French from 1893 to 1954. The latter date marks the defeat of the colonial forces at Dien Bien Phu and the Geneva accords, which followed. These accords set up separate Vietnamese states in the North and South of the country. The North was controlled by the Communists under the leadership of national hero Ho Chi Minh, and the South was provided with a succession of inept and corrupt leaders for two decades until 1975, when the Americans were forced to leave and the Vietnamese government was consolidated into a single entity.

The cultural, linguistic, and life-style differences between the North and the South are of some significance; there are, for example, the commercial and consumer tastes and customs affected in the South by the Americans. To say that the North and the South are separate nations is going too far, however, and this fiction is one that has caused the United States considerable trouble. Buddhism is the major religion of the country, although there is a significant Christian minority. Like Cambodia and Laos, Vietnam is a nation of beautiful temples and Buddhist monuments. The city of Hue, situated in the south-central part of the country, is a traditional center of Buddhist culture; it was once the national capital.

Decades of war have undone much of the economic and social fabric of Vietnam. The battle for independence from the French got its start in the 1920s; the Paris government was therefore under some pressure to get out of Vietnam for at least thirty years. The country was occupied by Japan during World War II, and the French were never really able to reassert their control after the war. U.S. military activity has left its mark on the society and culture, but the bomb craters and the naked jungles created by chemicals are less obvious today.

One of the most remarkable facts about the war prosecuted by the United States is the involvement of several presidents and administrations. It was President Harry S Truman who decided that the French should be given weaponry to assist their resistance to the independence movement. Dwight D. Eisenhower was the first president to send in troops, nearly all of whom were "advisers" to the South Vietnamese forces. John F. Kennedy enlarged the troop commitment to approximately eight thousand, giving the United States its first important presence in the country. Lyndon B. Johnson, who was president when the war was at its crest, raised this number to half a million. His utter determination to prevail was, in the long run, a

Fig. 7.8
Vietnam

Gross national product per capita	$220
Gross domestic product growth, 1993	8.0%
Annual population growth rate	2.3%
Infant mortality per 1,000 births	37
Literacy	88.0%
People per doctor	2,857
People per telephone	386
Population	73.4 million
National capital	Hanoi
Major trading partners	Former USSR, Japan, Singapore

Sources: United Nations, World Bank, and various publications

terrible mistake. Johnson also was the first president to bomb the North, a task undertaken on a massive scale in 1965. His successor, Richard M. Nixon, supposedly had a plan to end the war but we have never been able to find out just exactly how this would have worked. He reduced the U.S. commitment of troops as he sensed the national dismay surrounding the war effort in the late 1960s and early 1970s. Finally, President Gerald Ford presided over the final debacle of U.S. defeat and withdrawal. What is most instructive about these mistaken approaches, piled one upon the other, is that they demonstrate, among other factors, a lack of U.S. knowledge and appreciation of Asian culture and the practical realities that might flow from such knowledge and appreciation.

Vietnam clearly has a policy of celebrating the war. It has a museum that contains American weapons such as tanks and jet fighter aircraft. It urges tourists to enter the tunnel system in a location just outside Ho Chi Minh City so they can appreciate the successful techniques of guerrilla warfare carried out by the Communist side. And the defoliation of forests and the napalming of its people are graphically discussed and displayed.

Today, however, the emphasis seems to be upon economic development rather than upon the sufferings and glories of the past. The fast growth, heavy trading activity, and enthusiastic consumer involvement clearly show that the United States and other nations have opportunities here (see Fig. 7.8).

The less-developed nations of Asia and the Pacific Rim, then, are a mixture of suffering and hope. Nations like Sri Lanka, Nepal, Burma, and Cambodia have a long way to go, and many political changes to make, if they are to enjoy a prosperous future. Countries like Vietnam, on the other hand, may be on the brink of the take-off stage. Much will depend upon the political evolution of these countries and the form it takes. Some of their fate, however, will depend upon the reactions, approaches, and opportunities sought by nations like the U.S., Japan, some of the new Asian "tigers," and the European bloc.

Further Reading

Anderson, David L., ed. *Shadow on the White House: Presidents and the Vietnam War*. Lawrence: University Press of Kansas, 1993. Readings that seek to set out the roles of the various Chief Executives who were involved in Vietnam war policy.

Bhutto, Benazir. *Daughter of Destiny: An Autobiography*. New York: Simon and Schuster, 1989. Provides insights into the complex disarray of Pakistani politics from the standpoint of an important party leader.

Blaikie, Piers M. *Nepal in Crisis: Growth and Stagnation at the Periphery*. New York: Oxford University Press, 1980. Sets out the important social and political conditions that were later to lead to crisis.

Brown, T. Louise. *War and Aftermath in Vietnam*. New York: Routledge, 1991. One of the more up-to-date treatments of current trends in Vietnam.

Chandler, David P. *The Tragedy of Cambodian History: Politics, War, and Revolution Since 1945*. New Haven: Yale University Press, 1991. The whole sad story.

Falla, Jonathan. *True Love and Bartholomew: Rebels on the Burmese Border*. New York: Cambridge University Press, 1991. An in-depth and sometimes controversial look at the Karen rebellion against SLORC and previous central governments. Timely and well written.

Hamilton-Merritt, Jane. *Tragic Mountains: The Hmong, the Americans, and the Secret Wars for Laos, 1942–1992*. Bloomington: Indiana University Press, 1993. Like the Falla book (see above), this is a remarkable presentation of little-known aspects of larger Asian conflicts.

Hess, Gary R. *Vietnam and the United States: Origins and Legacy of War*. Boston: Twayne, 1990. A balanced treatment of issues that still raise great controversy.

Kapur, Ashok. *Pakistan in Crisis*. New York: Routledge, 1991. A recent survey of the many political imbalances and problems that plague this country.

Kyi, Aung San Suu. *Freedom from Fear and Other Writings,* edited by Michael Aris. New York: Penguin, 1991. Essays and thoughts of the Nobel Peace Prize winner; she stands as a symbol of a future free Burma.

Spencer, Jonathan, ed. *Sri Lanka: History and the Roots of Conflict.* New York: Routledge, 1990. Articles and essays with a focus mostly devoted to the Sinhalese-Tamil conflicts besetting the island.

Steiglitz, Perry. *In a Little Kingdom.* Armonk, N.Y.: M. E. Sharpe, 1990. A useful introduction to Laos.

Chapter 8

ASEAN: A Future Asian Community of Nations?

by Ardeth Maung

Much of the world has seen the promotion and development of supra-national levels of organization during the past fifty years. The preeminent and most successful example of these organizations has been the European Community, which has made strides toward a free market area; a unified court system; an embryonic but still largely powerless parliament; and a considerable unity of cultural, educational, and employment opportunities. Various other regions of the world—North America, Africa, and Central America are examples—have been experimenting with forms and arrangements aimed at economic, political, social, and cultural frameworks of supranational scope.

Asia and the Pacific Rim have also been the scene of such efforts. An association of South Asian nations (ASA) has held some formal meetings, though India's noncooperation has stymied these efforts. Broad-ranging economic and potentially political organizations are currently being proposed by this or that country in the hope that, at the least, a large free trade area can be launched. Earlier in this century, an aggressive and militarist Japan saw a "coprosperity sphere" of complementary economies developing in Asia in which it would serve in the dominant position.

More recently than this, some of the nations of Southeast Asia sought to organize themselves into an economic and trading bloc. The first of these experiments was ASA, the first Association of Southeast Asian Nations, founded in July 1961. Its members were Malaysia, the

Philippines, and Thailand. A month later saw the establishment of Maphilindo with its membership (as the name suggests) made up of Malaysia, the Philippines, and Indonesia. A U.S.-sponsored and -led security community, the Southeast Asia Treaty Organization, or SEATO, was established in the 1950s during the "pactomania" period. This faded away, however, in the aftermath of the Vietnam War, even though the United States remains committed by treaty to some of its members, such as Thailand. All of these organizations were ill-fated; but ASEAN, the Association of Southeast Asian Nations founded in 1967, has managed to last for more than a quarter of a century with the support of its six members—Brunei, Indonesia, Malaysia, the Philippines, Singapore, and Thailand. Asserting that this is a regional organization of great strength, however, would be clearly wrong.

The Seeds of Unity

The seeds of a plan for regional cooperation were sown in the early 1950s. The scars of colonial conquest and exploitation had imprinted a shared perception among Southeast Asian countries that many current problems are, or were, a consequence of colonialism. This provided, at the least, a bond of bitterness.

Among the many problems perceived at the time were anachronistic geographic boundaries foisted upon the colonies by their European masters, and consequent economic, social, and cultural dislocations, which had only suited colonial interests. The Indonesia-Malaysia-Singapore area, for example, which shares many commonalities of race, religion, language, and life-style, suffered greatly from this disruption.

The fact remained, however, that the formerly British spheres of Malaya, Singapore, Sabah, and Sarawak did not wish to be absorbed by the larger and formerly Dutch sphere of Indonesia. This irked President Sukarno and his followers, who saw Indonesia as the natural core, a place to which the others could "come home." The reality that the region was perhaps permanently divided, however, had been understated and ignored by most Asian leaders and nations. The imperialist heritage allegedly left another "disruption," the introduction of the Chinese into the Malay world. Some Malays, knowing that the Chinese had been imported to satisfy European needs for coolie labor during the nineteenth century, regarded these people as another negative legacy of the colonial era.

The ability to transcend such differences underlies much of the appeal of regionalism, and this thought occurred to leaders, peoples, and nations at a time of widespread Third World belief that collaboration between themselves was the only way to true independence and security against outside powers.

Neither ASA nor Maphilindo was able to mute nationalistic interests, and both were destroyed by rivalries that involved irredentism, challenges to the legitimacy of others, interference in the internal affairs of other nations, and, ultimately, Sukarno's campaign to crush Malaysia. But ASA, the first to collapse, foundered upon a Philippine claim that the North Borneo provinces of Sabah and Sarawak, which were about to be incorporated into the new nation of Malaysia, actually belonged to the former American colony. Maphilindo collapsed because its largest member and military power, Indonesia, did not recognize its limits and instituted its policy of *konfrontasi* against Malaysia. *Konfrontasi's* beginning is marked by the violent reaction of mobs in Jakarta in 1963 to the announcement of the annexation of Sabah and Sarawak by Malaysia.

The end of *konfrontasi* required a change of government in Indonesia to bring it about. A formal signing of the Bangkok Agreement in Jakarta in 1966 marked this end, although the eclipsing of Sukarno by Suharto in 1965 was the event that precipitated this rapprochement. The new regime in Indonesia saw Sukarno's policies as costly adventurism which were both futile and foolish.

The Establishment of ASEAN

The change of government in Indonesia was undoubtedly a key event in the establishment of ASEAN; and it was in fact this government that not only set out a broad policy of rapprochement, but also which solicited the nations who eventually became members to work in favor of the idea of regional cooperation. ASEAN thus came into existence in 1967.

This has not necessarily been a smooth existence, however; and no one should jump to the conclusion that ASEAN will necessarily lead to an effective supranational arrangement or even to something resembling a free trade area. So far it has not.

The strongest tendency within this bloc has been for nations to go their own way economically, politically, and militarily. This was most obvious during the early years of ASEAN, from 1967 to roughly 1976, when the organization seemed to be operating or, more precisely, not at all operating, in a more or less dormant phase.

One reason offered for this, which may hold considerable merit, is the dominant role of the United States in the region at this time. The Vietnam War was being fought, and the surrounding areas were scenes of a mighty U.S. naval, air, and armed troops presence. Bases in the Philippines, Thailand, and various nearby Pacific islands were active centers of widespread U.S. operations. The effect of this presence may simply have inhibited any local development of initiatives, since it probably encouraged ASEAN members to free-ride on the strength and activism of the Americans.

Only with the forced withdrawal of the United States from Vietnam in 1975 did the leaders of the ASEAN group appear motivated to reassess the reasons for their union and the possible future direction it could take. This marked a new period for ASEAN, lasting until 1987, in which attempts were made to revitalize group efforts. This was not a wholly successful period by any means; but the new hopes gained by the great economic performances of Malaysia and Singapore were undoubtedly important in adding stimulus to these efforts. A world-wide trend toward the development of trading blocs was also in evidence at this time, providing its own stimulus. It was not the case, however, that any meaningful integration of these six societies took place during this period nor, for that matter, was any significant progress made on trade or other economic arrangements, human rights, mutual defense, or any other concern.

The third ASEAN summit, held in Manila in 1987, saw the initiation of a new phase in the history of this group. For the first time a nonmember, Japan, was formally invited and allowed to participate in the deliberations. Since 1987, other nations—the United States and Australia, for example, and, recently, Burma and Vietnam—have also sought to enter the picture, and ASEAN has not turned any of these away.

The generous approach of ASEAN members toward the participation of influential and other nonmembers must be considered in light of grander and broader ideas expressed by some of its leaders and, sometimes, by other Asian leaders as well. Prime Minister Mohammed bin Mahathir of Malaysia has been proposing the formation of an entity he calls the East Asian Economic Caucus, or EAEC, which would surely include the present membership of ASEAN but might also bring in such nations as South Korea and Taiwan. Most significantly, Mahathir advocates a leadership role for Japan in this organization.

This design fits the Eastern direction that Malaysia's trade and economic development patterns have taken in recent years, so it is not merely a casual idea developed by Malaysian leaders; the pages of the *New Straits Times*, the government-influenced newspaper, have been full of articles promoting EAEC in 1993 and 1994. An even larger regional grouping presently called CAN, the Community of Asian Nations, has been discussed in *Asiaweek* and other publications; this organization would presumably include China, India, and virtually all of the countries that are the concerns of this book. For the moment, at least, nothing more than aspiration seems to be supporting the CAN or EAEC ideas; and the integrative motivations and other factors at work in these broad schemes have not been analyzed.

Not to be overlooked in this category of regional schemes is APEC, the Asia Pacific Economic Conference, which held its first meeting of fifteen Pacific Rim nations in Seattle in late 1993. A second conference was held in Jakarta in November 1994. An idea first set out by Canada, APEC is clearly the vehicle the United States hopes will be adopted for trade cooperation and perhaps for other purposes as well. But even though this new grouping has established a secretariat in Singapore, it cannot be said to have taken on any permanent shape or form. At the moment, the United States, for political reasons, must deny that it is anything more than a discussion group; it would run into flak if it characterized APEC as a future trading organization. Even with this modest format, APEC saw Prime Minister Mahathir of Malaysia, the architect of EAEC, absent himself from the Seattle meeting.

The only organization of this type that has taken any permanent form to date in Asia, then, is ASEAN. It has a variety of solid evidences of its existence: a secretariat based in Jakarta, meetings of its members, and, until recently, small tokens of group orientation and mentality. Singapore's official travel book, to cite one example, has small sections in its final pages urging visitors to also go to the other five nearby states in order to see their sights and spend some money there. No visa is required of visitors from one ASEAN state who go to another. Universities cooperate in new endeavors; one example is a 1993 conference scheduled in East Malaysia that was cosponsored by universities of two ASEAN countries and ASEAN itself. Some big cooperative economic ventures, like a new Malaysian car factory in the Philippines, are giving a strong impetus to a region-wide awareness. The vitality of ASEAN can be traced to the speeches and policy positions taken by leaders of the six countries. "Growth triangles" stressing regional economic cooperation have been developed under

ASEAN auspices and much is expected from these. And an ASEAN consciousness seems to be setting in: the term can be found in shop and business names, for example, and in special sections of newspapers devoted to coverage of the ASEAN nations.

Regional Integration Studies and Their Application to ASEAN

Three fundamental approaches to regional integration have been developed over the years: federalism, neofunctionalism, and in communications theory. All of these, in turn, can be viewed in terms of their accommodation to political, economic, or social integration; and all have been demonstrated to be powerful tools in defining the variables at work in the complicated processes of integration.

Federalism emphasizes representation and elections, a proper division of powers between the federal, national, and local authorities, and a tension balancing a measure of independence of subordinate units with the supremacy of the federal government. Communications theory, especially in the form of transactional analysis, implies integration of nations through such activities as frequency of telephone or mail patterns and other informal patterns of behavior. It is our impression that the more recent literature of communications theory has tended to emphasize epistemic patterns of communications flow; that is, the diffusion of knowledge, usually in specialized form, through the informal networks of communications established by academics, business people, and other actors who share a cross-cultural set of perspectives on scientific, financial, or cultural information.

Scholars such as Karl Deutsch believe that communications technologies serve as both agents and indices of integration. Whenever it is the case that a population shares values, preferences, life-styles, common memories, aspirations, loyalties, and identifications, such people can be expected to communicate with one another—in other words, transact—frequently and over a broad range of concerns. The boundaries of these transacting communities are marked by "discontinuities of transaction flow," which just means that interaction with peoples outside the subject communities is minimal or nonexistent.

Many critics argue that contrary to standing as evidence of an integrative thrust working between peoples, transactions cannot be looked upon as either an awareness of interdependence nor as some kind of acceptance of mutual obligations. They therefore fail to provide any measurement of the growth of a sense of community. The riposte of Joseph Nye and perhaps other scholars to this charge is that any number of types of nongovernmental transactions with important interpersonal communication connotations can be used to measure social integration (depending, of course, upon the marginal costs and benefits of obtaining such data). Social integration is therefore a process that involves personal contact and interchange; but this is not necessarily a conscious awareness of mutual obligations that may arise from it.

This assessment of the application of communications theory to ASEAN, then, is that this is not very useful at the present time for a variety of reasons, including perhaps a lack of applicable data. It should be briefly pointed out, however, that communications theory has updated its approaches in recent years so that the promise of analytical success is now much stronger. This is because communications theory today looks at underlying technologies of communications as well as the communications themselves; because interactive media as well as one-way media are increasingly the subjects of research; and because the emphasis of development communication has been switched away from mere persuasion.

Neofunctionalists, like communications theorists, have enjoyed some success in predicting mutual responsiveness among actors. The members of ASEAN have not always responded to each other in the kinds of ways one finds in an optimal neofunctionalist model. But even though the fulfillment of roles by the individual members of the association have not taken on full flower, some kinds of interactive patterns, as pointed out above, have begun to emerge. Neofunctionalism stands for the principle that certain roles and functions can be expected in any kind of viable political organization; and these roles and functions are carried out because it is to the advantage of the actors involved. To a great extent, it remains identified with Professor Ernst Haas, a pioneer in the field of integration studies who continues to contribute to this academic dialogue. It is a scheme that has been applied, and with some success, to the European Community, where integrative forces have been at work much longer and much more in earnest than in the case of ASEAN.

It can be fairly concluded, then, that neofunctionalism is the most promising approach in existence at the present time for analysis of this association of nations; this does not, of course, preclude the use of other approaches and modes of analysis in the future.

ASEAN'S Exceptional Features

One of the practices most disliked in the study of comparative politics is that of giving up explanatory theories or models on the grounds of the singularity—the uniqueness—of the phenomenon studied. There is a strong preference for employing existing models, such as federalism and communications theory, or the roles and dynamics one might expect in a neofunctionalist model, in analyzing a regional grouping like ASEAN. This is because political science and the other social sciences place the greatest value upon the development of generalizations of importance. But it is practical to observe that ASEAN members possess characteristics that sometimes make them less well suited to these particular analytic models. There are satisfactions to be found, however, in the literatures on symbolic politics, on the nature of regimes, and on political culture, for these appear to provide useful insights into the past and future development of this supranational association.

The exceptional features of ASEAN that deserve comment and exploration, then, are: (1) culture as an emphasis upon formal procedures; (2) the authoritarian nature of the six regimes; and (3) the ethnic, religious and cultural diversity found in these nations. One of the cultural predispositions found among ASEAN members is an emphasis upon symbolism, which in turn represents each member's preference for indirect approaches to conflictual situations. Murray Edelman's work *The Symbolic Uses of Politics* states that the symbolic side of politics requires attention, for people cannot know themselves until they know what they do and what surrounds and nurtures them. He distinguishes the purposes of rite and myth which reinforce the meaning of symbolism in political institutions. Ritual is motor activity that involves its participants symbolically in a common enterprise, calling attention to relatedness and joint interests in a compelling way. It thereby invokes conformity and even satisfaction in the joys of conformity. Myth, says Edelman, serves the same purpose as rites so that each reinforces the other.

It is through the reaffirmation and conformity brought on by symbolism that the members of ASEAN derive their consensual agreements. While individualism is often seen as the dominant value in Western cultures, collectivism appears to be more important, if not always dominant, in many non-Western cultures; and certainly among the latter are many Asian cultures. While Western societies stress a need for emotional detachment, personal goals, confrontation and self-reliance, Asian cultures are more likely to perpetuate the ideals of group orientation, shared responsibility, and harmony. The importance of consensus building, consensual knowledge, and group orientation in Asian diplomacy and regionalism have been pointed out by any number of authors. This need makes the use of nongovernmental, informal, and therefore unofficial channels more attractive.

This nonthreatening posture has been particularly compelling to members of existing subregional intergovernmental bodies like ASEAN, who fear that the diplomatic gains of their own organization could be overwhelmed within a larger framework dominated by industrialized states, which, after all, have cultures and attitudes with which ASEAN members are not altogether comfortable. A clearly analogous case can be seen in the rise of Japan as a power in Asia and the Pacific Rim, for it has been aided by a nonthreatening, informal, consensus-seeking, and often unofficial approach. The key here is adaptation to circumstances and surroundings or, as Ernest Haas would prefer to call it, learning. This does not mean that ASEAN has no problems. One of the first complaints filed with the new World Trade Organization created by the GATT Treaty has been brought by Singapore against Malaysia.

The Character and Purposes of ASEAN

This fits well with what Michael Anatolik has observed about the formation and operation of ASEAN. In a non-Western pattern of organization and activities, ASEAN has developed in an ad hoc fashion. There are no treaty commitments concerning political or security matters, though there is now good evidence that these are in an embryonic stage, and politics appears veiled by an economic-cultural organization. A consequence of this is that participants are subjected only to a gradual and incremental form of change.

A negative effect is that participants and observers develop varying expectations of the process, most notably in economic matters. Anatolik's *ASEAN and the Diplomacy of Accommodation* regards the organization as neither an actor nor a confederation but as a consultative process. ASEAN summits, he believes, will continue to be infrequent and ad hoc because they are not intrinsic or vital to the work of the regional organization or to any political processes associated with it.

Despite the rhetoric about regionalism, members seem to be content with those ASEAN benefits that have already been achieved—peace, stability, and security—because these allow them to pursue independent paths rather than pursuing more cooperative or integrative paths. There is an irony at work here, of course, since the formation and continuation of ASEAN would at first appear to be a thrust toward regionalism; but it can hardly be this if it is seen as a means of freeing up members to pursue their particularistic aims. The commitment of the members to the ASEAN organization rests therefore not on hopes for the future, but on past experience; this past experience created the common awareness that competition, especially of the very hostile kind exhibited by Sukarno, is futile, foolish, and costly.

A successful ASEAN grouping, then, is based upon principles of restraint, respect, and responsibility, according to Anatolik and other commentators. Ambiguity is the handmaiden of consensus, so the language of ASEAN is one that allows participants to achieve common stands and then, subsequently, to hold and develop their own interpretations of these common stands. Common foreign policy stances have had a slow and guarded development because divisions of opinion and perception within ASEAN made it difficult to find compromises. These same factors explain why ASEAN states have not moved toward a collective defense arrangement.

On some occasions, however, the cooperative work of ASEAN produces results that are seen by all of the member states as useful or beneficial. A human rights document produced and signed by the six in 1993, for example, sets out the thesis—familiar to anyone who knows these countries—that human rights cannot be defined merely in individual terms, as is clearly the tradition in the West. Human rights matters must also include a doctrine of social responsibility that assures that individuals do not overstep themselves in a headlong rush toward a mere assertion of their rights. The great difficulty with this point is that it serves these governments well.

Murray Edelman points out that governments that have the greatest need for reassuring symbols are often the ones that most outrage their citizenry or force unwelcome changes in their behavior. Although the formal institutions of government found in the ASEAN nations resemble Western and democratic structures, largely because these are part and parcel of the colonial legacies, the actual style of government, reflecting deeper social traditions, is authoritarian. This authoritarianism ranges from paternalism, as in Brunei, Malaysia, and Singapore, to outright military rule, which has been the case at various times in

Indonesia, the Philippines, and Thailand. Freedom of speech and press can run counter to the personal interests of an authoritarian ruler; and a variety of incidents have proved that these freedoms have damaged intramural ASEAN relations. As long as newspapers remain under government control, there is a marked lessening of danger that comments will be taken as insults in other ASEAN governments or societies. This rule of silence has been as important to ASEAN politics as it has been to the domestic politics of the various member states; and this raises the question, still to be answered, of how the ASEAN process, like the member societies, will hold up during any future transitions toward democracy.

Some Major Problems on the Road to Democracy in ASEAN Nations

The role of the military can be an important element in the life of ASEAN countries. Generals have often intervened in the political arena and have sometimes stayed on for a very long time. On a broader level, one of the main criticisms of military-sponsored development plans has been their failure to stimulate political participation, a factor that has retarded modernization and deepened the gap between the rich and the poor. Recent developments in the Philippines and Thailand provide some reason for hope that the presence of the military in ASEAN regimes may now be in decline. The major military member of the association, Indonesia, will see no such decline for a long time.

Violations of human rights are all too common in ASEAN countries. All six members have had prominent examples of such violations in their records in recent years. In response to intensified attempts of the developed world to impose Western norms of human rights, ASEAN members have recently vowed to take a common stand on human rights issues. Some pressures on this vital matter also come from the United Nations and other international organizations and groupings; and, perhaps significantly or perhaps not, the first all-Asian conference on human rights was held in Bangkok in 1993 with forty-seven Asian nations in attendance. Deputy Prime Minister Abdul Ghafar Baba of Malaysia stated in a *New Straits Times* article published in June 1993 that the differences in the legal systems of the various members should not be allowed to stand in the way of greater ASEAN strides in human rights. The development of a realistic and humane approach to this deep problem, however, has yet to occur.

Recent years have seen some mutual security discussions. The six members, as well as potential new members, of the association apparently believe that prospects are good for development of a treaty or, at the least, an informal set of undertakings in the cause of regional defense. ASEAN followers, and perhaps especially the Southeast Asian press, which often reflects official views, seem to be optimistic about this even though these matters are only in a beginning phase.

There are serious cleavages—economic, ethnic, racial, and cultural—at work in all six of these nations. Suspicions are found among Malay, Chinese, and Indian populations. There are subtle tensions and differences that exist within peoples of the same racial heritage. There are regional differences that exist within the same ASEAN member but also between countries. Religious rivalries are found to exist, for example, between Muslim and Christian groups and among other groups as well. In addition, there are serious territorial claims that have never been settled, such as the Philippine claim to Sabah and the claims made by several ASEAN members to the potentially oil-rich Spratly Islands. Above all of these considerations is the problem of an inherent contradiction between the pursuit of both nationalist and collective aspirations. There is little question that, so far at least, the former have held sway.

√ ASEAN Progress on Economic Integration

Economic interdependence among nations serves as an indispensable measurement in the evolution of regional integration. Joseph Nye, in his book *Peace in Parts,* states that the most successful area of regional integration is often the economic sphere, where problems, in his view, are often less highly politicized, more divisible, and more amenable to progress in stages.

Scholars appear to show parallel and almost consensual approaches in their definitions of economic cooperation, but their concerns for the process of economic integration seem to vary from one thinker to another. Some distinguish economic integration in a negative form or, in other words, in terms of the removal of restraints from the free flow of goods. (A few of these, it is safe to say, are a bit overly enthusiastic about the free market as a solution to all problems.) But these same writers also see integration in a positive form, namely the formulation of functional institutions and policies at a collective level. Others express concern about the consequences that can follow the unification of policies of member states. Nye, for example, states that he believes that formation of a regional transnational economy involves considerations of both welfare and interdependence, and these tendencies often come from quite opposite arenas of concern. A degree of protection, he points out, may create a transnational economy among a group of countries by increasing factors of production and also thereby increasing independence in a trading position; but if this protection results in diverting trade patterns in an inefficient way, a net loss of national welfare can be the result.

Controversies over collective policies resulting from increasing integration will remain a subject of debate. Our concern here, however, is to show how regionally integrated ASEAN members have become in terms of their economic interdependence. To measure ASEAN economic integration, we can use Balassa's categories of economic integration as basic tools in defining whether ASEAN has reached a higher level of integration in its quarter of a century of existence. The chief concern in investigating economic integration, according to Balassa's theory, is the degree to which reductions of barriers have influenced domestic policies of the nations which are subjects of the study. The Balassa model proceeds on the logical assumption that increased levels of economic integration will result in an ever-stronger complex of economic institutions which can eventually lead to full economic integration (see Table 8.1).

Even though Balassa's theory has some limitations, his basic idea of economic integration can be applied to the present status of ASEAN

Table 8.1
The Balassa Model

In a model worked out by development scholar Ben Belassa, two sets of forces are simultaneously at work in the processes of political and economic integration of societies. One of these sets of forces is policy; the other is the achievement of new institutional frameworks as a result of these policies. He believes that five sets of policies can be seen to develop over time—the abolition of tariffs among the partners in this relationship (as in ASEAN or the European community), common external tariffs, the free flow of factors (i.e., free trade and other contacts), harmonization of economic policies, and, finally and usually much later, unification of policies and political institutions. The institutional arrangements that accompany these initiatives are first, a free trade area and customs union; then a common market; then "economic union," which might include such important measures as interest rate policy or the adoption of one currency, and, finally, total economic integration.

See Ben Belassa, *The Theory of Economic Integration* (Homewood, IL: R. D. Irwin, 1961), p. 128.

economic cooperation. It is true that at this time ASEAN has not even reached a free tariff system, the first level of economic integration. The implementation of the 1989 PTA, or Preferential Trade Arrangements, negotiated by the six countries has reached only a 20–25 percent margin of tariff preference on items with an import value up to $10 million U.S.

This lack of progress toward integration does not militate against the Balassa model, however, because the latter charts a path that, in the normal course of our expectations, might be expected to emerge. It is therefore a good set of indicators by which to judge future progress or, perhaps, a continued lack of progress.

Economists are expressing increasing doubts that the ASEAN free trade zone, which is to be phased in over fifteen years, will ever get off the ground; a beginning for collective action is seen as a requirement if ASEAN is ever to mean anything. But such skepticism is natural since the global economic slowdown may be affecting Southeast Asia, and officials of a number of the countries are responding to pressures from powerful industry groups for protectionist measures. Such measures would undermine efforts to build a barrier-free ASEAN market of more than 330 million consumers for trade in all goods except unprocessed agricultural commodities.

The ASEAN countries' consistent use of nontariff barriers poses another problem. Many exporters to Thailand, Malaysia, and Indonesia, for example, frequently encounter customs-related problems and excessive bureaucratic procedures. Singapore is renowned for its stringent health, sanitation, and safety standards.

Economic integration can actually be said to be more successful in terms of the global system and its relationships with individual ASEAN members. Since member nations are perhaps overly dependent upon foreign trade and investment, the regional organization remains a fragile undertaking. Any leader of an ASEAN nation can frankly say that his or her country does not owe its economic growth to any supposed integration of ASEAN members into a free trade area, a customs union, or a common market. The quality and very high growth rates of exports have been, and still are, fostered by foreign investments and imports from target market countries.

Precise measures of the growth of trade within the ASEAN group of nations is provided, at least in those relationships where such data are available, in Tables 8.2 and 8.3. The six charts present all of the data available for export and import trade for selected years within the ASEAN community. (The 1990 figures are the latest available at this

Table 8.2
Asean Exports

| | Main destinations of exports 1975 | | | | |
	Indonesia %	Malaysia %	Philippines %	Singapore %	Thailand %
Indonesia	--	--	--	--	3.7
Malaysia	1.0	--	--	17.2	4.8
Philippines	--	--	--	--	1.5
Singapore	8.9	20.3	1.4	--	8.4
Thailand	--	--	--	3.5	--
U.S.	26.3	16.1	29.1	13.9	10.3
Japan	44.1	14.5	37.1	8.7	25.6
Main destinations of exports 1987					
Indonesia	--	--	--	--	--
Malaysia	--	--	2.1	14.1	3.3
Philippines	--	--	--	--	--
Singapore	7.0	18.2	3.4	--	9.0
Thailand	--	2.9	--	4.2	--
U.S.	19.9	16.6	36.2	24.5	18.6
Japan	43.8	19.6	17.2	9.0	14.9
Main destinations of exports 1990					
Indonesia	--	--	--	--	--
Malaysia	--	--	--	15.0	--
Philippines	--	--	--	--	--
Singapore	7.5	23.0	--	--	7.0
Thailand	--	--	--	6.3	--
U.S.	13.1	16.9	38.0	19.7	23.0
Japan	42.5	15.3	19.9	8.7	17.0

Source: Country reports of the Economist Intelligence Unit, 1992.
Note: Figures are not available in all categories.

Table 8.3
Asean Imports

	Indonesia %	Malaysia %	Philippines %	Singapore %	Thailand %
Main destinations of imports 1975					
Indonesia	--	--	--	--	--
Malaysia	--	--	1.6	11.6	--
Philippines	--	--	--	--	--
Singapore	7.2	8.5	--	--	--
Thailand	0.7	4.0	--	--	--
U.S.	14.0	10.7	21.8	15.7	14.43
Japan	31.0	20.1	28.0	16.9	31.5
Main destinations of imports 1987					
Indonesia	--	--	--	--	--
Malaysia	--	--	4.0	13.9	3.8
Philippines	--	--	--	--	--
Singapore	7.7	14.5	--	--	7.7
Thailand	--	3.5	--	3.1	--
U.S.	11.4	18.8	22.1	14.7	12.5
Japan	29.1	21.8	16.6	20.4	26.0
Main destinations of imports 1990					
Indonesia	--	--	--	--	--
Malaysia	--	--	--	15.2	--
Philippines	--	--	--	--	--
Singapore	5.8	14.7	3.9	--	7.0
Thailand	--	--	--	--	--
U.S.	11.5	16.9	19.5	15.8	11.0
Japan	24.3	24.1	18.4	21.3	31.0

Source: Country reports of the Economist Intelligence Unit, 1992.
Note: Figures are not available in all categories.

writing.) It can be seen that, in general, there are few discernible increases in activity through the past two decades. It is true that Indonesia now imports a great deal more from Singapore than it once did; but trade activity has mostly been increased, if it has been increased at all, with partners in the industrialized world. These charts, then, represent and illustrate the results of low (or no) levels of action on the trade front within the ASEAN bloc.

Another negative effect hindering the growth of ASEAN integration is that most of the members produce identical or similar products and have similar domestic economic structures. This limits complementarity in trade. It raises the barriers for foreign producers as well, because each country tries to support its own industries through credit subsidies and other direct support schemes.

The greatest of all obstacles to ASEAN economic integration is ultimately found in nationalist sentiments. These are aimed either at protecting domestic industries or resisting the loss of sovereignty or national decision-making power to an ASEAN arrangement. Unless ASEAN addresses such issues as nontariff barriers and harmonizes its trade and tariff regulations among its members, its efforts to build an ASEAN free trade area will remain highly vulnerable. This also brings into question the ideas about adding new members. Longer-range hopes for social and perhaps eventual political integration will have to await the growth of a broader supranationality—in other words, a common identity—of the peoples of the area. The ASEAN nations have hopefully learned from past experiences that military competition is futile, foolish, and costly. The association's orientation toward peace and stability has doubtless had the effect of downplaying any regional need for military alliances. This points up an advantage of ASEAN that may be understated in studies of the organization; for however slow the movement toward regional integration may be, striving for cooperation through consultation and collective management creates an atmosphere in which conflicts and hostility among the members and with other Asian countries becomes less likely.

Further Reading

Acharya, Amitav. "Regional Military Security Cooperation in the Third World: A Conceptual Analysis of the Relevance and Limitations of ASEAN." *Journal of Peace Research* 29 (1992): 7–21. A reexamination and reevaluation of ASEAN regional security in the 1990s.

Antolik, Michael. *ASEAN and the Diplomacy of Accommodation*. Armonk, N.Y.: M. E. Sharpe, 1990. This summary of regional diplomacy among the six member states of ASEAN provides some insight into what it considers the most successful experiment in regional cooperation anywhere in the developing world.

Balassa, Ben. *The Theory of Economic Integration*. Homewood, Ill: R. D. Irwin, 1961. This early work on economic integration has stood the test of time well and can be found to be applicable to integrative phenomena today.

Broinowski, Alison, ed. *ASEAN into the 1990s*. New York: St. Martin's Press, 1990. Nine scholars and experts on ASEAN address issues such as the economies, regional security, foreign relationships, and the past, present, and future roles of the regional organization.

————. *Understanding ASEAN*. New York: St. Martin's Press, 1982. Comprehensive treatment of ASEAN by ten scholars who look at the origination, associations, economic and foreign policy, refugee problems, and future of the organization.

Edelman, Murray. *The Symbolic Uses of Politics*. Urbana: University of Illinois Press, 1964. Groundbreaking work on symbolism, which has been shown to have many uses in political science, psychology, and the other social sciences.

Haas, Ernst. *Where Knowledge Is Power: Three Models of Change in International Organization*. Berkeley: University of California Press, 1990. This pioneering author in this field explores the dynamics of how international organizations learn through their past experiences.

Leifer, Michael. *ASEAN and the Security of Southeast Asia*. New York: Routledge, 1989. Leifer's work is the most comprehensive volume to date on the organization, its history, its accomplishments, and its limitations.

Lindberg, Leon N., and Stuart A. Scheingold, eds. *Regional Integration: Theory and Research*. An important set of readings which contributes to our understanding of this important and complex concept.

Rieger, Hans Christoph. *ASEAN Economic Cooperation: A Handbook*. Singapore: ASEAN Economic Research Unit, Institute of Southeast Asian Studies, 1991. Provides basic information on the Association of Southeast Asian Nations, its organization, and the various cooperative activities associated with it; emphasizes the organization's economic cooperation.

Simon, Sheldon W. "United States Security Policy and ASEAN," *Current History* 89 (March 1990): 97–132. Exploration of how social and economic dynamism in the region is forcing the United States to reevaluate its security needs there.

Sudo, Sueo. *The Fukuda Doctrine and ASEAN: New Dimensions in Japanese Foreign Policy*. Singapore: Institute of Southeast Asian Studies, 1992. Attributing Japan's active involvement in Southeast Asian affairs to the Fukuda Doctrine of 1977, this study traces the origins of Japan's political role in the region and analyzes the development and effects of the first postwar Japanese policy doctrine.

Chapter 9

Coming to Terms with the New Realities of Asia

The rapid pace of change in the Asia-Pacific area today will obviously require American policymakers to fashion intelligent responses. The various interested U.S. publics, whether they are in labor or business, human rights activism, communications media, education, or are citizens who simply want to be aware of the world, will hopefully be given some voice, at least indirectly, in this policy making.

These responses cannot be drawn up on an ad hoc basis. Even when the United States held relatively greater power in Asia than it does today, it was not possible to operate in this way and retain a prudent balance of goals, interests, and objectives. There is a need for an overall approach to this part of the world that is coordinated, feasible, sensible, and, most assuredly, fitted within the realm of possibility for the United States. This means, first and foremost, that America must no longer see itself as a force policing the world in the name of democracy or freedom. Such a goal was probably never realistic. Democracy and freedom have not always been the goals, anyway; it might be more appropriate to think of such activities as the suppression of nationalisms the United States does not like.

Supporters of the massive U.S. war effort in Vietnam in the 1960s and 1970s were basically wrong in encouraging this policy path, but they were right when they said that the aftermath of a U.S. pullout or defeat would mean an ill-defined role for the nation in Asia. This has been the case since 1975 as we have witnessed developments that seem to erode the U.S. position even further:

1. There is the mighty commercial challenge of Japan and many

other Asian countries who have developed trading surpluses with us. We have yet to deal effectively with this.

2. The Vietnam aftermath included the scuttling of the Southeast Asia Treaty Organization (SEATO), which had been put together and encouraged by the United States to perhaps evolve as a broad formation of military and trading partners in the region. Asians themselves have since put together the ASEAN economic bloc, but the United States has apparently had little or no role in this endeavor. The effect of these events seems to demonstrate that the United States should see itself as a partner with Asian nations in building the world economy, but it should not regard itself as the overpowering major player which, all would concede, it once was.

3. The loss of bases in the Philippines was a defeat both from the standpoint of military logistics and, perhaps even more importantly, from the standpoint of the psychological importance attached to the U.S. presence there. These bases were probably not needed, but the forced exit from them has helped to worsen an already bad policymaking environment.

4. The leverage, prestige and, sometimes, the humanitarianism associated with American aid programs appears to have been lost over the years, and for a variety of reasons. Aid programs have not had well-coordinated overall goals, they are often dominated by military aid considerations and purposes, and, for the first time in post-World War II experience, they are sometimes overshadowed by the aid programs of other rich nations, such as Japan and some of the European powers. The evidence supporting this argument includes an overall review of aid programs now being undertaken by the Clinton administration.

5. The response of the American public and now, increasingly, American policymakers, to Asian immigration has taken on an unfriendly tone at times and a racist tone at the worst times. This cannot do the United States any good at all and new policies are going to have to delicately tread between purposeful, humane, and understanding approaches and the national demands for controls. This task can be complicated further if domestic political attitudes toward Asian-Americans are insensitive or uncaring.

6. The United States often fails to speak out on important human rights concerns, either because these issues are neglected or because it does not wish to offend important trading partners. China, India, South Korea, Indonesia, Pakistan, Burma, and other Asian nations have been guilty of serious violations of the liberties and rights of their peoples in recent years, and the American response has been

infrequent and inconsistent at best. At times we have seen American-based international corporations participate with repressive Asian governments in activities that are detrimental to people of the nation and to its environment. This has practical as well as ethical consequences.

7. Finally, it must be said that it is now the case that many Asian nations, especially the smaller ones, look to Japan for international leadership on any number of issues rather than to the United States. This situation has evolved quite naturally under the circumstances and realities of the world economy and it is based upon practical considerations as much as any other set of factors. Changing this fact is probably not possible at the moment nor in the immediate future, so it would be a good idea for Americans to simply accept this reality for the time being and to be aware of it.

The array of policies and actions that must be considered as we look at the new realities of the Asia-Pacific Rim area is quite daunting. Perhaps the biggest change that is needed in this regard is psychological. The United States has always been a part of a global economy, to be sure, but it must rely upon international trade and other contacts today to an extent never achieved in the past. The plain fact is that the country was able for a very long time, and especially in the first two decades following World War II, to dominate the international economy and to rely, much more heavily than is possible now, on the domestic economy to take it up the road to prosperity. Thus an attitudinal change in the business, labor, media, academic and other communities must be in place before the United States can again assert the appropriate responses to Asian and world conditions and events.

Any number of incidents can be cited to show this need. One of the best examples is the ill-fated trip to Japan undertaken by President George Bush and more than two dozen executives early in 1992. This effort had no yield whatsoever; but what is almost as bad is that it was put together in an amateurish and haphazard way that did not serve the nation (nor, for that matter, the president) well. The idea that such an entourage and format would yield results was doomed from the start. The visit of Vice President Dan Quayle to Malaysia late in 1989 is another example. Tired from his long trip, Quayle chose not to meet with any of the top government officials who had been assembled to talk with him about mutual problems of the two nations. The offended Malaysians, who could hardly be blamed for their disappointment, required considerable attention from the diplomatic corps in the days that immediately followed.

These events do not let the Clinton administration off the hook. Some of its officials have made statements and may even have considered policies that do not comport with a sensible or aware approach to the Asia Pacific Rim region. A great deal of briefing and education is going to have to be expended upon political appointees involved in trade, diplomacy, security issues, cultural and educational exchange, and other efforts if these matters are to be handled well. Retraining, updating, and upgrading the work of career personnel should be an ongoing priority as well.

Beyond attitudinal changes, the most profound question is exactly what U.S. goals should be established for this part of the world. Keeping in mind the relatively new and certainly realistic idea that there are limits to what can be done, the economic, security, and other policy goals developed by decision makers can be expected to fit within certain guidelines.

The Lewis model used throughout this book, for example, demonstrates that the United States is faced with a severe and long-term problem of providing jobs for its own people in the face of low-wage competition from Asian and other nations. This will mean heavy emphases are in order for priorities such as research and development, technological innovation, export promotion and incentives, and job retraining schemes. These are areas in which the United States has historically excelled, and there is little reason to think that the nation cannot seize its opportunities in such endeavors.

Trade policy becomes a paramount concern of anyone who realizes that it can enhance these strengths or, if it is badly carried out, it can scuttle our best efforts. The U.S. skills of technological innovation brought about recent inventions such as the compact disc, videotape recorder, and semiconductor. But it has been Japan and, sometimes, other Asian nations that have developed the most effective manufacturing and marketing skills for such products. Patent and copyright protections are a given of any effective trade policy, and these are still absent from the general Asian and international scenes despite the new GATT agreement and structure. It is conservatively estimated that at least half of the income that would justifiably be derived from some protections is currently being lost because of violations.

A major hindrance to American trade negotiators for a decade or longer has been the complaint—a justifiable one—that the United States has thrown serious imbalances into the international economy because of its heavy government budget deficits and, even more to the point, because of its refusal to do anything about them. President Bill

Clinton, however, has been able to enjoin such worries, for the time being at least, with the claim that he is in fact doing something about this. The analyses following the 1993 Group of Seven meeting in Tokyo made this point and seemed to emphasize the strength of the United States at this conference. (It is also true that Clinton was in much stronger political health than any of the leaders he was conferring with, including the soon-to-be-ousted Japanese prime minister, Kiichi Miyazawa.) The administration's apparent long-term success in reducing the size of the bureaucracy will also add budget-balancing strengths.

A new stance on trade policy, which is becoming increasingly important, is U.S. insistence on gauging progress of Japanese imports of American goods. Although some Japanese leaders and experts say that this is not feasible, the current U.S. trade policymakers insist that it can be done. This remains to be seen, of course, but it is perhaps refreshing to many Americans to see a firmer approach taken by their government on this matter.

This stance should probably be incorporated, all the same, into a broader and more comprehensive policy scheme for the United States to carry out in this twenty-nation area. Such a scheme would seek to coordinate economic, security, aid, development, environmental, human rights, cultural, and diplomatic approaches for the region for the first time since 1975. It could be argued, perhaps, that the alternative of continuing a variety of ad hoc approaches does not necessarily mean that policy in the region will tend to drift; but that is a danger, and the generally unsuccessful experiences of America in Asia over the past two decades seems to confirm this. The United States clearly needs to decide what kind of role it seeks to play in the Asia-Pacific region, what its strengths and limitations are, and what goals it wants to achieve. Some goals are probably more obvious than others. We can, and we should, encourage and promote the causes of democracy and human rights. We can provide useful forms of aid to poor Asian nations. We can pressure American-based multinational companies to use better judgment than they have in the past about cooperating with tyrannical regimes. We can demand and fight for fair trade policies rather than falling into the wistful rhetoric that has characterized the past decade and a half. We can expect earnest efforts to protect the Asian and world environments through responsible policies on air and water quality, the threat of deforestation, labor and health policies, and related issues. We could even undertake policies to discourage the growth of the current Asian arms race.

The Asian scene in the first two or three decades after 1945 was one in which the United States saw its major limitations in strategic matters in which the Soviet Union was interested. Aside from these considerations, the United States held sway in all, or nearly all, policy concerns in the area. A 1966 gathering of Asian and Pacific leaders with President Lyndon B. Johnson in Manila saw the Chief Executive describing his colleagues as "my prime ministers." That day is now far behind us. But there are real advantages to be found in an atmosphere of mutual respect. We can hope that these can be enjoyed as we work in liaisons and partnerships aimed at making this a better world.

Index

Index

About the Author

Gerald L. Houseman is a professor of political science at Indiana University–Fort Wayne. He is the author of eight political science books and many articles and he has traveled extensively in Asia. He served with the Indiana University program in Malaysia in 1989–90 and again in 1995 and was a Fulbright scholar in Indonesia for 1993–94. His major areas of study are political economy, legal systems, and Asian political culture.

Ardeth Maung, author of Chapter 8 in this volume, is a native of Burma. She received her M.A. in international relations from Yale University in 1995 and is a Ph.D. student in political science at the University of Wisconsin.